Black Male Adolescents:

Parenting and Education in Community Context

Black Male Adolescents: Parenting and Education in Community Context

Edited by

Benjamin P. Bowser

California State University at Hayward

Lanham • New York • London

University Press of America®, Inc.
4720 Boston Way
Lanham, Maryland 20706

3 Henrietta Street
London WC2E 8LU England

Printed in the United States of America
British Cataloging in Publication Information Available

Library of Congress Cataloging-in-Publication Data

Black male adolescents : parenting and education in community
context / edited by Benjamin P. Bowser.
p. cm.
Includes indexes.
1. Afro-American teenage boys. 2. Parenting—United States.
3. Afro-American teenage boys—Education.
I. Bowser, Benjamin P.
E185.86.B5256 1990 305.23'5—dc20 90–45066 CIP

ISBN 0–8191–7975–2 (alk. paper)

The paper used in this publication meets the minimum requirements of American National Standard for Information Sciences—Permanence of Paper for Printed Library Materials, ANSI Z39.48–1984.

Contributors

Benjamin P. Bowser
Hardy Frye
Mindy Fullilove
Robert Fullilove
Lawford Goddard
Peter Harris
Ronald Hudson
Joyce King
Anthony Lemelle, Jr.
Grace Massey
Faye McNair-Knox
Caroyln Mitchell
Loften Mitchell
James Moss
Daphne Muse
Herbert Perkins
Alvin Poussaint
Walter Stafford
Robert Staples
H. Tee Sweet
Muata Weusi-Puryear
Omanike Weusi-Puryear

Contents

Section Three: Education for Survival and Success

Section Four: Development of Cultural Identity

ACKNOWLEDGMENTS

This book is result of the work, professional skill and dedication of numerous people. I am most appreciative of Dr. Reginald Jones, University of California, Berkeley, for his encouragement, to Ann Ingram for her copy editing and suggestions, and to Fred Felder of Cragmont Publications (Oakland) for typesetting and text preparation. Very special acknowledgment goes to the Black men of The Consortium for Effective Black Parenting, Inc. (Palo Alto, Ca.) for inspiring and calling for this book. It is dedicated to all of our fathers and sons.

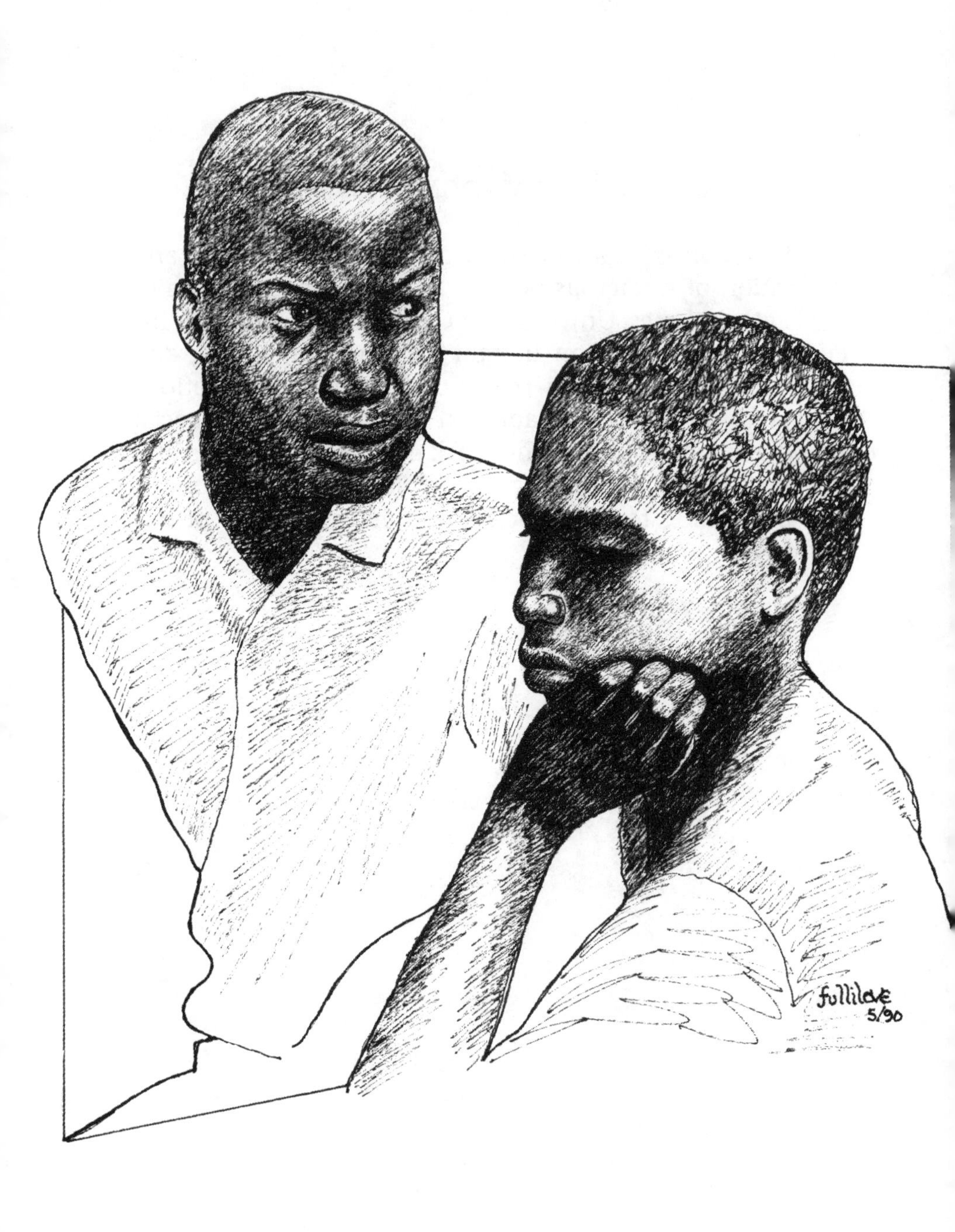
fullilove
5/90

Foreword

Alvin Poussaint, M.D.

THE TASK OF EDUCATING AND REARING the Black male adolescent is among the greatest challenges now facing the Black community and, for that matter, the nation. If we as a society do not rescue young Black men from the disaster that threatens them and nurture them adequately during their teenage years, there will surely be further deterioration of the Black family and enormous social cost to the country. We can no longer ignore what is now obvious: many of these young men are in deep trouble, particularly those living in extreme poverty in our urban ghettoes.

This volume on the Black male teenager is particularly welcome because it focuses on that one vital issue. Rather than generalizing about the problem of Black youth, it pinpoints a critical subcategory of concern. For too long, we have lumped all "Black" problems together without distinguishing among socioeconomic class, gender, age, or other demographic factors that influence and affect specific segments of the Black community.

The approach utilized in this book allows us to concentrate our attention on the specific issues that are relevant to the development of Black males. Young Black women face problems that are similar in some respects but quite different in others; this means that the proposed remedies may be different as well and another similar volume should be devoted exclusively to them. A goal of this, and any subsequent work, should be to analyze and assess possible solutions and then incorporate the most promising of them into social policy initiatives and community programs.

Over the past decade, newspaper reports and magazine features have zeroed in on the plight of the Black male with singular emphasis on the Black male in the so-called underclass. Black writers in particular have turned out a multitude of articles which can be generically titled, "The Black Male:

An Endangered Species." This increased interest is both welcome and necessary as we seek to examine the hopes and dilemmas confronting all young Black man.

Some readers may wonder why there should be special emphasis on the adolescent years: don't problems originate much earlier in life and simply become exacerbated and more overt during the teen years? It is true that many problems seen in adolescence derive from earlier childhood; while we must study the origin of these difficulties, we must also understand the special tensions that surge forth and are magnified during the adolescent stage of life. No one should read this book without reflecting carefully on the life cycle of the Black male child.

The socialization of the Black boy from the time of his birth deserves close scrutiny. What is the effect on him, for example, of growing up in a single-parent household headed by a women (which is the case in close to 50% of all Black families)? How is the little boy affected by the absence of a father or another adult male? What are the social forces that impact upon him and induce him to adopt antisocial "macho" attitudes that he thinks will enhance his male identity? What burdens does the community impose on this child to carry on certain Black traditions in music, sports, and dance? How many of these boys feel obliged to be "cool" and "hip" and to be able to "rap"? Finally, how do these and other psychological forces affect Black male adaptation to schooling and employment in a society that continues to single out the Black man for unique forms of discrimination?

From slavery until the present time, white people have greatly feared Black male aggression and independence; hence, Black men were required to shuffle, act simple-minded, and generally play the clown in order to appear less threatening. They were forced, for their own safety, to relinquish evidence of their very maleness; and there is, even today, pressure on Black men to be passive and to avoid speaking out forcefully. White men have long been obsessed about the potential sexual access of Black males to White women. Lynching, murder, and general mayhem have been committed against Black men—all under the guise of protecting the purity of White womanhood. These sentiments persist even now, in lesser (but not necessarily more subtle) forms. The ultimate goal of White racism in America has been to emasculate Black males; ironically, it has been the innate and rebounding potency of the Black male which has enabled him to make the gains he has achieved. But even with this resiliency, many Black men are psychologically and socially trapped within a destructive cycle that is very difficult to break.

It is appropriate, therefore, that this book focus on the teen years, because that is the beginning of both real and symbolic manhood. The question is: What obstacles remain and must be overcome for the Black boy to reach a dignified and productive manhood? The answers and solutions are multifaceted, and in some cases very complex; battles must be waged on many fronts.

This book is properly comprehensive. We must study the entire range of socialization of the Black male within dramatically changing family and community patterns. We have to consider the possibility that society's automatic assumptions of his criminality, and the "outsider" status often forced upon Black youth, have contributed to a mind-set that makes him resistant to mainstream morality. We must examine various educational approaches for their effectiveness in reaching out to the young Black male. How, for example, should parents go about instilling acceptable human values in young men who are growing up in unacceptable surroundings, with inadequate educations and limited opportunities? It is important to look carefully at those Black families whose children have achieved well against the odds—to try to identify and analyze their successful methods of parenting, and to transmit them to other families.

Among the core issues that must be addressed are the many obstacles to acquiring and keeping jobs and advancing within employment situations; these difficulties result, all too often, in the perpetuation of a cycle of poverty and dependency and the breakdown of Black families. We should also look into the ramifications—scarcely studied until now—of teenage fatherhood. Finally, this book provides some insight into antisocial behaviors that often end in vicious and self-destructive acts. The high rate of suicide and the astounding escalation of Black-on-Black homicide among teenagers and young men attest to the severity of these problems.

We need massive, bold, and creative intervention programs to address the urgent needs of one of the most maltreated and underserved segments of this country's population. The approach should not be hit-or-miss, but must be based on sound theoretical principles and research. This volume of essays on the adolescent Black male is a strong and important interdisciplinary beginning to what must become an ongoing commitment to this national crisis by ourselves, by government, and by the community at large.

Introduction: From Crisis to Action

Benjamin P. Bowser

There is talk of yet another crisis in the land. Black men have been assailed in the popular mind as having abandoned their wives and children, as being dangerous and troublesome in virtually every institution they participate in. These men are now an "endangered species." At the rate that Black men are being overwhelmed by what many would consider self-inflicted pathologies, they may soon join the eagle, rhinoceros, elephant and polar bear in near-extinction. On virtually every indicator of well being—health, education, crime, death-rate, homicide, incarceration, unemployment and drug addiction—Black men are disproportionately represented. A friend asked half-jokingly, "Will we be on display at local zoos and will affirmative action be required for us to be displayed with the monkeys and apes?" The descriptions in front of the cages may read "Here is what is left of the once-dangerous Black man. He defied almost everything." Implicit in all social crises is the need to do something to reverse worsening social problems. But in this case, it may be presumptuous to assume that there is a consensus on keeping Black men around, given the public image and record of trouble.

The popular press has called the circumstances of Black men a crisis. Where has the press been? Blacks have been saying that Black men are in special danger for a long time. This private concern became public in the late 1960s with the Black Panther Party programs to protect the community from the police and to assert Black manhood. Everyone took note of the disproportionate Black casualty rates in Vietnam and the rising numbers of Black men in prisons. This was in the early 1970s and before the new conservatism. Samuel Yette's *The Choice: The Issue Of Black Survival In*

America (1971) outlined the danger and was well received, but quickly forgotten. It seemed that only the very bitter and paranoid could really believe that the new objective of racial oppression was Black extermination. Subordination and the maintenance of inequality was one thing, but genocide was something else.

Black survival has always been hard work, but since 1970 it seems more desperate than ever before. The dramatic change was accelerated when OPEC put America on notice that oil was no longer nearly free. OPEC did more than raise the price of oil. They broke the spell of American invincibility in the world community in a way that touched everyone's lives and pocketbooks. The shock might have been even greater than the loss of the war in Vietnam. With the nation's basic identity in question, the business elite scrambled to maximize their profits and reassert their control. The restructuring of the American economy which had been in progress since World War II was accelerated. This meant rapid disinvestment from cities, withdrawal from social welfare goals and removal of domestic working-class jobs to overseas markets. As a consequence, large numbers of the nation's poor and working class were left behind in unemployment.

By 1980 the nation's conventional behavior followed the business community, and selfishness and individualism were openly celebrated. There was a call to return to basic values as if the past were morally superior to the present. And then the desire to roll the clock back was legitimized by the Reagan presidency. The struggle to make America into what Martin Luther King, Jr. called the "Beloved Community" was for the moment routed and belittled as just another special interest and outcome of liberal permissiveness. In this atmosphere, Yette's book should have received renewed attention from a worried Black community. To this day the possibility of Black extermination from social class inequality and from being simply jettisoned from the economy is certainly not far away from the viciousness displayed by corporations and the federal government for poor people's legitimate rights and needs.

If genocide is not inconceivable, then two concerns

come to mind. What form will it take and what is its timing—how and when? This is not an issue of ovens and concentration camps, but rather of benign neglect and simply holding to the current course. Nathan and Julia Hare's *The Endangered Black Family* (1984) took the possibility of genocide seriously and attempted to answer the hows and whens. The Hares suggested that black oppression will not continue in exactly the same way as in the past. The new way is by making it economically impossible for Black families to survive in general and to keep black youth from gaining economic mobility in the critical transition from youth to adulthood in particular. The Hares' claim was met with disbelief and bewilderment—it could not be so.

Then came Jawanza Kunjufu's *Countering The Conspiracy To Destroy Black Boys* (1984). The Kunjufu work quickly joined the Hares' in the outer world of disbelief. He added that the primary mechanism for the destruction of Black youth was psychological and cultural. Destroy any positive self-concept Black youth may have and then replace it with white images of Black inferiority. Black youth will then destroy themselves and their community more effectively then any army of occupation. Furthermore, the victims will blame themselves since the real power and money interests, who create and sustain the psychological and physical conditions, are not immediately apparent in the destruction.

Voices in the wilderness have an uncanny tendency to become prophetic. I would venture to say that the majority of both White and Black people do not believe that the current destruction of Black youth and communities is the result of anyone's intentional or unintentional decisions outside of the community. Mobs of Whites are not attacking Black communities as they did in 1919 Race Riots. The mobs and attacks are coming from within. But for anyone who cares to look, there is a consensus that the destruction is vast and, if unchecked, could mean the eventual end of any significant Black presence in the U.S. Finally, even statistical indicators show enough consistency to suggest that Black youth are indeed endangered. Social scientists have now joined the prophetic voices in describing the seriousness of the moment. A thought-provoking discussion of these indicators is found in the essays in *Young, Black And Male In America* (1988), Jewelle Gibbs et al. (eds.).

Community in Crisis

Depending upon your point of view, the Black community appears to be in a series of discrete crises. Newspapers and magazines are particularly good at conveying this impression. Each Black crisis lasts for a time, is popularized by the press and then disappears from view. At last count there have been the crisis of the inner city, the crisis in the schools, the crisis in academic achievement, the crisis of teen pregnancy, the housing crisis, rising crime, the heroin crisis, the crisis of prison overpopulation, the crisis of the black family and the crisis of Black leadership—or lack of it. Now there are the AIDS crisis, the crack cocaine crisis and the crisis of Black males. There will undoubtedly be others. All of these crises are very real.

But when public attention moves from one crisis to the next, it is not because the former crisis is solved. It is still there. What is missing is a willingness to realize that all of these crises have been with us for a long time, are outcomes of other events, are on-going and closely related. By taking a comprehensive view it is very apparent that the causes of all of these crises are related and that any solution will have to be also comprehensive. Even if there were the willingness and resources to address any one of these crises, the impact would be minimal unless the other crises were addressed as well.

To run from crisis-to-crisis and not take a comprehensive view is a form of denial. What is being denied is the gravity of the situation and the scope of real solutions. To run from crisis-to-crisis is also a good way to obscure the root causes of the crises and the responsible parties who have the power to make changes. In contrast, a comprehensive view leads to three conclusions. First, the crises are the result of systematic institutional-level decisions and actions. Widespread neglect and contempt from enough decision-makers in government and the private sector have produced the decline in Black life and community we are now experiencing. The riots in the 1960s were in response to just this sort of strategic neglect (Kerner 1968). Second, past discrimination set the stage for displacing large numbers of Blacks from a changing national economy which is now phasing out labor-intensive functions. In addition, the demographic structure of the Black community—the large number of young people approaching the age of employment—is aggravating an already desperate situation (Wilson 1987). This means that, a league of current decision-makers, such as teachers, businessmen, bankers and others, are in no way directly responsible for the Black condition due to the effects of past racial discrimination. Or finally, Black people, and Black youth in particular, have simply gone mad and want to destroy themselves. It's plausible that any one or two of these crises may be a result of some failing of an institution or of the victim himself—dependency on welfare; ignorance of drug addictiveness; lack of morals, role models, orientation to the future, work ethic; unrealistic expectations; lack of knowledge of study skills and contraception. But it is implausible that multiple, simultaneous, on-going and related crises are happening without considerable involvement and reinforcement from many institutions in and outside of the Black community.

A Different View

A comprehensive view of all the crises shows the extent to which the entire Black community and Black presence are under siege—people, institutions, traditions, resources and values. It is my contention that the conditions that have drawn Black young people in as agents of self-destruction were created by government neglect, by intentional private sector policies to disassociate itself from Blacks and the poor, and by crime organizations—drug traffickers—which are covertly supplied and sanctioned by the federal government. Our government officials decry drug addicts and traffickers, yet the Central Intelligence Agency has been a major player in domestic drug trafficking for some time

(Kunnes 1972). But neither the siege on Black life nor its special effect on young Black men are new. What is new is the effectiveness of the current assault. Although, the immense cruelty of American slavery is a given, but in one sense it may have been less destructive than the present because at least then we knew the cause of our deprivation and could see who was really responsible. That is not the case today. In 1834, a ten-year-old wrote:

> Dear Sir: This is to inform you that I have two cousins in slavery who are entitled to their freedom. They have done everything that the will requires and now they [owners and overseers] won't let them go. They talk of selling them down the river. If this were your case, what would you do? Please give me your advice (Aptheker 1970, 116).

During slavery it was clear that slavery and racial discrimination were at the root of Black family separation, poverty, lack of education and confinement in northern cities. Under these circumstances, the education and parenting of young people could not be taken for granted. Then, parents had a purpose and a goal. But today it is no longer clear what it is that we are struggling against. Each problem and the people caught up in that problem are presented as if they are solely responsible for perpetuating their own deprivation. Furthermore, the community has no apparent purpose or reason for hopefulness. This context for our present situation was developing at the turn of the century. Freedom from slavery brought with it a new basis of subordination where the mechanisms of control became indirect and no group of people were visibly responsible. Even then, Black men were particularly marginal to this new system. In 1899 W.E.B. Du Bois pointed out that Black women outnumbered men in Philadelphia's Seventh Ward. He explained:

> There were a considerable number of omissions [in the community survey] among the loafers and criminals without homes, the class of lodgers and the club-

> house habitues. These were mostly males . . . (Du Bois 1899,64).

Du Bois went on to suggest that if these men had been included in the population count, they would still not outnumber women. Furthermore, an incredible 41% of the men living in the Seventh Ward were never married or divorced. Du Bois also gave us some sense of the plight of their children and families. Nine percent of Seventh Ward families were considered "very poor" and needed public assistance in order to live. In addition, "there were a number of persons who from time to time must receive temporary aid, but can usually get on without it. In time of stress as during the year 1893 [depression] this class was very large." Furthermore, the Black children who came to the attention of the Children's Aid Society were delinquents, deserted babies, orphans, half-orphans (due to their mother's delicate health, "worthless" fathers or the "worthlessness" of both parents), from the almshouse (abandoned), abused and "from [the] county poor boards" (Du Bois 1899,273). Du Bois's observations in 1899 could describe in 1988 the particular crises of Black families, children and males—the crisis of the entire community.

But there were major differences between then and now. Du Bois was very clear on the basis of the causes and from where solutions would have to come. He warned against viewing the "Negro Problem" as single issues without reference to one another or as hopelessly complex. At the heart of the new Black condition was the nation's unwillingness to grant them the same humanity which was begrudgingly extended to European immigrants. He wrote:

> The difference is that the ancestors of the English and the Irish and the Italians were felt to be worth educating, helping and guiding because they were men and brothers, while in America any census which gives a slight indication of the utter disappearance of the American Negro from the earth is greeted with ill-concealed delight (Du Bois 1899,389).

Nineteenth century humanity was not something to be granted Black people. Du Bois asserted that any solution to the modern social problems of the ex-slaves would require Blacks to focus on self-improvement and Whites to broaden "the narrow opportunities afforded Negroes for earning a decent living (Du Bois 1899,389)." In addition, Whites would have to examine their opinions. Blacks are not inferior as a people, but may appear so due to their conditions. Since Du Bois's classic study, two generations of scholars, teachers, social workers, newspaper writers and leaders have given testimony to the continuing Black condition of economic and social ghettoization. Until this decade, there was a consensus regarding the causes of these conditions based on fact, not ideology. The facts were that discrimination in the workplace and Whites' belief in Black inferiority were primary factors in maintaining the Black condition. A thirty-year-old male drug addict is quoted in the prologue to Kenneth Clark's *Dark Ghetto* (1964,1):

> You know the average young person out here don't have a job, man, they don't have anything to do. They don't have any alternative, you know, but to go out there and try to make a living for themselves. Like when you come down to the Tombs [jail] . . . they're down there for robbing and breaking in. They want to know why you did it and where you live, but you have to live. You go down to the employment agency and you can't get a job. They have you waiting all day, but you can't get a job. They don't have a job for you. Yet you have to live. I'm ready to do anything anyone else is ready to do—because I want to live—I want to live. No one wants to die. I want to live.

This testimony, given over twenty-five years ago, is still true today. The context for our problems is the same today as it was at the turn of the century. A "ghetto" is still more than a physical place. It is a psychology and formula for indirect control. Perceive and treat an entire class of people as inferior, confine them with one another, cut enough of them off from meaningful participation in the economy and from the means of survival, and more than a few individuals will come to self-destructive behavior. The root causes are the same as those identified by Du Bois almost one hundred years ago—narrowed opportunities by neglect and discrimination and by a continuing belief in Black inferiority.*

But if this condition is not enough to destroy a people, the desperation and neglect are now being exploited by an underworld of drug trafficking which has created an alternative economy out of Black genocide. The U.S. government is not as benign and innocent as the current administration claims.

The context of whatever solutions are to be developed since Du Bois's study has not changed either. As Du Bois pointed out it will require black efforts toward "self-improvement," a real broadening of opportunities, and a fundamental change in Whites' beliefs. But now it will also require an end to the strangle-hold the covertly sanctioned drug trafficking has over black communities. While the Black condition has gotten worse with predictable outcomes, the most crucial change is in the absence of any comprehensive view of the various crises. The present may be the first time since the end of slavery that there is no overall consensus among Blacks on the causes of their conditions, its solutions and the parties who are responsible. There lies the real crisis.

A Focus on Young Black Men

Whatever is going on in Black communities today is taking a special toll on young Black men. When compared to young Black women or to White youth, young Black men

---

* Recent public opinion surveys indicate that white beliefs in black inferiority have declined. See Sniderman and Tetlock, 1986. But somehow a softening in belief has not changed basic behaviors. Possibly, the general public is more sensitive to expressed racism but has not changed its fundamental beliefs?

are overrepresented among academic underachievers, school dropouts, men in jail and the unemployed. When compared to any other group, Black males murder and are murdered more frequently, are more commonly involved in drug abuse and are sexually more active with predictable consequences. This is only a partial list of the problems. Young Black men are heavily involved in most of the crises threatening Black life. There is an obvious need to better understand what is going on with this group and why. But given the vast and crisis-oriented attention to young Black men, how they are viewed is equally as important as why their behavior is so destructive.

There is a need to give a new and hard look at young Black men within their community context and not as a social problem. What they become and what they do is intimately related to what happens to them in schools, in their immediate community and in the worlds beyond their community. Young Black men or any other group cannot be abstracted from their social context—to do so is to deny their humanity. To look at young Black men in social context is a way to better understand them as well as the conditions that are now shaping the Black experience in the U.S. In studying this one group in their social context, we also contribute to the more comprehensive view which Du Bois advocated. This is not to say that by omission other groups of Blacks—women, older men and children—are less important. There is also a great need for new work which focuses on them in their social context as well.

Research focusing on young Black men in community context might uncover insights on the particular character of contemporary racial dominance. The mechanisms of control and the way in which current inequality is maintained are directed at young Black men in particular. The reader has a lot of material to draw on in the social and behavioral sciences as well as in the popular press. But the vast majority of these articles and books take the social problems and crisis perspective. The reader rarely gets a sense that behind the stories or studies there are real people who are conscious, who make choices and whose circumstances are conditioned. Most of what is communicated to us about young Black men is also victim centered—some deficiency within the group is the cause of their destructive behavior and repairing that deficiency is the solution (Ryan 1976). It is the objective of this collection of essays to depart from victim and crisis centered thinking. These conventional perspectives do not define the problems and causes, nor do they lead to viable, long-term solutions. To view the crisis of Black youth from within the community and from the young people themselves is to study "the crisis" in social context. It is my belief that such an approach is consistent with the pre-World War II studies of Negro youth and is a more fruitful line of investigation.

References

Aptheker, H. 1970. *And Why Not Every Man?* New York: International Publishers.

Clark, K. 1965. *Dark Ghetto.* New York: Harper and Row.

Du Bois, W.E.B. 1967. *The Philadelphia Negro.* New York: Schocken Books (1899).

Gibbs, J. et al. (eds.). 1988. *Young, Black and Male in America.* Dover, MAn: Auburn House Publishing.

Hare, N. and J. Hare. 1984. *The Endangered Black Family.* Oakland: Black Male-Female Relationships Books.

Kerner, O. 1968. *Report of the National Advisory Commission on Civil Disorders.* New York: Bantam Books.

Kunjufu, J. 1984. *Countering The Conspiracy to Destroy Black Boys.* Chicago: Afro-American Publishing Company.

Kunnes, R. 1972. *The American Heroin Empire: Power, Profits and Politics.* New York: Dodd, Mead and Company.

McAdoo, H. and J. McAdoo. (eds.). 1985. *Black Children.* Beverly Hills: Sage Publications.

McAdoo, H. (ed.) 1981. *Black Families.* Beverly Hills: Sage Publications.

Ryan, W. 1976. *Blaming the Victim.* New York: Vantage Books.

Sniderman, P. and P. Tetlock. 1986. "Symbolic Racism: Problems of Motive Attrition in Political Analysis," *Journal of Social Issues*, 42(2), 129-150.

Wilson, W. 1987. *The Truly Disadvantaged.* Chicago: The University of Chicago Press.
Yette, S. 1971. *The Choice: The Issue of Black Survival in America.* New York: Putnam.

About this Book

Benjamin P. Bowser

This edited work did not begin over conversation at a faculty club nor did it come from foundation support. During the fall of 1987 a small group of Black professional men began meeting at De Anza College in Cupertino, California, to discuss what we could do as a group to more effectively address the issues facing Black youth and families. All of us were deeply involved in black communities across the San Francisco Bay Area. Most of us also had teenage sons. The issues that concerned us were not simply "out there" in the community or a subject for research. We were dealing with these issues at home as well.

Our relatively fortunate circumstances did not exempt us from struggling to educate our sons to be successful in school and to value themselves, their heritage and their community. Parenting Black sons is more than an afterthought. It is a hard uphill struggle against adversaries who would have Black young people be smaller persons and play smaller roles than they are capable of. When those of us who met were young men, lesser places had been also assigned for us in the minds of teachers and others who mattered. Our parents had the same struggle as we have today with our sons to make more of ourselves than what we and others thought we could be. Despite all the history which has happened between our youth and our sons', the fundamental experience has changed little.

Our meetings led to conversations with other Black parents and, for those of us at universities, to extensive library research. It soon became clear to us that there was virtually no written record of the struggle we and other parents were experiencing in raising young Black men. Adolescence is the most critical period in educating and parenting. A parent can do it all perfectly prior to these years and still find themselves struggling to have a say among the many new voices telling their son who he is and what he can and cannot be. Our first conference was held in May 1987 on "The Education and Parenting of Black Male Adolescents." The conference was a great success in both attendance and seriousness of purpose. Parents, service providers, teachers, school officials and others who had simply heard of the conference came from all over the Bay Area. Most of the papers in this collection began as presentations at that conference. It was clear to us from the beginning that the work which came to the conference was far too valuable to be left as conference proceedings.

The most important related works are Harriette and John McAdoo (eds.) *Black Children* (1985); Harriette McAdoo (ed.) *Black Families* (1981); Kerby Alvy's *Black Parenting* (1987); Jewelle T. Gibbs et al. (eds.) *Young, Black and Male in America* (1988) and Reginald L. Jones (ed.) *Black Adolescents* (1989). The McAdoos' works are important because they bring together current research on Black family and children. The Alvy work documents the need for and issues in Black parent training. The Gibbs' reader is a thorough reader of the social indicators of Black male status and the Jones essays are an equally thorough review and discussion of the psychosocial dimensions of Black adolescence. All five works are written primarily from a researcher's point of view. Black parents and teen sons are the subjects of investigation. But current research does not tell the whole story. What is clearly needed are ways to discuss the social contexts of parent and teen experiences. This need does not separate research from practice and experience. Instead research can draw on both. Praxis— combining research and practice— would also mean giving both parents and teens a voice by viewing their experiences as meaningful and legitimate. Finally, wherever possible, our objective is to provide parents with guidance based on successful practice.

The Authors and Chapters

In order to reflect both practice and research, it was necessary to assemble a group of writers who cut across all segments of the Black community. They had to have experience as well as knowledge about young Black men. Insight would have to come from university and community-based researchers, counselors, activists and creative artists who know and work with Black teens. We were fortunate enough to get such a diverse group to contribute to this collection. Their challenge was to do work which showed young Black men in social context, to ground their work in both research and experience and, if appropriate, to be prescriptive. All except the Staples essay are original and unpublished. The first drafts of these papers were reviewed by three people: a university researcher who looked for academic soundness, a practitioner who looked for experience, and a parent who looked at the level of discourse and for prescription of action. Our authors were challenged. Several dropped out because the task of relating across experience and research boundaries was too demanding. They were replaced. The end results were second, third and fourth drafts. Consequently, there are insights, excitement, potential controversy and new ideas in these chapters.

In the first section, "Up Against The Odds," Robert Staples begins this collection by focusing on the effects of the new "Jim Crow" on the Black community and Black men. The destruction of Black communities and the desperation evidenced in self-destructive behaviors are the consequence of large numbers of Black people being pushed to the margins of the economy. Walter Stafford extends Staples' discussion by outlining the process by which young Black and Hispanic males are sorted and tracked away from opportunities to meaningfully participate in the economy. This is not some impersonal demographic or economic development. What he describes is the "northern" cousin of Jim Crow who has proven to be an even more effective oppressor. In the face of the structural conditions outlined by Staples and Stafford, there are prominent social analysts who do not take the internal strengths and resources of the Black community into consideration in efforts to reverse the tide of self-destruction (Wilson 1987). In the third essay in Section One, Hardy Frye suggests that those who take this view are out of touch with Black communities. Very slowly our communities are beginning to organize and assert themselves. We are in the early stages of a new movement of Black self-assertion. In our darkest hours Black people have the remarkable ability to counter the odds.

The new social system that sorts Black men out of opportunities to participate in the economy has a direct impact on young Black men. To be an "outsider" looking in affects self-identity. Young Black men have no illustrations about how the world of work and opportunity see them. In the final essay in Section One, Anthony Lemelle looks at the world from how young lower-class Black men see it. After years of "assumed criminality" a culture of resistance has developed where they seek to authenticate their experiences. The mainstream denies them opportunities, expects them to be trouble and then punishes them for both resisting and becoming what they are expected to be.

Section Two is devoted to parenting. Grace Massey provides us with a description of Black unwed fathers from the eyes of the young women who have had their children. From the mothers' point of view, these young men turn out to be very different from the conventional portrayal. In prior times, these young men would have certainly formed families. The current main barrier to their exercising greater responsibility is the lack of real opportunity to form and support a family. In the second essay, Joyce King and Carolyn Mitchell have written original and ground-breaking material. They have done social scientific analysis of mother-son interaction by using Black literature, working from an Afrocentric perspective. The result is revealing about the socialization of sons and the inner struggle that Black mothers face in rearing their sons. This chapter is also a significant methodological contribution and challenge to future research.

In the third chapter of *Parenting*, one of the deans of the Black theatre, Loften Mitchell, writes from personal experience about an important black tradition that has been lost. The Black community used to be an "extended parent" in the rearing of young men. Mitchell's essay explores what older Black people remember about their life in the community and contrasts their memories with the present. But here again, those like Loften Mitchell who are close to the community have surprises. The tradition of community co-rearing is not completely gone and might very well be renewable.

Section Three is on education. In research done specifically for this collection, Bowser and Perkins organized in-depth focus groups with academically successful Black and Hispanic teens. We let the young people tell us their experiences and what factors contributed to their success. There is a lot of information on why Black teens fail, but there is very little on how and why they succeed. Again the reader will find surprises. What these young people reported is absolutely consistent with Lemelle and Stafford's earlier essays. But academic education is not enough. There are two things all Black parents are very concerned with— their children's values and motivation. Lawford Goddard outlines his experience in developing a training program that addresses both concerns. Goddard's work is very much in the tradition articulated by the father of the Afro-American movement, Carter G. Woodson. Black parents and community have to assert their right and the necessity to define their own values and then educate their young people in these values. This is not only an issue of self-determination. It is also one of making demands on school systems and the government for resources. Anything less will maintain the kind of chaos we now have.

Next Robert and Mindy Fullilove talk frankly about the potential collision course young Black males are on with AIDS. Young Black men's sexual attitudes and practices will have to be altered quickly if yet another and potentially more lethal form of destruction does not overtake them. The final education chapter outlines an alternative form of education which some Black parents may have to give serious consideration to. Omonike and Muata Weusi-Puryear have educated their sons at home. They have been able to exercise greater influence and have minimized the destructiveness of the expected "sorting and tracking" of young Black men. But in order for this alternative to work, it requires a total commitment to an alternative life-style. There is much here from which all parents can learn whether they choose to educate their children at home or not.

In the final section the focus is on the important issue of identity. What every author in this collection would agree on is that virtually every aspect of the stigmatization, sorting and tracking of young Black men requires a successful assault on their self-concept. The assault occurs at all levels of schooling and then on into the world of work. Fay McNair-Knox looks into the language that Black young are creating and evolving. Listen carefully and they will tell you in their own words about their inner life— what they are concerned about, what they fear and who they think they are. One of the very best sources of insight and knowledge about our young people is right in front of us if we will listen. Tee Sweet sketches us a picture of young Black men who have attained success in education and at work, but at a price— their identity. She very carefully traces the willingness of these young men to abandon their identity to the informal expectations of their employment and, surprisingly, of their families.

In the third essay by Ronald Hudson, the same issues are explored based on his long experience in counseling Black male high achievers. Then psychoanalyst James Moss carefully outlines the complexities and varied impacts of powerlessness on the Black male's sense of self. He presents an important new model for conceptualizing the relation between identity and social power. These are important essays because they explore the psychological effects of an oppression which is benign, covert, elusive and takes its toll at all levels. There is something concerned parents and educators can do. In the last essay in this section, Daphne Muse discusses the importance of using Black literature to counteract the stereotypes and subtle destructiveness young Black teens experience in everyday life. She also provides an excellent bibliography of materials which can entertain as well as authenticate a Black male's self-worth. Finally, Peter Harris, the editor of *Genetic Dancers*, the only magazine in the U.S. devoted to Black fathers, gives a passionate plea for action, renewal and hope.

In the concluding essay, I provide an overview of our authors' work and briefly discuss the implications of their insights, research and experiences. As the editor of this collection it was a privilege to work with such talented and committed people. Most of these articles were written while the authors maintained crushing personal and professional obligations. This work was produced from virtually no resources other than commitment and care. Each of these chapters is a work of love and a call to all of us to come together and work toward a better future for all of our children and the coming generations.

Section One:

UP AGAINST THE ODDS

IN THE FIRST ESSAY OF THIS SECTION, Robert Staples focuses on the social structure that has created the condition under which young Black men are struggling. Walter Stafford continues Robert Staples' line of investigation by describing the strategies used to sort young Black and Hispanic men out and separate them from opportunities for social and economic participation in American Society. In the third essay, Anthony Lemelle looks at the circumstance described by Staples and Stafford from the eyes of young Black men. What he shows to us is the culture of resistance these young people have developed in order to survive and maintain their sense of personal worth. In the final essay, Hardy Frye calls to our attention evidence that Black communities are beginning to fighting back and that we may be on the threshold of a new movement for organized resistance against the new barriers and self-destructive behaviors.

Chapter 1

Black Male Genocide: A Final Solution to the Race Problem in America

Robert Staples

THROUGHOUT THE AGES, philosophers have wrestled with the concept of reality, how we construct it out of our own experiences and location in a particular society. When these perceptions of reality collide, that conflict often derives from the interests a group has in the definition of social reality. At no time has there been such a gap in the interpretation of the Black situation as in the 1980s. Despite current and increasing Black deprivation, a noted white economist seriously wrote, "The greatest irony of Reaganomics is that its most vociferous opposition has come from the two groups—women and Blacks—who have benefited most from its policies" (Brookes 1986). After citing figures which ostensibly show that since 1982, Blacks have far outstripped whites in employment gains, this economist claims that "the economic recovery of 1982-1986 has been mainly an 'affirmative action' job explosion, with white males badly trailing women and blacks, both male and female" (*ibid.*).

The Gallup Poll's 1987 survey on the community's treatment of Blacks shows that 64% of the nation's Whites believe Blacks are treated as well as Whites and three % say Blacks are treated badly. Conversely, 52% of Blacks say they are treated badly or not very well (Gallup 1987). The above survey did not measure the beliefs of a substantial number of Whites who think Blacks actually receive preferential treatment over Whites (Reichwein 1983). Since past years have revealed racial discrimination as the reason for the low status and discriminatory treatment of Blacks, it seems practically an absurdity for a majority of Whites to think that Blacks have achieved equity with Whites in the U.S. While all Blacks—men, women and children—are burdened by the persistence of institutional racism, the situation of Black men has especially deteriorated to the point of their being called an "endangered species."

Endangered Species?

Newsweek magazine began a cover story on Black men with this statement: "Black men are six times as likely as white men to be murder victims. They are two and a half times as likely to be unemployed. They finish last in practically every socioeconomic measure from infant mortality to life expectancy . . . black men in America seem almost an endangered species" (Monroe 1987). *Time* magazine had largely reached the same conclusion when it wrote, "Perhaps as much as 50% of young black males in certain cities still find themselves cut off from the American mainstream. Unemployed and undereducated, they seem unable and in some cases unwilling to fit into the broader society" ("New Generation" 1986).

If the White-controlled news magazines can make such apocalyptic claims about the status of Black men in America, the alarm in the Black community is considerably greater. According to Reverend Floyd Rose, a former president of the Toledo Chapter of the NAACP, "We have lost our children. When they get to high school age they are not in school, and they are not in jobs; they are on the streets. By the year 2000 it is estimated that 70% of all black men will be in jail, dead or on drugs or in the throes of alcoholism" (Herbers 1987).

Echoing the same concern, a Black newspaper columnist quotes a Black medical doctor as saying:

> Judging by today's statistics, unless a cure is found for AIDS and unless black people stop taking drugs to the extent they are, we won't have to worry about integration or equality at all; we'll be extinct as a race in

less than a century. We won't be around to celebrate the 200th anniversary of our own emancipation (Robertson 1987).

The statistics, as dismal as they are, would seem to substantiate both of the above statements. Among the problems confronting Black men in the 1980s:

1. While Black men account for only six % of the population in the U.S., they make up half of its male prisoners in local, state and federal jails.
2. The majority of the 20,000 Americans killed in crime-related incidents each year are Black men.
3. Over 35% of all Black men in American cities are drug and alcohol abusers.
4. Eighteen % of Black males drop out of high school.
5. Twenty-five % of the victims of AIDS are Black men.
6. Over 50% of Black men under the age of 21 are unemployed.
7. Forty-five % of Black men between the ages of 16-62 are not in the labor force.
8. About 32% of Black men have income levels below the officially defined poverty level (Staples 1982).

While there is no shortage of theories to explain the aforementioned statistical trends, ranging from change in the economy to the breakdown of the Black family, two older theories seem most applicable to the understanding of what I will call Black male genocide. One of these explanations lies in W.E.B. Du Bois's prediction in 1902 that the problem of the twentieth century would be the color line (1961). A combination of social and cultural forces have brought about a social movement for domestic Black liberation and in the international world for wars of national liberation in Africa, Asia, Latin America and the Caribbean islands. These liberation movements are in response to two centuries of European economic and political exploitation. The most recent development in this context has been the internationalization of the world's labor force which has resulted in domestic job flight.

White Misconceptions

The second explanation for Black decline was articulated by Samuel Yette in his book, *The Choice.* Yette predicted a choice between accommodation and extinction for the Black population of the U.S. His prediction of genocide for the entire Black population diverges slightly from current trends, in that it is Black men who are most vulnerable to the ravages of an unbridled and dying American capitalism. For most Black men accommodation is simply no longer an option.

The statistics on Black male progress belie the racial millennium perceived by a majority of the nation's Whites. What accounts for this dichotomy in the two races' perceptions of the status of Black Americans? First, the development of a substantial and highly visible Black middle class has led many whites to generalize about Black "progress." On the basis of that premise, it is easy to reject the notion that there are any serious barriers to Black achievement. Present inequities can be rationalized as reflecting the pathologies of the Black underclass and no longer the fault of individual Whites or White-controlled institutions.

Secondly, the White male has experienced some downward mobility from his former monopoly on all high-paying jobs in U.S. society. Between 1979 and 1983, five million families headed by White males were added to the poverty rolls for much the same reasons that Black males dropped out of the labor force (Harrington 1987). The bulk of the new and lower-paying jobs created in the 1980s went to women and the international labor force. Yet, to a White working-class person indoctrinated with racism, the natural tendency is to scapegoat Blacks as a source of all White problems. A member of the Ku Klux Klan noted that there are more Klansmen from the North now than there are from the South. He asserts, "Basically, they're from Illinois and Michigan, the northern industrial states. Most of them have lost their jobs. They blame it on the blacks. I don't know how they tie it in" (Clendinen 1987).

Virulent Racist Attacks

The decline of industrial jobs and the shift to a service and information processing economy favored female workers, pushing the traditional labor of Black and White males out of the center of the economy. The Reagan administration cleverly manipulated a propaganda campaign, notably through inflammatory and erroneous statements from the late Clarence Pendleton and Edwin Meese, to convince White workers that they were being discriminated against in favor of Blacks. But this campaign runs deeper than Reagan. The Black liberation movement was quieted by the imprisonment, assassination or co-optation of its leaders. Attempts at racial equality have been successfully channeled into more easily controlled institutional forms (such as Black politics and capitalism). By default segments of the conservative White ruling class have gained the ideological initiative. The ruling class shifted the ideological focus to issues of reverse racism and the victim's culpability for his own plight, diverting attention away from challenges to racism and capitalism.

Research studies and official pronouncements all encouraged the perception that the pathology of the Black underclass—unemployment, crime, welfare dependency, family dissolution, the breakdown of societal values—is attributable to Blacks, not poverty. Not only are the victims of racism blamed for their poverty, White society projects social pathology on all Black men and singles them out as indolent, violent and irresponsible. In reality, the negative behavior of Black males is the specific consequence of their powerlessness and economic isolation. The result of this campaign has been an outpouring of violence against Black men by working-class White males. There has been a plethora of racial incidents beginning with the shooting of four unarmed male youth in New York City by Bernhard Goetz. These include:

- The beating of three Black men by Whites in the Howard Beach section of Queens, New York, which led to the death of one of the victims.

- The order by a Louisiana sheriff that Blacks passing through White neighborhoods be routinely stopped;
- The hazing of a Black cadet at the Citadel Military Academy; and
- The taunting of Blacks in marches at the time of Martin Luther King's holiday in 1987 (Gallup 1987).

The racial climate created by Ronald Reagan and his minions has led to an unprecedented number of attacks on Blacks in White neighborhoods, college campuses and public streets. Racial slurs by public officials are becoming commonplace, lending some observers to claim, "It looks like open season on Blacks" (Marable 1987).

Economic Transition

What underlies white desperation and willingness to listen to conservative nonsense are major changes in the economy. In the post-World War II era, the role of non-white nations has largely become that of reserve labor supply. Now entire industries have been abandoned in the U.S. and passed over to the Third World—notably auto, steel, textiles, shoes and assembly work. Jobs in U.S. corporations are exported to Third World nations in the Pacific Rim and Caribbean. This movement of jobs has impoverished the domestic White and Black working classes.

The movement of domestic jobs overseas has not enriched the Third World. Since World War II, the U.S. and some of its European allies have been busily engaged in maintaining non-white nations in a semi-colonial status. Exporting jobs to them helps to maintain their dependency, not to mention exploiting their cheap labor. In addition, the U.S. and its allies have intervened in two wars of national liberation, Korea and Vietnam, in order to prop up American puppet states. Additionally, they have supported oligarchies in Latin-American and Pacific Rim countries that have developed internal resistance movements and created massive dislocations of indigenous populations. This has happened in Cuba, Nicaragua, Chile, Haiti, Panama, the Philippines and now Burma.

In reality what has happened in the last decade has been the enrichment of the wealthy and the impoverishment of lower-income groups. Only the upper class in this country has really benefited from the internationalization of domestic jobs and industries. The income of the richest one-fifth of families increased by 14% in the last six years, while the poorest one-fifth of American families had their share of the total income of all families reduced by one-third (Ehrenreich 1986). It is apparent that most Blacks are concentrated in the poorest one-fifth of all families, and the upper one-fifth is overwhelmingly White. Income, however, is not the only measure of the racial difference in wealth. When accumulated assets that can be converted into cash, such as stocks, bonds and property, are included, the median wealth of White households is twelve times that of Black households (O'Hare 1986). Although average income and poverty rates can be useful, they actually overstate the gains made by Blacks and disguise the fact that 99% of the wealth in the U.S. is held by a relatively small group of Whites.

Additional Consequences

Economic internationalization and support for repressive foreign governments have given impetus to successive waves of immigration to the U.S. by collaborators in the colonial effort, such as Filipinos, Vietnamese, Cambodians, Cubans, Nicaraguans, Salvadoreans and Chileans. Other immigrants are fleeing war-torn conditions of their countries and the harsh economic climate created by American-supported dictators in Third World nations. These immigrants often take menial and low-paying jobs traditionally held by Black Americans. Immigrants typically take the lowest paying jobs as more established ethnic groups move up the economic ladder. After 400 years, Black males have not moved up in large numbers and find themselves locked into the bottom of the socioeconomic scale, now by the latest group of immigrants. While the victims and collaborators of American imperialism replace Black male workers in the

U.S., American capital chases the cheapest labor. Also, exporting jobs to friendly Third World dictatorships serves a variety of purposes. The most important purpose is that it has created a cheap pool of labor within U.S. puppet states such as the Philippines, Haiti, Mexico and Taiwan, labor that can be exploited by multinational corporations. American workers, after all, earn a guaranteed minimum wage, insist on occupational safety rules, and belong to labor unions that call strikes to protest oppressive working conditions.

Third World Workers

Workers in impoverished and debt-ridden Third World nations consider themselves lucky to acquire jobs at seventy cents per hour in unregulated plants. In such plants output quotas are often increased, hours lengthened, wages reduced, industrial pollutants ignored, and nascent dissidents fired. If workers organize to protest such conditions, the army may be used to intimidate or terrorize them. This increasing practice of exporting jobs abroad provides graphic evidence to counter the notion that capitalism creates jobs for its native labor force. Despite the growing problems of a displaced Black male labor force, the image inculcated in White consciousness is that Blacks have succeeded in American society. Certainly the symbols and role models of Black male success are abundant at the top levels of society, with Black male presidential candidates, mayors of large cities, astronauts, sports heroes, highly paid entertainers and more. To the unenlightened White public, no more evidence is needed that the American dream applies to everybody willing to play by the rules and work hard.

The reality of Black male achievement in the U.S. is that with the exception of entertainers and athletes, most black males in successful positions are examples of the most egregious tokenism and possess little power that cannot be vetoed by a White male in a superior position. As Theodore Cross has noted:

> Almost without exception, black people in the United States are born into a state of powerlessness. Even when their professional, management, or business attainments are very great, individual blacks are seldom in a position where they are feared, obeyed, or greatly respected by whites (Cross 1984).

Economic Disenfranchisement

Beginning with economic power, Black men are disenfranchised in the capitalists' own arena. Black businesses, largely owned by males, take in less than one % of all U.S. business revenues. For those who hope to make it to the upper echelons of the White corporate world, the statistics reflect the scant chances of their succeeding. Among senior executives of the nation's 1,000 largest companies there are four Black males. Even the comparatively conservative group of Blacks holding Master of Business Administration (M.B.A.) degrees attributes the Reagan administration's attacks on affirmative action as a major reason for that low number. In one survey, 40% of Black M.B.A.'s felt their company was reluctant to accept Blacks, and 41% believed their company was patronizing to them.

Other surveys indicate their feelings have validity. A report revealed that not only are Blacks underrepresented at senior corporate levels, they have lost ground within the past seven years. One corporate manager summed up the situation nicely with this assessment:

> Chief executives aren't picked because they have fifteen years of this experience, ten years of that. They're picked to fit into the group that's already there. And, just as it was twenty years ago, that group is primarily white and male ("Wall Street" 1986).

The paucity of Black male executives is so pervasive that they play by rules peculiar to Black men in a White world. Generally those rules are: (1) Do not question the impact of the company policy on the recruitment and advancement of racial minorities and women; (2) Insist that your company demands only hard work and competency for upward mobility; (3) Question the competency of Blacks who have not made the normal progression to the higher ranks of management; and (4) Avoid any intimate associations with White female employees.

Political Arena

Not only has playing by these unwritten rules failed to elicit the expected rewards for Blacks in the corporate world, it has not worked very well in the political arena either. One such attempt was that of William Lucas to become the nation's first elected Black governor in Michigan. Running as a Republican who supported conventional Republican policies, Lucas only attracted 23% of the overwhelmingly Democratic Black vote and 30% of the White vote. A post-election analysis indicated that 30% of the White Republicans crossed party lines to vote against Lucas. As a political researcher summed it up, "Republicans didn't take into consideration that there are two sides to a racial question. Blacks voted their party and their interests. The Blacks didn't fall for it (racial manipulation), and the whites voted by race. They voted for the White male" (Tyson 1986).

The hypocrisy of the White position that achievement should be based on merit is the fact that it entraps Blacks into playing by formal rules while Whites often employ informal methods for getting ahead. Whites can use intra-company social and business relationships with White peers and superiors to gain advancement in their companies, whereas Blacks rely heavily on educational credentials and performance of their job descriptions to attain the same and more elusive goal.

Alternative Economy

A final consequence of the economic transition and Black disenfranchisement is the formation of an alternative economy. According to a U.S. census report, 54% of Black males, 18-29 years old, are living with their parents (Glick and Lin 1986). Some of them may find temporary shelter with a Black woman who is eligible for public assistance (if no adult male is living with her). Apart from these two options, all that is left is homelessness and public begging or participation in the underground economy. Increasingly, the sale of drugs to alienated and powerless young Black men has produced an alternative economy which can provide high wages and self-esteem to young men denied both in mainstream America. With the lack of equally successful role models in the inner city, drug dealers often become heroes to ghetto youth.

A combination of miseducation and drug trafficking alone threatens to institutionally decimate much of the Black male population. The public schools fail to provide them with marketable skills in today's economy. Increasing competition among a variety of cultural groups for the scarce jobs available places Black males among the most vulnerable groups to unemployment. For those with no job, hence no legitimate income, the commission of street crimes can lead to a lifelong career of crime and occasional imprisonment. Those who survive by other means are still left with nothing meaningful to do in a society where money and work define masculinity. For many, self-destructive behavior will be the order of the day. These same men will instead define their masculinity by siring children they cannot support, and will defend their masculinity by violence.

Racial Images

Even in the 1980s racial images shape the Black male's access to upward mobility in the corporate structure. One Black male, a designer in a print shop in Chicago, requested to go out and work in sales for his company. His supervisor's response was:

You know, I really believe you could do some sales, and I'd like to work with you, but I think you're too big and too black, and you might intimidate our clients (Winfrey 1987).

Because the gap between aspirations and achievement is so great for even highly educated and some high-income Black males, racial membership becomes burdensome for all but those who deny that it still has some significance in American society. Studies have shown that higher income and status are not a shield against heart disease for blacks as they appear to be for whites ("Black Doctors" 1986).

Writing in *The New York Times Magazine*, former tennis superstar Arthur Ashe revealed:

> Early on I learned that white society would tolerate only so many of us in one group at any one time; only so many or none in some places—"nice Negro families" in a previously all-White suburban neighborhood; only so many in certain public schools; only so many in white colleges. When I got in any of these, I was supposed to feel lucky (Ashe 1986).

Ashe goes on to say that middle-income, professional Blacks pay a heavy price if they cling to the myth that success in America is independent of racial membership. Many of them, he observes, are barely able to tolerate the stress. Nearly all of them, he says, are hypertensive and many are visiting psychiatrists.

Black Entertainers

One of the greatest contributors to the Black success myth are Black entertainers. Because they are paid huge sums of money, are very visible, and highly publicized, they serve as role models for Blacks who seldom see or know of Black successes in other fields. They are also a major source of Black images for Whites, who are unlikely to know members of the Black underclass and come into contact mostly with the token Blacks placed in highly visible positions. In the three dominant media, television, movies, and music, Black males are extensively represented but limited in the roles they play. In both television and movies, Black males are confined to comedies or assigned roles as sexually neutered sidekicks to White male actors.

Black women have fared even worse. They are either absent or given a limited range of roles, such as a household servant (usually obese and sassy) or a degenerate prostitute. In the music world, Black male singers represent flamboyant and androgynous characters who could not possibly symbolize the sexual romantic fantasies of White female record buyers. For the 1980s, Black male media stars seem to have fallen into two character typologies. One is the larger-than-life caricatures such as Mr. T. and "the Refrigerator" (William Perry), who can be merchandised and not taken seriously by the White public. Their female counterparts would be Whoopi Goldberg and Oprah Winfrey. Even the brilliant and angry Black comedians such as Richard Pryor and Eddie Murphy have been reduced to playing stereotyped street-smart, ghetto males with little or no meaningful involvement with a girlfriend, wife or children.

The other type is the "safe" Black male, who represents no threat to the White supremacist system. The ultimate safe Black male image is exemplified by Bill Cosby on television's "The Cosby Show." Cosby has made major contributions to Black causes. Probably more Whites are exposed to him as a positive Black male model than anyone else in America. Yet, his television show portrays a Black family that is the epitome of Black middle-class success, contrary to the reality of the daily lives of most Black Americans. Perhaps because the program's Huxtable family is a paragon of family and economic stability, one has to question the reality of the characters at a time when a growing consensus is emerging that Black males are an endangered species. Certainly, Black male dominance in sports has to be a bright spot in an otherwise bleak picture. But a closer look reveals that while Black males are engaged in injury-producing sports that result in short, albeit lucrative careers. In contrast, Whites have equally lucrative and greater longevity in sports such as golf, tennis, and bowling that the more economically deprived black males seldom have the opportunity to play. Even the dominance and progress of Black men in the major sports (baseball, football, and basketball) are diminished by the persistence of racial discrimination in media treatment of Black athletes. There is also segregation in football positions and the lack of opportunities for Blacks as managers or in front office jobs in sports organizations. This last deficit was brought to public attention and controversy by a statement on a nationally televised program by Al Campanis, then-general manager of the Los Angeles Dodgers.

Despite the visibility of Blacks in baseball, Campanis said that Blacks lack the intellectual skills to be major league baseball managers and high level executives. While his statement implied acceptance of every stereotype about Blacks, praising their physical abilities and displaying contempt for their mental abilities, his comments only reflected the tip of an iceberg. As sports columnist Glenn Dickey observed:

> The color line has been broken on the field but it's still largely intact when it comes to managers and executives. There have been only three black managers. There are no black general managers. But that only hints at the problem, which is a system that virtually locks out blacks on all levels. At the top, the general manager hires people throughout the entire system. Whites hire whites. It's as simple as that (Dickey 1987).

Profits, Not Jobs

The Black male is blamed for his high rate of unemployment and underachievement because he has allegedly failed to prepare himself to compete in a technological society. It is estimated that as many as 44% of all Black males can be classified as functional illiterates, i.e., unable to read or comprehend complex written material (Kozol 1985). Such a high percentage of functional illiteracy begs the question of why the public school system allows that many males to reach the tenth grade or graduate without marketable reading and writing skills. Is this simply a nationwide coincidence or is it that these Black men are obsolete in a modern economy, and schools are only reflecting and justifying this fact? After all, many of the jobs they could perform have been exported to countries that will employ non-English speaking people who are functionally illiterate in their native language.

According to Clyde Taylor, a much lower level of literacy is needed for job performance in Third World countries than is demanded by the American occupational structure. Taylor cites evidence showing that in Third World countries, only mass education at the elementary level for 30-50% of the population is needed, far below the level of "functional illiteracy" now available in the United States (Taylor 1983). Other students of the subject have claimed that Black men have less incentive than White men to acquire an education since data show that the same amount of educational investment yields considerably less return in the form of superior occupational status or mobility to non-whites than to Whites.

Because the productive forces of U.S. capitalism are geared toward making products for profit, not social needs, the work that Black males could perform has a low priority among industrial leaders and marketeers. Even the federal government is directing its resources toward a massive military buildup that will drain much of the capital needed for the reindustrialization of America's manufacturing stock. As a result, Black males are selected out of the labor force by the educational credentials allegedly needed to compete for jobs in our technological society. The jobs they could do without the credentials, such as rebuilding the infrastructure of the U.S. (dams, bridges, highways, etc.) have been relegated to lower funding priorities than the building of sophisticated missiles and other objects of human destruction.

Under mature capitalism, the job most typically offered to uneducated and young Black males is that of the minimum wage security guard, an occupation that entails protecting the property and person of affluent Whites from other underclass Black males. The leaders of American society appear to have made the decision to spend a hundred billion dollars a year more for protection against the underclass rather than to educate and provide them with jobs.

White Settler Societies

This morbid situation in the U.S. is not unknown or unprecedented in the history of White settler societies. The American Indian is a prototype of a similar form of genocide in this country. Similar parallels can be found among the Maoris of New Zealand and the Aboriginals of Australia. All these groups had in common a forced coexistence in a white-dominated culture that had appropriated their land or their labor. Because their conformity to Anglo-Saxon demands could not be assured, American Indians, Maoris and Aboriginals were perceived as continuing threats to the existence of white rule. As the capacity of the economy to function without them developed, they became excess baggage and a competitive threat to the privileges of White males.

For many Black men, forced idleness and impotence have encouraged self-destruction created through the use of alcohol and drugs, fratricidal violence and suicide. The out-of-context criticism of this behavior itself by Black female authors like Michelle Wallace, Ntozaki Shange and Alice Walker is used by Whites to give further justification for Black male genocide. For the moment, capitalism in America has declined in its ability to provide the White male worker with the unchallenged monopoly he once had on the highest-paying jobs, best housing, education, women, etc. Now his overriding concern is to cling to his declining status and racial monopoly. Only in this way do unenlightened White male workers believe that they can maintain their privileged place in a changing world. The dominance they hope to acquire will be through voting for a president who ostensibly represents their interests. This means putting Blacks in their place by whatever means necessary—including higher education requirements for unskilled jobs and through promotion of Blacks on the basis of merit only.

Let us be clear, however, that an epitaph for all Black men is premature. Many of them remain valuable commodities to American capitalism. As athletes they are twentieth century gladiators without peers. In the entertainment world, they provide amusement and escape from reality for the White citizenry and role models for Blacks. Indeed, entertainment may become the opiate of the twenty-first century.

Alternatives to Genocide

If America is to avoid the specter of a nuclear holocaust, conventional warfare will require large numbers of Black males to fight its wars of containment against the oppressed masses of Asia and Latin America. Certain sectors of the economy will still require Black labor. Although new immigrants will accept lowpaying, dirty jobs when they first come to the United States, they will not be content to stay in those positions for 400 years as Black Americans have been forced to do. Thus, unless there is a constant flow of immigrants, the dirty work will still have to be done by men of color.

Another scenario is possible. The contradictions of world capitalism are reaching a crisis point, and its ability to use racism to divide workers is at the point of diminishing returns. Disenfranchised White farmers and steel-workers may discover their commonality with unemployed Black teenagers in Harlem. In this case, they may stop scapegoating Blacks.

Already the White jobless in Europe are experiencing poverty and economic dislocation because of the declining ability of capitalism to provide them decent jobs. Even the welfare state, or its measures, will be unable to pacify members of the working class who realize there is work to be done and wealth to be shared in a society not based on class rule.

But only the strange mixture of racism and sexism could have motivated American White workers to elect a President whose policy was to help the wealthy, claiming that the benefits would trickle down to the working class. The competition for jobs among Black and White and male and female workers may prolong the divisions in the working class somewhat longer than in Europe. But economic justice is an idea whose time must come. Black men may not only survive to participate in it. They may lead the struggle for it.

References

Ashe, A. 1986. "No More Zero-Sum Game." *The New York Times Magazine.* August 31, 26.
Brookes, W. 1986. "An Affirmative Action Explosion in Employment," *San Francisco Chronicle.* October 7.
Clendinen, D. 1987. "Behind the Hatred." *San Francisco Examiner and Chronicle.* February 8.
Cross, T. 1984. *The Black Power Imperative.* New York: Faulkner.
Dickey, G. 1987. "What's Sad Is That Many Think Like Campanis." *San Francisco Chronicle.* April 10.
Du Bois, W.E.B. 1961. *The Souls of Black Folks.* Greenwich, CT: Fawcett. (originally published 1902).
Ehrenreich, B. 1986. "Two Americas: Are We Becoming a Nation of Haves and Have-nots?" *San Francisco Examiner and Chronicle.* November 23.
Gallup, G., Jr. 1987. "How Blacks, Whites View Blacks Treatment." *San Francisco Chronicle.* February 19.
Glick, P. and S. Lin. 1986. "More Young Adults Are Living with Their Parents. Who Are They?" *Journal of Marriage and the Family.* 48; 107-112.
Harrington, M. 1987. "White, Male and Poor." *San Francisco Chronicle.* March 15.
Herbers, J. 1987. "More Blacks Slip Into Poverty." *San Francisco Chronicle.* January 28.
Jet. 1986. "Black Doctors Have High Rates of Heart Disease." April 13, 36.
Kozol, J. 1985. *Illiteracy In America.* New York: Morrow.
Los Angeles Sentinel. 1986. "Wall Street: Racism, Inc." September 4.
Marable, M. 1987. "Open Season on Blacks—Again." *Los Angeles Sentinel.* January 8.
Monroe, S. 1987. "Brothers." *Newsweek.* March 23, 55.
O'Hare, W. 1986. "Wealth Data Puts Black-White Gap in Sharp Focus." *Focus.* August, 4.
Reichwein, J. 1983. "Whites on Blacks: Opportunities Plentiful." *The National Leader.* February 17, 12.
Robertson, S. 1987. "Drugs, AIDS and Blacks: A Catastrophe." *Los Angeles Sentinel,* April 2.

Staples, R. 1982. *Black Masculinity: The Black Males Role in American Society*. San Francisco: Black Scholar Press.
Taylor, C. 1983. "The Politics of Illiteracy." *Institute for the Study of Educational Policy Monitor*. 7: 3-4.
Time. 1986. "New Generation of Native Sons." December 1, 34-35.
Tyson, R. 1986. "Lucas' Race was Factor in Margin, Analysts Say." *Detroit Free Press*. November 6.
Winfrey, O. 1987. "Prejudice Against Black Men." "Oprah Winfrey" Television. Air date: January 23.
Yette, S. 1971. *The Choice: The Issue of Black Survival in America*. New York: Putnam.

Chapter 2

Pushed Out of the Dream: Sorting-Out Black Males for Limited Economic Mobility

Walter Stafford

EACH GENERATION OF ADOLESCENTS is unique in the dilemmas and contradictions it presents to society and attempts to resolve. Adolescence is not only a chronological period for youth reaching adulthood. It is also a period in which adults attempt to determine if society's and their own expectations can and have been met through the ways in which young adults are socialized to take advantage of opportunities.

Adolescents mirror society's institutions and begin to see their own future: they have their clearest glimpse of the groups who will share, compete and support them in the future. In the past, the network of informal and formal rules and procedures for socialization and control have been sufficient to withstand past challenges. But in the 1980s and 1990s youth and adults are having to make more adjustments than in any past post-war decade. For now many adults look in the mirror and they see African-Americans, Latinos and Asian-Americans in their future. These are the fastest growing groups in the labor force that will make the ultimate choices about many of the benefits the present generation of adults hopes to enjoy.

The Issues

More than ever there are two major questions. First, what should be the proper balance of opportunities extended to these growing numbers of minorities? And how can these groups be controlled in the present and future? The ultimate issue is whether adult decision-makers and established interests want groups of color, especially young men of color, to participate in the very institutions that African-American, Hispanic and Asian fathers were excluded from. If the answer is "yes," how does one now socialize and also control these groups? How does one include groups which historically have been viewed with disdain and fear? If the answer is "no," how do you maintain control over the growing minority population and what resources will it take? What are the repercussions and strains of maintaining control for society? And how can the necessary innovations in social control be justified?

It could be argued that most systematic knowledge about African-American men in this country is focused on how society can control them and protect itself from them. In contrast, there is much less knowledge about increasing institutional opportunities. And for Blacks this knowledge is primarily in sports and is not transferable to other aspects of American life. Thus, for a broad change toward real opportunities to occur, most of the knowledge about institutional changes and African-American men needs to be altered. This is not immediately realistic. My hypothesis is that more likely society will utilize the professionals in the social welfare state to "claim" that they have a body of knowledge of how to deal with African-American men, in which case, the professions will become the primary agents of social control. Therefore, ideas and symbols of control will continue to outweigh alternative ideas of how to increase socialization for opportunities for social mobility in the near future.

The Shape of the New Institutional Adjustments

The adult White society and many African-Americans are already making choices about the balance between the opportunities to be extended and the necessity of controlling young African-American men. Each decade the percentage of African-American males who serve some time in prison increases (McGhee 1984). More prisons are being constructed than at any other time in U.S. history (Staples 1984,63). It is also clear that the economy will not present a wealth of "good job opportunities." Governmental and private job projections suggest that new and future jobs will earn primarily low rather than high wages (Mishel and Simon 1988). Contrary to the media's focus on labor shortages, planners are increasingly worried about the prospect that groups that have been traditionally excluded from the labor market will not be willing to accept future low-wage jobs (Costrell 1988; Levitan and Shapiro 1987).

This is a time of uneasy questions. However, the questioning does not mean that decisions are not being made. The historic belief that African-American men are to be controlled is now a virtual reflex. And this reflex continues to characterize decisions about the balance between making new opportunities possible and needing to control African-Americans. The difference now is in the nature of the political economy and the symbolic opportunities promoted by dominant interests.

The new procedures of control are administered through networks of private and public agencies which constitute the social welfare state. The emergence of the social welfare state and the end of state sponsored racial segregation has been accompanied by an important change. The stereotypes and symbols that were utilized to "justify" separation of the races prior to the end of de jure segregation have been transferred to symbols of "deviancy." The procedures for giving African-American men a status as America's primary "outsiders" is now controlled by professional experts. In essence a more sophisticated "sorting-out" process has emerged in the modern social welfare state. Instead of White mobs, police and southern landowners enforcing the de facto exclusion of African-American men from American life, this is now the job of "professionals."

The actual "sorting-out" process is not apparent to many African-Americans because of the pervasiveness of symbols of opportunity. The rise of the new social welfare arrangements and the globalization of the economy have been accompanied by the promotion of symbols of opportunity when very little real opportunity exists. The principles of equality and of open opportunity are being promoted as never before. The need to extensively promote these symbols is necessary in order to make it more difficult for advocates of African-Americans, and African-American men in particular, to make "claims" on the basis of racism.

The promotion of new symbols has meant that young African-American men have been reared with different myths than their fathers about their prospects in society. Unlike their fathers, they are not being reared with the myths of separate-but-equal. Theirs are the myths of opportunity. African-American parents now face a more difficult task because the myths of opportunity, when compared to reality, are much more difficult to explain. Moreover, the locus of control for interpreting Afro-American reality in many institutions has been removed from the Black community. Black people are now more reliant on interpretations by "experts" for their children's problems. More often, the interpretations of the experts are behavioral and emotional. The experts rarely look at social structure or the decisions of power brokers who create the conditions African-Americans have to cope with.

Generational Differences

The changes presented thus far are only a piece of the puzzle describing the new machinery of oppression. Consider some of the essential differences of this generation of young African-American men and those born in the 1940s:

- This is the first generation of African-American men who have not faced going to war. Clearly, no war has been a benefit for African-Americans and society. Vietnam left a scar on American history that will never be erased. The war was a major factor in compromising the vitality of African-American men who are now 35 to 42 years old—young men in the prior two decades.

Look at the experiences of prior generations of African-American men. Other questions about the symbols of equality have to be examined. African-American men have always been forced to raise questions about this nation's inequalities during and after periods of war. World Wars I and II and Vietnam provide ample historical examples.

- This is the first generation of African-American men that has not been a part of a collective demand for equality or equal rights. This generation of youth has increased its share of their age cohorts. However, they have very little apparent purpose and ideology and this is not their fault.

In prior decades there were political and collective mentoring processes that constantly centered on an end to separate but equal segregation, restrictions of voting and changes in power relationships. Young African-American men did not simply emerge untutored in the 1960s. They were the products of churches, black colleges and youth organizations.

The "racial" problems of the 1980s are not the same. Institutional racism is not readily identifiable for protests. Moreover, many of the civil rights groups which raised the problems of racism no longer exist. Indeed, there are few structural mechanisms for youth to get a perspective on the political inequities of the system. The family is now the only place to get race-conscious socialization. And most African-American parents are limited in their understanding of the differences between the myths of separate-but-equal and the myths of opportunity.

- This is the first generation that will not enjoy the benefits of separate Black educational and religious institutions which represented symbols of excellence for African-American men and symbolic exclusion for Whites. African-American men can be found and readily identified in many of the sectors where they had proven their excellence but were barred from in the prior generation. They are most notably present in sports, the dominant symbol of excellence of African-African men from which they were excluded until the 1940s and 1950s.

Another area of male symbolic exclusion that has changed is politics. African-American men are mayors of key cities in the nation and they are key symbols in the House of Representatives. Although their numbers are small in relationship to the total elected positions in the nation, the major transitions have been made.

The results of these changes in sports and politics are quite obvious. African-American men are dominant in sports at the collegiate and professional player levels and they can be pointed to in politics as symbols of progress. The key for this current generation is becoming the "transitionals" in areas less familiar to the public, such as in science, technology and management which require altering different types of "old boy networks"—those based on exclusionary access to knowledge.

- This is the first generation of African-American men that is probably at ease in interracial dating and friendships. Undoubtedly this reality affects only a small proportion of the community but it is significant.

This is the first generation since WW II that is likely to face downward economic mobility. There has been a shift in production centers from domestic U.S. localities to global markets. This shift has been accompanied by a decline in manufacturing and a rise in low-wage service jobs.

- These transitions in the economy have lowered the chances for African-American men to become upwardly mobile. Since the 1960s there has been an increase in the number of African-American men in their twenties who have dropped out of the labor market (U.S. Department of Commerce 1983). As a result, the real wages of young African-American men declined more than any other group during the last decade (U.S. Department of Commerce 1986).

At the same time, African-American men have not been

able to diversify their economic base in the expanding service economy. The net effect of these problems is that younger men have limited opportunities to earn high wages and find good jobs. Instead they find themselves competing with women and immigrants for the few available low-wage jobs.

A Conceptual Focus of the New Arrangements

In a recently completed study of the economic mobility of African-American and Puerto Rican men, I developed a framework for explaining the institutional factors which result in the exclusion of these groups. That framework describes the "sorting-out" of African-American and Puerto Rican men from alleged opportunities. The fact of continued and even deepening inequality for these groups is not new. But implicit in the concept of "sorting-out" is the manner in which American institutions have come to maintain racial inequality.

Simply stated, professionals and managers within institutions distinguish between groups based on the assumed interests of society at large. The "sorting-out" process encompasses stereotyping, labeling and stigmatization—the production of social deviance. This is done without a stated policy of class and judicial racial separation. Few would deny that stereotypes about African-American men are pervasive in almost every professional discipline and are ultimately reflected in discriminatory policy. In isolation, stereotypes can be muted, since they are often individually based. However, stereotypes also influence decisions about labeling which is collective action carried out and justified on the basis of professional expertise.

The decision to label occurs in response to the "deviant" actions or attributes of the designated out-groups. As Howard Becker notes, social groups create deviance by making the rules whose infractions constitute deviance (1963). The ability to label is in fact a reflection of the power to determine how a group will appear as well as how their behavior will be interpreted. If the out-group is negatively labeled and stereotyped on a continuous basis, it is unlikely that they will be extended opportunities for upward mobility or best positions in the mainstream. Exclusion from mobility and opportunity is further reinforced through stigmatization.

Sorting-Out in Institutions

In constructing this framework I have borrowed heavily from perspectives on labeling in criminology and mental health. In studies of both arrests and juvenile delinquency, labeling does influence decisions by officials (Smith et al. 1984). Because of the presumed criminality of African-American youth, other studies of arrests show that the police are often reacting to the demeanor of the youth. The youth's "demeanor" is really the preconceived stereotype of the police about how African-American men in lower-income communities behave toward authority. Studies by Elliot show that in self-reported data, young African-American men are no more likely to engage in criminal activities than their White cohorts (1982). However, the young men are very likely to receive harsher sentences or recommended treatment for committing the same or similar offenses as Whites. Also young African-Americans are more likely to be referred to public detention facilities while White youth are sent more often to private care facilities or hospitals.

There is a similar body of knowledge about "sorting-out" in education achievement and outcomes. Studies show that teachers disproportionately refer young African-American men to special education classes (Tucker 1980). These referrals are not based on knowledge about emotional problems but rather come from stereotypes about these men in general. This process is very apparent in the disproportionate numbers of African-American males believed to have learning disabilities. Most of the youth referred to special education classes were simply unruly.

The "sorting-out" framework can be applied to the economy as well. According to segmentation theorists, labor markets are divided into core and peripheral industries and jobs. In the core sectors, the jobs pay higher wages. The benefits are more extensive. There are articulated ladders for mobility and the turnover rates are low. In the peripheral sectors, there is little training, high turnover, few benefits and low wages. With the demise of official racial discrimination, African-American men are now "sorted-out" in the labor market by their alleged lack of access to core industries and jobs.

For whatever reason, the historic pattern continues in the present. African-American men have only had open access to the secondary jobs and industries. Once in these industries, it is difficult, if not impossible, to shift to the core sector. Even if they gain access to the core sectors, studies show that they are the least likely to gain access to training and the divisions that have extensive job ladders (Wilson 1986; Stafford 1985). A key finding of segmentation theorists and observers to changes in the economy is that a growing economy does not ensure jobs for African-American men. If their job base is narrow and in secondary industries, as it is in many cities, then African-American unemployment rates will rise even during periods of economic growth.

There is further evidence to a "sorting-out" process in political economy. Critical to understanding "sorting-out" procedures is the manner in which business, social welfare organizations, government and the university have integrated and coordinated functions in the last twenty years. The modern social welfare state is still emerging and very little attention has been given to how it controls race. However, it seems clear that with each victory in the political arena or in the courts by African-Americans, new institutional procedures have been developed to foster racial and class differences, in which case, demands for more effective and radical solutions have been attenuated.

For example, various "sorting-out" procedure adopted by individual schools or school systems were instituted after the Brown Decision in 1954. Institutions showed their resilience in separating groups along lines paralleling race, and the Supreme Court has had to clarify its rulings several times to give any semblance of "all deliberate speed."

Similar trends of sorting and re-sorting within the labor market were evident after the 1964 Civil Rights Act. To alter these practices the Supreme Court also had to rule against biased attitude tests and other devices for screening and sorting workers.

Controlling Race in the New Welfare State

The desire of Whites to hold on to power and privilege was not the only motive for selecting "sorting-out" as the way to maintain and justify racial inequality in the new welfare state. The welfare state was expanded to manage programs addressing poverty, urban blight, low educational achievement and poor health care. Not so incidentally, almost all of these problems were directly attributable to racism. However, the creation of these programs produced a demand for new professionals. And here is where an additional barrier to equality emerged.

These professional groups, notably teachers and social workers, claimed that they had special knowledge and expertise to deal with the problems of clients. But in reality their knowledge emerged only after the proliferation of programs. One consequence is that these professionals established themselves on very limited knowledge about their clients. Their knowledge about African-American men, African-American families and African-American communities continues to be limited. However, because they are credentialed and certified, these groups became the "experts" within public and private sector bureaucracies. They are now the groups responsible for programmatic labeling and for incorporation of definitions of deviancy into administrative guidelines.

Another factor that has helped to establish "sorting-out" as the means for controlling African-Americans was the growth of interest groups making claims on the state for resources and revisions in society's definitions of their cultural and sexual identities. These interest groups were often interchangeable with the new professional groups. The feminist movement set the pace for claims. They defined themselves apart from the late 1960s' civil and human rights groups. In doing so, they indicated that it was every group for themselves in making claims for rights and definitions (Chaffee 1988). Feminists effectively utilized the universities by gaining new departments, challenging established theories, establishing themselves on faculties and publishing articles, books and monographs. They also effectively utilized affirmative action laws to break barriers in the private sector and government. As the social welfare state emerged, these women played a significant role in altering established views of women (usually white) as effective administrators and professionals. It was of great significance that they were in the position to challenge ideas and stereotypes that could lead to women being labeled as deviant.

Notably absent from the groups shaping the new welfare state were African-American men. The fact that Afro-American men did not organize effectively to make claims around their economic oppressed status is in part the reason for their current plight. Thus, the stereotypes used to reinforce the reasons for racial segregation prior to desegregation remained unchallenged during the proliferation of the new professional networks or the transformation of stereotypes to other forms. Stereotypes, according to many observers, do not fade away with education or increased awareness of groups. They usually become assigned to other characteristics and symbols (Gilman 1985). If any lesson has been learned from the feminist and gay rights movements, it is that groups have to organize and become a part of the professional and managerial network to alter the symbols of deviancy.

African-American Men and The New Arrangements: Why No Claims Were Made

The reasons why African-American men did not and have not organized specifically around economic oppression are important. The first, and probably the most crucial reason, is that African-American men saw themselves as a politically oppressed group. They believed that access to jobs came first: then economic oppression could be reduced. This view turned out to be very naive. Although leaders in SNCC and Martin Luther King, Jr. openly challenged the fallacy of separating politics from capitalism, the traditional civil rights organizations did not. As a consequence, the economic oppression of African-American men was never defined in terms of lack of resources, except for job training. There was never any discussion about direct welfare relief.

The second reason why African-American males did not mobilize around economic oppression and prevent themselves from being declared deviant is linked to the first. It is difficult to define oneself as "male" and at the same time see oneself as oppressed and then demand benefits. The ethos of this country remains supremely "macho," even as men increasingly recognize their own independency and fragility. Peter Starns, in research on men and changing industrial patterns, has noted:

> The only common currency among the diverse interpretations of manhood now available is a sense that masculinity is sorely troubled in modern society, both in concept and practice . . . Maleness has long been in crisis . . . The advent of an industrial society challenged some key cannons of manhood and made the fulfillment of others increasingly difficult. (Starns 1979, 1).

Clearly, if there were any group whose concept of manhood was challenged, it was African-American men. The now glorified protest movements of the 1950s and 1960s were very deceptive. African-American men eradicated their "Sambo" images in the media. But Sambo was replaced with the symbolic "savage" during the height of the Black Power and Black Panther agitations. It was no coincidence that this country was unable to recognize African-American men as leaders in their own right and as legitimate and effective fighters against racial and economic oppression. The federal government undertook major covert operations to paint

African-American male leaders as "womanizers" and "savages" thereby reaffirming existing and new stereotypes.

The third reason for lack of mobilization was African-American men's relations with African-American women. White men were forced to readjust or change their symbols of white women by the feminist movement. In contrast, African-American men and women forged, for a very short period, a consensus about their general oppression. But no consensus developed about how this society specifically oppresses African-American men and women as separate genders. As a result, a division developed within the race along gender lines as African-American men and women could not agree on their unique experiences within racial oppression. Where there is no agreement, there is certainly no solution. The problem was simply that the debate required a much deeper sense of history than Whites had to examine, and the resolution required power and resources that African-Americans did not have.

The final reason for lack of African-American mobilization is the phenomenon in the African-American community of "sins of the father, curse of the son." Over the years a curious expectation has developed and is reflected in our churches, families and schools around African-American men. The essence of this belief is that a significant proportion of each generation of African-American men has to be sacrificed. No one will say it that bluntly. But in essence, there is an expectation that we have to write off a significant segment of each generation of men and put our energies into the next. This expectation that has been in existence for so long that it appears to be virtually taken for granted. However, it is an admission of the powerlessness of the community to change or to develop intervention strategies for men after they reach a certain age.

Conclusion

This and the coming generation of African-American men are not likely to effectively address their status as outcastes and deviants without a refocusing by the African-

American community on issues of economic inequality. This will mean recognizing that the social welfare state is not benign. It is as oppressive as southern Jim Crow, if not worse. This will also mean breaking the "claims" of professionals and their power to stigmatize and "sort-out" young African-American men and women.

Currently, there is a stalemate among the African-American leaders on how this nation's political economy should be addressed. This stalemate exists in part because many of our "allies" have helped set the course of African-American oppression in the welfare state. Equally as important, African-Americans themselves are all too often the expendable foot soldiers of the welfare state. It is assumed that social welfare arrangements are "good" in contrast to the conservative alternative—no benefits at all. However,the conservative-liberal contrast is only part of the problem that must be examined. More fundamental questions revolve around who plans the arrangements of the state, which groups define deviants and who makes decisions about establishing frameworks for control.

Ultimately, a major share of the blame for not making claims on the system rests on adult African-American men, especially those who have the knowledge, credentials and know-how: the middle class. As gender has become parallel to race in decisions about allocation of resources, African-American men have maintained their voices about racial injustice but have not confronted their own humanity and the issues around their "maleness." This is of course a sensitive area. However, it is all too clear that knowledge about African-American men is distorted in the social science literature where professionals base their claims. Indeed, there has been more than twenty years of governmental and foundation funding of social scientists to study the conditions of Blacks. African-American men have generally been excluded from this work. In addition, less is known about African-American males today than in the 1960s. There has been no major contribution to understanding African-American men. At best, careers have been made for a few individuals.

There is a need for an independent voice of African-

American men to emerge in the development of social policy. We are outsiders. No matter how much African-American men may think they are included in the mainstream, the stereotypes and doubts persist. But until major changes can be brought about, our "voice" should remain that of outsiders. We should not, as Franz Fanon and generations of African-American novelists have noted, interpret our conditions as outsiders in the language and concept of institutions that minimize our humanity. When by necessity we utilize the language, our goal should be altering the system. The language of the professionalized state is often a cover-up for lack of knowledge and interest in only social control. The designations of differences between African-American males and others come out of the ambivalence of professionals toward African-Americans in general and men in particular.

We should remain true to the excellence of the outsider. Recognition of this status has been our strength. We should cherish, as Richard Wright noted, the "gift" of double vision. As Richard Wright acutely observed, our existence is based on the dreadful objectivity of simultaneously being inside and outside of American culture. It is a legacy we pass on. To deny this vision and legacy of coping and resistance for today's young men may be our greatest negligence.

References

Becker, H. 1963. *Outsiders: Studies in the Sociology of Deviance.* London: Free Press of Glencoe.

Chaffee, E. et al. 1988. *Collegiate Culture and Leadership Strategies.* New York: MacMillan Publishers.

Costell, R. 1988. *The Effects of Industry Employment Shifts on Wage Growth,* 1948-87. Washington, DC: U.S. Goverment Printing Office.

Elliot, D. and D. Huizinga. 1982. "Social Class and Delinquent Behavior in a National Youth Panel; 1976-1980." *Journal of Criminology.* 21, 149-177.

Gilman, S. 1985. *Difference and Pathology: Stereotypes of Sexuality, Race, and Madness.* Ithaca: Cornell University Press.

Levitan, S. and I. Shapiro. 1987. *Working But Poor: America's Contradiction.* Baltimore: Johns Hopkins University Press.
McGhee, J. 1984. *Running the Gauntlet: Black Men in America.* New York: Urban League.
Mishel, L. and J. Simon. 1988. *The State of Working America.* Washington, DC: Economic Policy Institute.
Smith, D. et al. 1984. "Equity and Discretionary Justice: The Influence of Race on Police Arrest Decisions." *Journal of Criminal Law and Criminology.* 75, 234-249.
Stafford, W. 1985. *Closed Labor Markets: Underrepresentation of Blacks, Hispanics, and Women in New York City Core Industries and Jobs.* New York: Community Services Society of New York.
Staples, R. 1984. "American Racism and High Crime Rates: The Inextricable Connection." *The Western Journal of Black Studies.* 8(2), 62-72.
Starns, P. 1979. *Be A Man! Males in Modern Society.* New York: Homes and Meyer.
U.S. Department of Commerce. 1983. *Census of Population.* 1980. U.S. Summary. Detailed Characteristics, Tables 87, 334. Washington, DC: U.S. Government Printing Office.
U.S. Department of Commerce. 1986. *Money, Income of Households, Families, and Persons in the U.S.: 1984.* Washington, DC: U.S. Government Printing Office.
Wilson, J. 1986. *Black Labor in America.* New York: Greenwood.

Chapter 3

Changing the Inner City: Black Urban Reorganization

Hardy T. Frye

In Black urban America, trends are emerging that reflect shifting community attitudes and changing patterns of behavior. Residents are concerned with various social problems that are plaguing their communities and they are seeking ways to improve the quality of life in their neighborhoods. These trends are partly in response to the male and youth centered symptoms which are so visible.

These emerging trends are an early stage of a developing general social movement. This movement is fueled by the question that is nagging most Black people: Should members of the Black community increase their participation in self-help projects to solve their community's problems? Significant help in addressing the social ills of the Black urban community is not now forthcoming from the larger White society or from the various branches of government. There will be no significant help until there is further growth in Black political power and the community develops the ability to leverage this new growing power in the arenas of local, state, and federal policy-making. The continuing absence of such external help has led many Black inner-city residents to believe that self-help is essential.

This developing social movement appears to be unnoticed by many scholars and urban experts writing on the Black inner city, scholars such as William J. Wilson (1987), Charles Murray (1984), Ken Auletta (1983), and Richard Nathan, et al. (1987). As a result, this movement and its corresponding community activism have not been included in the analyses of scholars who argue for large macroprograms to solve the communities' problems.

Experts and scholars have described the social pathologies of the urban Black communities in great detail, but they have ignored attempts by Black residents to address them. These experts have suggested that such communities lack a noticeable class infrastructure that would allow local community people to begin addressing these pathologies. Wilson (1987) argues that migration of the Black middle and working classes from these urban communities has led to the collapse of their earlier infrastructures. When experts and scholars do acknowledge some of the self-help and community organization activities that attempt to address these social problems, they quickly suggest that such efforts do not possess sufficient resources.

Instead, the experts and scholars suggest, the major social problems of Black urban communities can only be addressed successfully with macroprojects established by the state or federal governments with strong support from the private sector. These writers usually advocate higher welfare benefit levels, guaranteed jobs programs, more manpower training programs, adequate housing programs, better law enforcement, stiffer sentences for criminal behavior, and so on. In other words, they seem to believe that the local people are irrelevant in helping to solve the most pressing problems of their own communities. I would not argue with the assertion that improvements in job training, housing, and other programs should be implemented at the macrolevel by the various branches of government and that in some situations we need better law enforcement. But I also believe that in the Black community a general social movement is growing that reflects shifting attitudes and behaviors as community problems are dealt with at the microlevel. This shift in attitudes and behaviors is surrounded by a general discussion within the community concerning its declining quality of life.

Some efforts by local Black urbanites have already begun to create a new community infrastructure. This new infrastructure of leaders and activists is addressing the community's social problems and will either hinder or support similar efforts made by federal, state, and private policymakers. Community input will determine the reception given to the efforts of planners and policy-makers when they finally do begin to deal with the Black community's needs. And so any analysis and planning for actions by such agencies must provide an accurate description of what is being done on the local scene by local people. Only then can effective programs be designed to work in conjunction with local community efforts.* Policymakers, advocates, and analysts need to include in their observations an analysis of the changing attitudes and everyday activities of people living in these urban enclaves.**

The social movement I describe here is producing indigenous leaders who promise to be key players in the restoration of urban communities. These leaders and their communities will generate their own ideas about what is to be done and how to do it. This general social movement of community residents will lead to an exciting growth in organization that could have a major effect on the urban quality of life and could reestablish the community control movement, which seems to have died when many of the aspiring Black middle-class and working-class folks left. The new community control thrust is very different from the thrust of the late sixties and early seventies in terms of its class origins and focus.

The earlier community control movement was made up mostly of Black middle-class and working-class people. They focused on controlling the outside agencies that brought programs into their midst—police, school boards and teachers, social workers and social welfare agencies. Those outside

---

* During the 1960s, the War on Poverty programs were expected to solve the problems of Black urban communities. Most of those programs were developed by outside experts and planners with very little, if any, community input. Today such an approach would be politically unsuccessful because of the level of political and community consciousness emerging within the urban Black community.

** We also need a better analysis and understanding of the community activities being carried on by various Black organizations in the community. Childs (1987,16) has pointed out that there are literally hundreds of these organizations operating within Black communities that seek to serve their communities and to solve some of their problems.

agencies and their activities were seen as being oppressive toward the community.

The present thrust in community control is concerned with establishing new norms of behavior and with developing effective ways of addressing problems internally while working in conjunction with outside agencies. In many cases, local people are dictating the "style" in which such solutions are to be implemented. This newly developing general social movement suggests a maturing in the ways Black residents of urban enclaves think about the nature of their communities' problems and who should have the responsibility for coming up with the solutions.

Characteristics of This General Social Movement

Because of the accelerating growth in the social pathologies affecting urban Black communities and their effect on the quality of life, a response is emerging from a new set of activists and from reinvigorated former activists who are still in the community. Blumer, when discussing the origin of social movements, noted: "They have their inception in a condition of unrest, and derive their motive power on the one hand from dissatisfaction with the current form of life, and on the other, from wishes and hope for a new scheme or system of living. *The career of a social movement depicts the emergence of a new order of life*" (Blumer 1969, 8) [emphasis added].

The background for the development of such a movement is a gradual and persuasive change in the values held by people within the communities. Blumer called such a change in values a "Cultural Drift . . . a general shifting in the ideas of people, particularly along the line of the conceptions which people have of themselves, and of their rights and privileges. Over a period of time many people may develop a new view of what they believe they are entitled to" (Blumer 1969,9).

This new, indigenous movement is, in its present stage, similar to the early civil rights movement of the late 1950s and early 1960s. It is amorphous and without organizational structure. Participants are groping and uncoordinated. The interaction that occurs among similar movements in various Black communities is at an elementary level; most activities are somewhat spontaneous.

The participants in this new movement include revitalized Black community activists—individuals and groups—as well as new activists. How much does their activism reflect the developing character of the new movement at its present stage? And conversely, how great is the influence of these revitalized individuals and groups on this movement? Their earlier activities took place within a developed organizational structure, a body of customs and traditions and social values, with established leadership. How much of their past experience is influencing their present activism?

The general themes of this new social movement are self-help, community control, and improvement of quality of life. The new activists, long-established community groups and organizations as well as the general populations of urban enclaves, are caught up in public and political discourse and community protest surrounding these themes.

How have individuals, groups and institutions related to the thrust of this new movement? Since the days of the modern civil rights movement the church, an established community institution, has played a new role—now less concerned with the quality of the lives of its followers after death and more concerned with the quality of their lives today.

In many Black communities, residents are currently organizing and taking part in protest marches and demonstrations against drug use and drug pushers. Such marches, while they are the descendants of early civil rights marches, have a new target. Today's marchers seem to address four audiences—the larger society, elected officials and public agencies, Black youth, and drug pushers.

The marchers have four goals: (1) to inform the larger society about the concern with which they view the community's social problems, including the sale and use of drugs and the increase in criminal behavior; (2) to send a message to elected officials and various public agencies (including the police), calling for and expressing the willingness of community people to work with the police to solve the problems now strangling their communities; (3) to send a message to young people that, while the community needs their help in this endeavor, residents are determined to make changes, with or without their help; and (4) to tell the drug pushers, in strong language that reflects growing community unity, that residents want the pushers out of the community.

The new general social movement seems to be saying that collectively the Black community has the right and responsibility to establish behavioral norms acceptable in the community, and to do that through the institutionalization of community control. Describing the inner workings of the general social movement, Herbert Blumer noted:

> Such a movement is episodic in its career, with very scattered manifestations of activity. It may show considerable enthusiasm at one point and reluctance and inertia at another; it may experience success in one area, and abortive efforts in another. In general, it may be said that its progress is very uneven with setbacks, reverses, and frequent retreading of the same ground. At one time the impetus of the movement may come from people in one place, at another time in another place. On the whole the movement is likely to be carried on by many unknown and obscure people who struggle in different areas without striving and achievements becoming generally known (Blumer 1969, 10).

The Self-Help, Quality of Life, and Community Control Movement

As discussed earlier, this new social movement appears to have been activated by overwhelming pressure resulting from social disorganization occurring within the Black community because of the dramatic growth of social pathologies and the belief of many community people that the spread of these social ills must be brought under control by them if the community is to survive.

As Blacks within urban enclaves discuss these problems, and as attitudes change, a pattern is emerging of overt behavior by some Black community members toward individuals involved in the increasingly frequent criminal behavior. That criminal behavior is the most significant of the social problems currently threatening the urban Black community. Residents feel strongly that other social problems also need to be addressed, including teenage pregnancies, the high rate of unemployment among the young, and the high dropout rate among high school students. But at present the changing overt behavior of Black urban residents appears to be focused on the increasing criminal behavior—including drug pushing, general drug use, physical assaults, and neighborhood burglaries.*

In addressing the increases in crime, Black urban residents have made several shifts in previously held attitudes about criminal behavior and Black people. At the organizational level, they are involving themselves in city-wide political liaisons with potential allies who are concerned with crime both within the Black community in particular and in urban centers in general. These shifts and involvements of Black urban residents are evident:

1. They are beginning to accept types of institutional controls for those involved in criminal behavior that until recently have been shunned (particularly controls advocated/enforced by external agencies and groups).

* Although it is usual to base a scholarly discussion on research, here we have only newspaper accounts of this movement and its activities. Most of those stories report acts of collective behavior by community people who are trying to combat and respond to certain types of criminal acts. Thus, we do not know how far this movement has gone in its attempts to address other community problems. Also, in presenting an analytic discussion of this movement, we must separate the actions of this movement from movements and organizations that focus on other specific social problems.

2. They no longer make the racial framing of issues primary, particularly in relationship to neighborhood crime issues.
3. They work more closely with organizations internal and external to the community—for example, the Nation of Islam, church groups and the local police.
4. They are participating in coalitions with neighborhood, city-wide, and regional groups that have similar concerns.
5. They articulate their own approaches and solutions to the pressing social problems in their neighborhoods. In many cases these shifts and involvements overlap the activities of other more organized groups.

Enlightening Incidents: Cases in Point

One of the first shifts in attitudes toward the increase of violent criminal behavior was acceptance of control techniques that before now had been unacceptable, particularly when used by external agencies. Three incidents illustrate this point.

In Detroit, after several shootings at a high school, the local community accepted the installation of metal detectors at the front door of the high school—the door through which all students entering the school had to pass. Even when the ACLU objected, suggesting that this was a clear violation of the constitutional rights of these students, many in the community found use of the metal detector to be acceptable if it would prevent further shootings. The use of metal detectors to control possible violence in inner-city high schools has increased since then.

In Oakland, California, several Black policemen were charged with police brutality for beating community drug pushers, and the officers were brought before police officials for possible disciplinary action. Many community people protested, saying that the officers "were only beating drug dealers." They noted that the Black community has been subjected in the past to brutality by white policemen, and nothing was done about that. Why, they asked, were black policemen now being criticized for taking similarly strong action to *protect* the community?

In Washington, D.C., members of the Nation of Islam beat drug dealers and chased them from Mayfair Mansion* (now a low-income housing project) and were chastised by the police and some members of the local media for their actions. The community came to their defense, asserting that the Muslims had been able to do in a couple of days what the police had not been able to do over the past couple of years. Richard Bryant 3X wrote that one resident of the project, Betty Adams, head of the tenants' association, commented on the nation of Islam's Dopebuster patrol: "It's made a wonderful difference in all of our lives . . . I never thought that we would get those people out of here" (Bryant 1988,2).

Recently I discussed the level of neighborhood violence occurring in Compton, California with some local residents. I asked them if the violence of some young adults and gangs could be explained by the facts that the young people involved were unemployed, and that their unemployment was caused largely by racial discrimination in the job market. No one questioned that White racism toward the Black community still exists at unacceptable levels. But those I spoke with refused to view this increase in criminality as a result of white racism. They suggested that other factors were important, such as a decrease in the control parents have over their young adult children, unwillingness to work for the minimum wage, and lack of feelings of community pride.

In Compton, most local public officials (including the police) are Black, Whites do not appear to be directly involved in racial domination of the Compton inner city. Newspaper reports of criminal violence by various youth gangs contain interviews with local people, and the state-

---

* Columnist Ethel Payne describing the drug problem at Mayfair Mansion, noted: "The once affluent housing development was riddled with dope users and dealers who made life so hellish for the lawabiding. Residents were afraid for their own safety" (1988,30).

ments made by members of the local community seem strangely devoid of discussion of white racism or racial domination as factors that might explain such criminal behavior. This seems a far cry from the explanations of violent collective behavior that were expressed by community people during the late 1960s and early 1970s.

Black inner-city urban participants in the new general social movement are beginning to establish working relationships with groups and organizations internal and external to their communities—the police, various religious groups and churches, for example. In Washington, D.C., when members of the Nation of Islam formed their now-famous Dopebuster patrol in Mayfair Mansion, local community people asked the Muslims to maintain a permanent presence in the project. One result of this public plea was that the owner of a vacant apartment in the project allowed it to be used as a command post, so that the Muslims could continue administering the Dopebuster program. As a result of community support and pressure for the Muslim patrol, the mayor of Washington, the police chief, other city officials, and various community leaders from throughout the city joined in support of this antidrug patrol.

The *New York Times* published a story by Isabel Wilkerson about one of Detroit's poorest neighborhoods, a drug haven on the city's north side. There, *The Times* reports, "Some residents have resorted to vigilantism, setting crack houses afire or assaulting drug dealers, even as the police increased their raids."

Community concern was also expressed in other ways. One group of neighborhood people called on the local Twelfth Street Missionary Baptist Church for help. These residents joined with the church and a church-sponsored group, Reach, Inc., to buy up abandoned houses (most of which were being used as crack houses) in the neighborhood, renovate them, and sell them to community people in need of housing at a low price. "Crack dens are being replaced by green lawns and marigolds." Wilkerson further noted:

> The group went after the first problem house and its owner seven years ago, paid the overdue taxes and

> bought the house for $8,000. It has since tried to stabilize the neighborhood and fight the drug dealers house by house, slowly whittling away their home bases and replacing them with churchgoers . . . The neighbors have given the group a growing list of houses they want the church to buy, and some have signed up as potential homeowners."

One community person, describing the effect of this effort, noted: "I'm not going to say we've climbed out of the gutter yet, but it's quieter." Another remarked: "It's getting better because we're getting new neighbors" (Wilkerson 1988).

Lee P. Brown, former chief of police in Houston, Texas, (now New York City Police Commissioner) in an essay discussing innovative policing techniques used by his department in fighting crime growth, included the involvement of local people as a key component of his department's efforts. Describing one of the department's programs, the Directed Area Responsibility Team (DART), and the department's rationale for starting this program, Brown wrote: "We want to be able to maintain order by being a partner with the community. The citizens of the community therefore become part of the resources we have at our disposal to help us improve the quality of neighborhood life throughout the city" (Brown 1987, 131).

The DART program—with the police and neighborhood residents working together—addressed other community problems such as potential health hazards, as well as neighborhood crime issues. Houston's DART program and similar innovative efforts by police departments and social agencies in other urban areas suggest that there is growing recognition by such officials of the need for cooperative working relationships with local folks. The efforts made by urban community residents toward achieving closer working relationships with internal and external agencies are likely to be met by reciprocal desires. Clearly the Houston police department wants to nurture such a relationship. Brown noted: "The use of community resources is the umbrella under which we conduct all our policing activities, because the police alone cannot control crime. The community also must be involved. We can be the catalysts—the professionals—but the citizens of the community must be involved" (*ibid.*, 133).

I believe such enlightenment on the issues of community involvement in policing the neighborhood, as shown by Chief Brown, is encouraging. But it is important for public officials to understand that the police must have active community participants as the catalysts for cooperative ventures as they all search for solutions.

The shifts in attitude and the changing overt behavior of members of our Black urban communities and some of their organizations have also led to participation in community coalitions. Recent activities in Oakland, California, and nearby San Jose supply us with examples and some understanding of these community coalitions. Oakland community and church leaders along with 250 community residents recently met and made an urgent plea to their state legislators for help in this city's fight against a "drug epidemic." Oakland Community Organizations (OCO), an umbrella organization that includes 13 church and neighborhood groups, sponsored the meeting. Participants asked their legislators to come up with comprehensive solutions to the drug problem in Oakland's inner city. Later OCO participated in a joint news conference with People Acting in Community Together (PACT), based in nearby San Jose, to demand of several state legislators a comprehensive plan for addressing the drug problem.*

Throughout the nation such community coalitions are being built in our urban enclaves to deal with the drug epidemic. Thomas Owen (1988,6) states that the Citizens' Committee for New York City (CCNYC) has brought together and coordinated the activities of some 300 neighborhood groups to devise various techniques to use in combating illegal drugs in the communities.

---

* Clemmons (1988) stated that OCO claims to represent 7,000 families and PACT, 21,000 families. They suggest that they joined in a coalition "to increase their strength by combining forces."

Luis Overbea reports increased community involvement as residents patrol their neighborhoods to drive out drug pushers and prostitution in Boston, New York and other cities. He writes: "Black Muslims and Guardian Angels often receive the publicity when they patrol America's neighborhoods. But local citizens are banding together to help protect their communities, too" (Overbea 1988).

Neighborhood folks are patrolling, joining coalitions, committing acts of vigilantism, accepting types of controls long shunned in their communities, and choosing not to see the growth in neighborhood crime as attributable primarily to racism. More and more are beginning to articulate their own solutions to their social problems (at this time the major emphasis is on crime and its prevention) and the type of punishment that should be meted out. The solutions and the punishments they are recommending would appear in many cases to be extreme, in others to be appropriate.

This new social movement with much of its rhetoric and overt behavior, particularly as it relates to criminality, raises questions about whether the neighborhood groups are violating individual constitutional rights. This concern is likely to lead to a clash between the community folks battling the drug problem on the "front line" and those who are less concerned about how we deal with the drug epidemic but do not want constitutional rights infringed on. The civil libertarians will be closely watching the activities of the community groups and organizations. One might ask whether the civil libertarians are trying to impose middle-class values on the lower-class community residents. This is particular interesting since no attempts by mostly middle-class professionals to deal with the drug problem have been successful so far. We might at least consider allowing local residents to practice some self-determination in this area, as long as they do not go overboard in their denial of constitutional rights. Before long we will see philosophical discussion, and perhaps also court cases, to determine whether in these situations the rights of the criminals are being protected while the rights of the victims are being violated.

Constance L. Hays wrote about an incident that took place in Harlem. Some people of the community beat a man severely after he snatched a twenty dollar bill from a woman in a bakery. Subsequently the man died, and two men and five teenagers were charged with manslaughter. One of the defense attorneys, asking that the charges against his client be dropped, said: "You can't say my client was the cause of this . . . He was one of twenty or thirty people that took part in it." All of them were acquitted. One defendant who had the charge of manslaughter dismissed said: "I did what was right" (Hayes 1988).

C.T. Clemmons wrote that when the Oakland Community Organizations and San Jose's People Acting in Community Together met with their state representatives, they argued for:

> a comprehensive plan to fight the drug problem, a plan that will include increased prosecution of drug dealers, higher bail for drug-related crimes, and money for drug treatment.
>
> They want neighborhood "crack" cocaine houses closed down under nuisance abatement laws, and they want drug dealers' money seized and used for housing, education, and jobs.

Another participant at the news conference suggested: "State lawmakers are aware of the seriousness of the problem . . . but if we don't push them they'll become inattentive" (Clemmons 1988).

Clearly this articulation by community folks and community organizations of an approach to their pressing community problems and possible solutions represent attempts at self-help and community control. This is indicative in their attitude shifts and changing patterns of overt behavior toward drug pushers and other criminals. They are attempts to dictate new norms of behavior for the community. These efforts will eventually have the effect of enhancing the community's quality of life.

The Movement's Significance and Potential

This new general social movement, which has evolved in the urban Black communities over the past decade, represents a significant shift in the class makeup of a movement for social change in the Black community. It includes many more lower-class urban dwellers than did the movement of the 1960s and early 1970s. The major sociological factor that appears to have mobilized this segment of the Black community is the tremendous increase in drug-related crimes.

Although some middle-class and working-class Blacks have chosen to remain in the inner city, many of the former leaders of these urban neighborhoods (middle-class and working-class Blacks) have moved to previously closed suburbs, leaving the remaining inner-city dwellers to fend for themselves. Some might argue that these urban Blacks are beginning to mobilize because they must to survive. This movement also represents a groping for strategies and techniques, not only to address the crime problem but also to address other social ills in the community. This new movement is also evidence that the analysis made by some scholars and experts—those who say that inner-city urban communities and neighborhoods are devoid of any resources that might work toward the liberation of their communities—is erroneous. But what is most important about this new movement is that it represents a self-help approach by Black inner-city people to the social ills afflicting their communities.

It is difficult to predict with any accuracy the direction this movement might take or the outcome of its efforts. But clearly we can speculate on its potential for a reorganization of the Black urban community.

A general social movement of the nature described has the potential to rebuild the community infrastructure that Wilson (1987) and others suggest has collapsed in the urban inner city. This rebuilding process has begun, even though there has not been a mad rush back to these urban communities by middle-class and working-class Blacks. The infrastructure of new and revitalized leaders and lower-class residents are people who were excluded from leadership roles in the past. By using the general strategy of establishing community organizations, it is possible that the following changes can occur in urban Black communities:

- A renaissance of community activism emanating from the community itself;
- A redefining of the relationship between external public and private agencies and the neighborhood;
- A mobilization of both internal and external political, economic, and social resources;
- A development of approaches to neighborhood social problems that originates with residents;
- The establishment of new standards of normative behavior, arrived at collectively by community folks;
- A growth in community and regional coalitions to address not only the current social ills of the community but emerging problems as well.

All of the above changes emanating from this movement, as they occur, will bring about collective empowerment of inner-city dwellers. The empowered communities might join forces with external agencies and offer macroprograms to help solve the major urban social problems. This would allow for the reorganization of our urban enclaves in ways more acceptable to the inhabitants. And so they might establish, through practice, that it is not necessary for residents to accept and model their efforts for community revitalization on middle-class values and orientations as they address the social ills of our urban communities.

References

Auletta, Ken. 1983. *The Underclass.* New York: Vintage Press.

Blumer, H. 1969. "Social Movements," in Barry McLaughlin (ed.) *Studies in Social Movements: A Social Psychological Perspective.* New York: The Free Press.

Brown, L. P. 1987. "Innovative Policing in Houston." *The Annals of the American Academy*. 494(November):129-134.

Bryant 3X, R. 1988. "Dopebusters: Muslims' Anti-Drug Patrols Bring Calm in D.C." *The Final Call*. June 16, 2.

Childs, J. B. 1987. "Policy Implications of Current Research on the Black Community." *Social Policy*. 17(Summer):16.

Clemmons, C.J. 1988. "Oakland, San Jose Groups Call for State Action on Drugs." *The Oakland Tribune*. June 22.

Hays, C. L. 1988. "Charges Dropped Against Seven in Fatal Mob Beating of Man." *The New York Times*. June 28.

Murray, C. 1984. "Affirmative Racism." *The New Republic*. 192 (December): 18-23.

Nathan, Richard, et al. 1987. *Reagan and The States*. Princeton: Princeton University Press.

Overbea, L. 1988. "On the Street to Fight Drugs, These People Wear No Badge." *The Christian Science Monitor*. July 5.

Owen, T. 1988. "Citizen Patrols: Self-Help to an Extreme?" *The Christian Science Monitor*, July 5.

Payne, E. L. 1988. "Drugs out of Control." *The Final Call*. June 16.

Wilkerson, I. 1988. "Detroit Citizens Join with Church to Rid Community of Drugs." *The New York Times*, June 29, p. 10A.

Wilson, W. J. 1987. *The Truly Disadvantaged: The Inner City, the Underclass, and Public Policy*. Chicago: University of Chicago Press.

Chapter 4

"Betcha Cain't Reason with 'Em": Bad Black Boys in America

Anthony J. Lemelle, Jr.

THE PROBLEM WITH THE SOCIAL UNDERSTANDING of bad Black boys in America is that the theories that form our understanding of them are unrealistic and our goals are equally unrealistic. The standard theories of Black delinquency obscure the historical reality of Black boys being forced into criminality. Forced criminality viewed as an historical process results in a Black counterculture that will likely fail to correct itself through economic solutions. The common goal of social agents is to correct the problem of criminality in the Black community. The image the agents share of this criminality is a landscape of poverty and a subject of deficit: boys who are poor, living in the ghetto in a fatherless family.

Some authorities believe the boys to have deviant body types and low educational achievement ability (Wilson and Hernstein 1985; Banfield 1970; Moynihan 1965; Sheldon 1949). The powerful role models the boys emulate are Black pimps, hustlers, drug dealers, and street-corner men within their communities, and they see Black athletes and entertainers, soldiers and prisoners outside their communities (Staples 1982,135-146). Even the progressive literature stresses the economic factors that prevent Black boys from adopting middle-class attitudes and life-styles (Staples 1982,22). It is doubtful that free and just economic participation in American society will necessarily change the cultural values of Black Americans into what Whites find pleasing.

I intend to: (1) raise salient methodological problems in the study of bad Black boys; (2) define the American crisis of rewarding Blacks on a much lower level than Whites resulting in the continued production of a Black resistance culture; and (3) examine the temporal refusal of bad Black boys to commit themselves to American values.

Salient Methodological Problems

The dominant American ideology holds the view that with an increase in income the social values Black Americans hold dear will change, producing a mythological society where individuals receive social rewards based on merit rather than race, class and sex (Bell 1973; Young 1961). Implied in this reasoning is the belief that middle-class income results in White middle-class role behavior. In spite of the fact that the historical evidence contradicts this view, it is vigorously maintained in the social sciences literature and generally in culture. The studies that attempt to count numbers of delinquents, examine their rearing and economic backgrounds, other personal characteristics and attitudes ultimately fail the test of providing an emancipatory social theory.

An emancipatory theory would indicate the ways in which Black youth might realize their full potential in a society structured to accommodate the "unity of diversity" (Hegel 1955,24). Some theories intentionally, and others unwittingly, support a specific form of unacknowledged political domination. They do this by denying the central contradiction in the development of Black life in America. That is, Blacks have been systematically created as criminals by authorized agents in a politically organized society that claims a more perfect union of liberated and equal human beings. This means that in the final analysis, the empirical researchers that quantify the study of Black juvenile delinquents have a covert therapeutic agenda. Their goal is to cure the very victims of oppression whom they work so assiduously to identify, maintain, control, improve, and of course, they do all of this while earning ever-better incomes through their administrative performances.

Defining Professional-Managers

It is not enough to theoretically appreciate the deviant boys or have sympathy for their choice to become juvenile delinquents. This choice is due to economic and political history which has functioned, and continues to function, to place limits on their choice to be rational and cognizant. If there were realistic choices to be rational, all might choose to be authentic, altruistic, voluntary practitioners of the Golden Rule (Matza 1969; 1971). The historical condition of forced criminality produces a dynamic communicative discourse between the Black underclass and the institutionally situated professional-managerial class charged with the management of the status-quo.

Fueling this discourse is the condition where race and class have virtually become synonymous (Pinkney 1984,46-57).

For the purpose of understanding this perspective it is important to stress that the professional-managers represent an elite group that is located inside and outside of the race-class group—they are both White and non-White. The non-Whites are particularly interesting in that they represent a small social stratum that is gathered from the oppressed masses and retained primarily to articulate the various values and ideas of the oppressing class. The Black elite belong to this group and assist in administrating the underclass in the context of Western liberalism. In a real sense, they are the "good boys" of the empire. The popular press leaves the impression that there has been a major increase in this group.

The proportion of Black families in the middle-class range (between $15,000 and $24,999) declined from 26% in 1972 to 23% in 1975 (Pinkney 1984,103). Family income is a partial indicator of the numbers of Black professional-managers. It is necessary to consider which jobs include decision-making authority to determine whether or not the employee is a professional-manager. Although the professional-managerial class is a relatively imprecise stratification category, it consists of the upper levels of the Black middle-class. Their jobs have status and prestige as well as incomes which range between $20,000 and $45,000 per year. Most of the Blacks in this group are middle-level managers without full decision-making power. Census data for 1980 indicates that 6.6% of all professional-managers are Black while Blacks compose 12.6% of the total population (Blackwell 1985,17).

There are additional systemic flaws that make the behavior of most bad Black boys appear more rational than the behavior of most professional-managers. The difference between Black and White income is a flaw that is impossible to mask from Black youth. Black income is approximately 56% that of Whites, down from 60% in 1971 (Statistical Abstract 1985,422). What is more debilitating is the difference between income when educational and occupational levels are considered. Contrary to the idea that rewards are distributed in society based on merit, educational achievement fails to distribute equitable income at each level of schooling. The education of Black men results in much less income than does that of White men (Swinton 1983,45-114). The ideological position of the dominant professional-managers is incapable of resolving these contradictions. It would be similar to asking two teams of boys to play a game of basketball while crediting one team with two points for each goal scored and the opposite team with one point for each goal scored. Naturally antagonisms would develop between the two teams as a result of the unequal rewards for similar work. Eventually, the oppressed team would stop playing the rigged game because there would be virtually no chance of winning.

Types of Professional-Managers

The professional-managers may be identified on the basis of their commitment to the myth of meritocracy. On the other hand, it might be clearer if we organize the professional-managerial group into social categories of those who cooperate, compete, coerce and advocate conflict and exchange (Nisbet 1970). While various social situations will result in the overt expression of any one of these orientations of social interaction, it is reasonable to say that personalities tend to consistently perform roles in a specific mode. Cooperative professional-managers are indifferent to the inherent contradictions in the social order that cause Black youth great stress. They adhere to the goal of making the system work as it is currently organized. They often advise Black students to work hard and not to be too ambitious with their dreams. Above all, Black youth must stay in their place.

Conflict professional-managers advise Black youth to struggle for a greater share of social goods and resources by working against the powerful White social structure. Those professional-managers who joined the civil rights and Black Power movements are examples of the conflict mode of interaction. Professional-managers who work in the exchange mode adhere to the policy of voluntarily doing something for Black youth with the expectation that a reward will follow. Some White teachers in inner-city schools believe this mode is effective and encourage their students to behave accordingly. Inner-city policemen are a good example of coercive professional-managers. They usually force the youth to adhere to the group wishes of the status quo. Conflict professional-managers appear to provide the most potential for equitable social change.

But overall, the professional-managerial class projects fear of its inability to contain resistance in the underclass by creating the mythology of meritocracy and writing a mythic history of Black respectability. Through denial, the professional-managerial class has absolved itself of responsibility for the perpetuation of Black inequality. Through the culture of resistance the boys view professional-managers as being "in-on-the-take." The teacher in the classroom, for example, and others are on the frontline of the entrenched battle between Black culture and the professional-managerial culture. Knowing that Black students are commonly understood as disreputable, the teacher has to mediate between "just doing my job" and attempting to deal with the socially created category of inferior Black youth and bad Black boys.

Failure of Progress

To understand bad Black boys, it is necessary to be sensitive to the social context that produces them. It is also important to understand the roles available on the stage of their social lives. The boys will audition for specific roles and will be offered them if their performances are sufficiently reliable to produce the criminal career. The landscape of the "ghetto" or "internal colony" is interesting as a backdrop of inequality. The available roles for Black boys provide myths that the boys usually internalize during socialization. Social class might provide some insight into differences between one group of Black boys and others; that is, inequality is insidious. The life-long process of socialization to become a Black male in America means more than class or income. It includes a commitment to remote goals, ambivalent moral codes, and expectations that divine good will be manifested independent of their actions (Horowitz 1961). To be an American Black male is a value system and world view that has been created by social history. There is a functional role for the mythic Black male. The myth is often taken literally in a society to enhance, express and codify belief; to safeguard and enforce morality (Malinowski 1948).

America's paternalistic culture is more threatened by masculine youth than female youth. America, being both sexist and racist, has historically subjugated Black men because they can take the place of the male oppressor. White men of power anticipated that Black women would at best escape their defeminization and develop as sex objects with a social class, power and status comparable to subjugated White women. Black men posed a primary threat to White males as laborer, entertainer, sport competitor, sexual competitor and military competitor. The interest of White men favors a peculiar form of dehumanization and subjugation directed toward Black males. Notwithstanding this motive, the roles of Black females require them to accommodate the consequences of classism, racism and sexism as well (Marable 1983,69-104).

The system of Black male subjugation is an issue of income, status and power; simultaneously, Black youth inherit and produce a different cultural voice than White youth—this factor is equally as important. If we approach the economic factors from a sociological point of view, it exposes the expression of Black frustration and protest in Black culture. At every level of the economic hierarchy Blacks are discriminated against. This means that, if any class group (lower class, working class, middle class, upper-class) is examined, Blacks will form an aggregate at the bottom of the class category. At every level of stratification Blacks will be concentrated at the bottom. There is additional segmentation at the bottom of these classes as well since Black women, Black elderly, Black disabled and Black youth will be positioned at last in of the Black aggregate of each class (Bonacich 1976; Poulantzas 1975). Second-class positions in the stratification hierarchy have less power and status. Also, the resulting inequalities of daily living present distinguishable differences in style and quality of life. Differential rewards in the labor market produce jealousies, antagonisms and protest on the job between workers and against professional-managers. Conflict is also produced within the professional-management ranks due to its internal inequalities.

Failure to understand this relative poverty results in the specious reasoning that Blacks have made social and economic gains since the civil rights and Black Power movements. The reported gains in white-collar employment of Blacks between 1960 and 1980 do not take into consideration inequalities in discretionary decision-making power or relative salaries (Bowser 1981,307-324). This failure also eliminates the possibility of understanding developments in Black culture, particularly Black youth contribution to resistance elements within the culture.

The "Underclass" as a Culture of Resistance

Black culture has become inextricably linked to resistance and protest, redefined over time by professional-managers as criminality. Today's so-called underclass Black family culture, education, employment, crime and life itself are a composite of resistance. The mainstream is correctly viewed as illegitimate and grossly unjust. The legitimation crisis is real to many Black youth. An example among many occurred when a Black male youth, engaged in an argument with a high school counselor, pulled $900 in cash out of his pocket and then asked the counselor how much money he had on him. The counselor responded that he had $26. The unavoidable conclusion from this story is that the student has a reasonable understanding of America cultural and institutional systems (Jones 1986,16-29). He understands that money has become the omnipotent cultural production, and ideologies adhering to the moral justification of the system are merely rationalizations committed to the perpetuation of master-slave relationships.

Rejection of Key Institutions

At least 48% of Black households are headed by women. The majority of Blacks over the age of 18 are no longer married. Divorce rates alone underestimate the extent of marital dissolution. Separations are nearly as common as divorce among Blacks. About 47% of Black men and 56% of Black women are not married. Most Black children are born out of wedlock and are reared in poverty; 86% of Black youth live in poverty (NYT 1983).

The nuclear family is no longer the model applicable to Black families. The decline in Black nuclear families is not due simply to economics—being able to support such a luxury. It is also due to a gradual disenchantment with the ideology of the nuclear family after 1925; male-present households were the norm between 1880 and 1925 (Pitts 1982; McGhee 1984). Whatever the impact on the human growth and development of Black youth, it remains clear that many Blacks have rejected the ideology of the nuclear family. It has been reported that nuclear family organization is central to economic organization (Chodorow 1978). This ultimately means that while Black neo-extended families, or network structures, are more equalitarian than nuclear family organization, there remains the contradiction between what is needed for economic success in America and the Black family. It is likely that the rejection of the nuclear family is in fact a deeper rejection of capitalist economic organization (Rubin 1976; Eisenstein 1979).

In an equally powerful way Black youth have rejected American education. In New York City 72% of Black males drop out of high school. Nationally, the rates for the same population have ranged from 21.6% in 1968 to 16% in 1980 (Statistical Abstract 1982-83). Twenty-five % of Black children are being raised by high school dropouts. However, Black women fare better with urban education resulting in greater college enrollment. In 1981 more than 128,000 more Black females than males graduated from college. At this rate, in eight years there will be one million more Black female college graduates than Black male graduates (Blackwell 1985,150-193). One wonders if formal education is as important a factor in economic success among the masses of Blacks as we would like to think. The most successful Black Americans who began with small businesses are very often among the least and most poorly educated. Black youth have not failed to make this observation. The empirical literature reported this some years ago—it is old news: rearing background is the best predictor of educational success, in spite of test scores. Parents' location in the stratification hierarchy is the best predictor of childrens' future income (Bowles and Gintis 1972; Jencks 1972). Possibly, rejection of education is the rejection of inferior roles in the capitalist economic organization.

Black youth reasonably give little legitimacy to the labor market. In the decade between 1972 and 1982 labor market participation for Black males declined from 79% to 75%. There were 425,000 adult Black men who either never entered the legitimate labor force or were dropouts. In 1982 over two million of all Black males, 29% between the ages of 20 and 64 were either unemployed or not in the labor force. In 1982, 48% of Black teenagers were unemployed, as compared to 19% of White teenagers. It is estimated that 25% of the income of Black youth comes from crime. Much of Black labor is criminal labor. In 1981 there were more than two million arrests of Black males. In 1978 Blacks were 25% of approximately 273,000 persons in state and federal adult correctional facilities, and another 60,000 Black males were in local jails (McGhee 1984). Robert Staples summarized the situation: "Many blacks do not consider America to be a fair and just society, hence feel little obligation to obey its laws . . . .

The fact that America and South Africa rank as the world's largest jailers of racial minorities in the industrialized world gives eloquent testimony to the role of race in the criminal justice system" (Staples 1984,63).

Black males have indicated a consistent alienation from the American social system. The strongest evidence of this sense of alienation has been increasing homicide and suicide rates among Black males. The highest death rate from accidents and violence is represented by Black males compared to any other race or ethnic groups. There were 153 deaths per 100,000 Black males, while there were 98.6 deaths per 100,000 White males in 1985. Black males die from homicide at a rate which is almost six times that of Black females. In 1978 more than one-third of Black male deaths resulted from homicide in the age group of 20 to 24 years. Between 1970 and 1979 there were over 78,322 Black male homicide victims. There is a spiraling suicide rate among young Black males. Suicide is the third leading cause of death among young Black males. Black males had a 1979 rate of 11.6 suicides per 100,000 which was an increase from 8.0 per 100,000 in 1970.

Method: Recording Everyday Stories

No one in the "legitimate" world wants to know what bad Black boys think or to ask bad Black boys to give their reactions to particular criminal stories. For one point, the boys are aware of the expected line that they should give toward such stories. They have a cultural heritage of techniques to perform normative expectations. In the situations in which they are placed, they must select, check, suspend, regroup and transform the direction of their statements and behavior, given their experiences (Kuhn 1964; Blumer 1969).

I want to suggest a method of studying the boys which records their natural stories in everyday conversation. Researchers who engage bad Black boys cannot know if their preconceived ideas are correct or if they are getting straight information. Instead, the researcher should rely on the mythical history and biographies of the subjects. Otherwise, the researcher runs the risk of obfuscating the natural front the bad boy creates and the natural setting by the introduction of political considerations. The appearance and the manner of the researcher might significantly alter the manner, and in short, the reaction to the situation.

To generate mythical histories and biographies, the researcher should become emerged in the culture of the Black boys. Go to the places they go and become involved in the action in which they are involved. In this way, the researcher can come to see the world from the viewpoint of the boys. It provides the opportunity to listen to the natural stories the boys tell in their daily uninhibited conversations. Stories are narrations of events which take on a mythical character. The myths organize the world view for the community. Myths transmit the important style of life that is appropriate for youth with similar mind-sets or in similar social situations. This method takes on the world from the viewpoint of the subject, rather than from the perspective of an authority. The myth is organized in rituals that express the goals of the social group.

Ritual behavior is group communication in addressing the human condition. These behaviors are meaningful in the sense that the goals of the group are often expressed through rituals. The famous sociologist, Max Weber called "style of life" more than the categories of "matters of taste" or "appreciative standards" of appropriateness. Bendix wrote: "Weber's specific objective was to analyze the social conditions under which the charismatic inspirations of the few became first 'the style of life' of a distant status group and eventually the dominant orientation of a whole civilization" (Bendix 1962). To accomplish and maintain group membership, a commitment to the group's collective "style of life" is necessary. The commandments of the group becomes the individual's duty, or as Max Weber described it, his "sacred honor." The significant rituals that prescribe a "style of life" for bad Black boys are the disciplines of heterosexuality, it's-a-white-man's-world, and trickster. The agents of social control are committed to the ritual of I-caught-a-bad-nigger.

Heterosexuality

Bad Black boys are oblivious to the full significance of their development of masculinity. Socialization of Black boys in America sends competing messages in a peculiar way to the boys. On the one hand, boys are encouraged to identify with the privileges of masculinity while at the same time they are encouraged to remain boys for the rest of their lives. Essentially, it is a choice of career paths where many boys believe it is either "ball" or "time". They realize that any career choice will result in discrimination; that they will be unable to go as far as White boys. A cultural form of ambivalence toward masculinity is obvious among Black boys. Claude Brown's classic provides an example:

> The first time I heard the expression baby used by one cat to address another was up at Warwick in 1951. Gus Jackson used it. The term had a hip ring to it, a real colored ring. The first time I heard it, I knew right away I had to start using it. It was like saying, "Man, look at me. I've got masculinity to spare." It was saying at the same time to the world, "I'm one of the hippest cats, one of the most uninhibited cats on the scene. I can say 'baby' to another cat, and he can say 'baby' to me, and we can say it with strength in our voices" (Brown 1965,171).

On this point we should be careful. Cultural restraint in the boys' masculine socialization is not necessarily a fear of being called a "sissy." The boys are primarily concerned about the possibility of being exploited by peers, authorities, systems or situations. They are reacting to the oppression and repress the confrontations they face in those kinds of interactions. The boys must keep their pride in the face of brutal social images. They know that "sissies" are fair game for exploitation, as are their sisters. The boys are careful not to jeopardize their birthright of masculine privilege by becoming as exploitable as girls are in society. When the boys' desire for full masculine privilege is affronted by repressive authorities, they react bringing into practice their cultural dicta. One bad Black boy illustrates the meaning of "sissy" by suggesting that his sister was not a sissy, nor was anyone in his mother's house:

See, I doubt if somebody will grab me because if they grab me they got a fight. My mother didn't raise any sissies in the house. My sister, she can fight. She's nineteen. I know this dude that jumped on me. She whipped him so bad they had to take him to the hospital; he had a concussion.

It's-a-White-Man's-World

Commitment to delinquency in the context of the dimension of forced criminality features a ritualized reaction on the part of the delinquents. Black youth are alienated from the cultural values of the propertied and professional-managerial elite. This is most clearly illustrated in the contacts the Black youth have with the police. The police are often referred to as "the man" or "the rollers." "The man" has a double-meaning. First, it refers to the most prominent sexual power in a given situation. Secondly, it refers to the dominance of White men of power.

Black boys are primarily concerned with avoiding shame and guilt in situations with the police. Their relationship to the police is analogous to the settler class in colonized and neo-colonized Third World countries. While most Americans believe that the police function to protect and serve the community, Black boys perceive the police as settler agents whose intentions are to "set up", "hold down", and "roll on" the community. To avoid embarrassment, shame and guilt; in short, emasculation, the boys seek to neutralize the military-like systems that occupy their communities. As one boy described it:

> One night I was walking down (the street) on my way to the house and I seen my cousin and them (the police) in the wash house. OK! Then a helicopter starts flying around me and stuff. They put the light on me and I just kept on walking until I got into the wash house. When I got into the wash house, see I had some gloves on me, and I said these fools might want to come and get me. I handed my cousin the gloves. Just about a minute after I did that I was standing up there and the police came in there checkin' me. So I said, "Ah, what seems to be the problem, Officer?" He said, "Which way did you come down here?" I said, "I came down (the street)." He said, "Well, there's a lady up the street who says you were messing with her car." (I said), "Do you see a bumper jack or something?" Then he asked me do I want to go down the street. I told him no, on the grounds it might incriminate me. I wasn't messing with the car. I always keep gloves; I might have to bust a nigger up. I don't want to mess up my hands on those hard-ass niggers. After that, soon as I go walking down the street, Blood (the police) said, "We're going to get the lady to come down here"-where I was. So he got me standing in front of this big picture window like some kind of criminal or something. Then this other policeman comes down the street and tells him that the lady says that I was the one who did it. So I said, "Fool, I ain't no criminal." So they ran a check on me. So they said the lady said wasn't nothing missing out of her car. (The policeman said), "We're going to let you go but I'm going to take your name and send a record of you to the police." I said, "Go right ahead", they're never going to see me.

Trickster

Authority has always been a problem for Black Americans. As one commentator has pointed out, "It is not the dominator who constructs a culture and imposes it on the dominated. This culture is a result of the structural relations between the dominated and the dominator" (Freire 1970). A kind of anarchy emerges because authority must use fraudulent social relations to maintain its dominance. We have seen this false authority used in America's racist history. We have also seen the persistent revolt against American social control.

An illustration is that Black and White youth respond differently in public situations where authority is involved. The Black youth confront a public view that sees their distinctive racial, cultural and linguistic features as a source of public embarrassment. White youth come to social situations with a cultural heritage associated with glorifying the "lovely White." Black youth come to social situations with an attitude of having something to prove. This need is perpetuated by the cultural vestige that "a nigger ain't shit." Most Black youth know the myth and operate on it in their general appraisal of situations. The closer the boy is associated with the delinquent, the more certain we can depend on him to operate on the nigger myth.

Black youth view their social promotion as pilgrims engaged in struggle. On the other hand, White youth view their condition as a status of privilege, comfort and harmony. Even rebellious White youth have the privilege of race to clean up and rejoin the mainstream. White delinquents are treated differently than Black ones. Black youth believe they must fight for a place in given situations while White youth believe their status is guaranteed. Often, Black youth display an argumentative mode of conduct in situations which arise during a normal day. Authorities are alarmed by the level of aggressiveness. The authorities view the aggression as poor preparation for the rigors of civilized manners and style. The authorities point to biological, psychological, social or cultural differences; they seldom reason that the differences are ideological. In fact, the authorities have developed additional techniques to contain Black youth "mau-mauing."

While White youth value prosaic posturing related to their social achievements, Black youth value sport in their social presentations. Many Black youth will refer to the myth of the "sporty life"—social accomplishment should be done with adventure where style and chance determine goals. When the Black youth say that they have "scored", they mean that they have accomplished an intended goal in antagonistic circumstances. To "score a lid of dope" is similar to "scoring on that babe" or scoring in a class. White youth believe that they only score at play; Black youth play to score. These distinctions appear to be true even among delinquent White youth.

The Black boys rely centrally on the myth of the "player," "hustler," or "playboy" as a model for the expression of style and manner. The authorities view these roles as pretentious displays of virility. Each role is fundamentally a labor market orientation. For the Black boys there is great insecurity about their labor market roles. This insecurity translates into higher aggressive behaviors on their parts. White youth feel greater security in their labor market performances partly because the history of American political economy has provided "affirmative action" for White males. They did not have to compete with Black males for jobs since Black males were always excluded from the best jobs. Even today, this legacy is with us in the sense of relative deprivation.

The orientation to masculinity is not directed toward contributing to gross national production; it is tied to domestic labor production. The occupations are service-sector work where street culture serves as a highly competitive environment snared with the antagonisms inherent in systems where individuals sell their labor in a "free market." The goals of the boys' activities are to earn money, material and pleasure where all three are in short supply. The boys carry culturally transmitted trickster techniques to enhance their competition in the urban domestic street markets. We will see how the trickster technique functions in street communications.

Communication in urban domestic street markets requires rituals of performance and fronts. Information sharing is done through "signifying" where the communicator makes a verbal or gestural front which enables observers to place the communication in context. The observers are called on to agree with the performance of the communicator; that is, they engage in "certifying" the situational provocation of the communicator. If agreement exist with the social construction of the communicator, the observers initiate the ritual of "cosigning" where language and gestures of agreement are exchanged. The boys will verbally make statements, such as "right on" or "sho' you right", or engage in hand slapping ceremonies like "high five."

In a deeper sense, to signify means of repeating a sign retells a folk tale: "Blood, it's a white man's world; he is out to crush the studs." To certify the sign is to admit awareness of it in the moral universe: "Sho' you right, black." To cosign means to affirm the messenger, the message and the way of communicating: "I'm down with you, blood." Usually these signs are performed in the setting of "jive talking." For those communicating, it becomes a matter of "keeping the faith."

Construction of social reality in the urban domestic markets always includes turn-taking. A turn to express reality is taken and not earned. Actors in black culture are expected "to take his" which is done through "woofing"—the communicator attempts to convince the audience that his understanding will stand before challenge. Black boys who fail to woof will be viewed as less virulent with respect to achieving the rewards of money, respect and girls. These exchanges require careful management of aggression. The game for them is "to keep it all together" by remaining "cool" or by "chilling."

Black boys are also taught through male culture to portray docility. But their masculinity is tied to the ability to transform their docile appearance into a weapon against oppression. The grandfather character in Ellison's Invisible Man expressed this cultural dictum: "Live with your head in the lion's mouth . . . I want you to overcome 'em with grins, agree 'em to death and destruction, let 'em swoller you till they vomit or burst wide open" (Ellison 1972,19-20).

The primary device of the Black boys seeing themselves as "niggers" produces a moral commitment to the trickster, justified by their condition of forced criminality. To be a nigger entails more then operating as trickster only toward White authorities. It includes making adjustments in a variety of interactions, in fact, toward peers too. The nigger is hard and bad, possessing extraordinary sexual power. At the same time, the nigger is understated and docile, a hard worker for a style of life reflecting consumption of the "better things in life." The most respected pimp, for example, will work long hours to maintain his image and business organization. At the same time, he is expected to be well-dressed and have an impressive car. The pimp's role is usually adverse to other pimps who represent potential threats to his territory. The important ethic operating among pimps is to always avoid embarrassment.

Whether the boys are involved in pimping and pandering, drug dealing, robbery or prostitution, occasionally or as a regular, they rely on the trickster mode to accomplish the exchange. The ideal trickster is a magnanimous character whose intentions are malicious. Black youth malevolence is guided by the nature of the work they must do, simply, "It's a jungle" where every man is expected to take ideal and material power if granted the opportunity. Charles Silberman wrote an excellent description of the Black trickster (Silberman 1980,159-224). For our purpose, it is important to stress the Black cultural themes, given the historical and temporal reasons for having a commitment to those values.

The malevolent aspect of the trickster personality is directly related to the human condition that requires that the boys work or starve. That is, in a capitalist society, money is the mediation of exchange. Most of society limits what is understood as illegitimate. But the boys have had to revise legitimacy to make sense out of their reality. Life becomes "that fast life" where a "quick trick" emerges as the means and ideal of the good life. Easy money for them is the ultimate symbol of success, and easy money is always fast money.

Black culture disseminates a set of trickster techniques to

contend with the anarchy of inequality, imparting to its youth's rebellious style: "You might be poor, but you can always be clean." The appearance of leisure and of conspicuous consumption might at first cause us to reason that an anti work ethic exists among the boys. We realize with closer observation that the domestic work of the boys is hard work accomplished in a facade of leisure.

The boys, for example, who sell marijuana on the streets of the major cities are representative of the trickster mode. When the marijuana arrives in their neighborhoods, it is in bulk form. The marijuana must be weighed and packaged for distribution in the community. This work is tedious and requires attentive measures. The small packages are distributed to a team of street hustlers who must compete in the street market with spontaneous techniques, such as two-for-one sales or by "fixing-up" (increasing the weight of) the package. In addition, the individual seller must be on constant look out for plainclothes and uniformed policemen. The youth selling marijuana on the streets feel stress from the fact that the police or a rival might "jump out on you" at any time. Then there is additional stress from the risk of missing a customer.

The boy's language reflects the stress of the exchange. When they approach a potential customer, they will commonly set the parameters for the exchange: "Blood, it is hot out here." This indicates that the police are suspected of being in the vicinity. At the same time, the boys advertise their product, "This is the best lovely (a treated form of marijuana) in town." Regardless of the quality of the marijuana a boy is selling, he must "unload it." This condition intensifies the trickster activity on the street. Poor-quality marijuana at best sells where the seller can remain unknown and the boys will have to make a judgment when the issue arises.

I-Caught-a-Bad-Nigger

The most protrusive ritual engaged in by the professional-managerial administration is the activity of systematically organizing and justifying the failure of Black boys. The fact is that most crime is committed by the professional-managerial class. In spite of this, most arrests and prosecution are suffered by the underclass. While one can reason that the professional-managers class provides a necessary service in society it is more difficult to argue that they are directed by altruistic motives.

Most professional-managers are on the scene among the underclass primarily to earn an ever-increasing standard of living; therefore, if their salaries are taken away they have little reason to remain administrators over the oppression of the underclass. All this notwithstanding, the values of hard work, loyalty, strength, discipline, religiosity, fitness, patriotism and character are essential to the professional-managerial agenda. However, those values function to the specifications of racist mores and traditions. Given such a context, the value orientation of the professional-managerial class is applied to make the Black boys understand their status in society as a caste career of limitations and diminished potentials. The professional-managers must initiate status degradation ceremonies using their assumptions of the disreputable Black boys.

In Black culture we are left with the profile image of the professional-managerial agenda in Richard Wright's novel Native Son. The central protagonist, Bigger Thomas, is described in the story's newspaper account as a "Negro sex-slayer . . . looks exactly like an ape . . . gives the impression of possessing abnormal strength . . . is about five feet, nine inches tall and his skin is exceedingly black . . . His lower jaw protrudes obnoxiously, reminding one of a jungle beast" (Wright 1966,260). While it is hard to imagine the five-feet-nine boy being the animal he is described to be, it is relatively easy to understand why Bigger is imagined by the professional-managers to be the profile of a criminal. The work of the professional-managerial class is similar to the earlier work of the missionary in colonized countries: the colonizer must transform the heathen culture of the native into a supposed culture of repute.

The professional-managers are for the most part oblivious to the cultural vestige since they have been trained to believe that their system of government is the best in the world, where persons are presumed innocent until proven guilty. The professionalmanagerial attitude results in the anarchy of their administration; they operate as if the Black boys are guilty of incompetence, over-expressed athleticism, and delinquency. The boys, for their part, sense an indignation and feel that they have nothing to lose.

Conclusion

Acceptance of affinity for and affiliation with delinquency among underclass boys is motivated by the criminal anarchy of the administration of the professional-managers. Black culture is resistant to mainstream American social organization—our survival as a people has necessitated it. The boys run against the limits of the caste structure and if they attempt to transcend those limitations, they are checked by the professional-managers. The boys are not the problem; we have sufficient reason to believe they are forced to accept their expected and mythical role of "bad niggers."

Forced criminality produced by the structural relations fuels an apparent irrationality among bad Black boys who feel rebellious toward state rationality. Perhaps like Jacobins, the relatively deprived French revolutionists, the boys sense society's commitment to the proposition that "a nigger ain't shit." In my view, Tocqueville's prophecy that the possibility of revolution lies in the presence of Blacks in the United States is of major significance.

If American society is as I understand it, then we are left with three choices in our orientation toward Black youth. One possibility is to ask them to adhere to European American values, realizing that they will continue to be exploited. Not only will they be exploited, but to prosper in the context of American capitalism means to exploit people of color in the international Third World. For Americans to live at a higher standard of living means that the labor of poorer nations and their natural resources must be appropriated by American multinationals at a profit. Profit is the labor of a laborer not paid to him or her. Profit is kept by someone who has not labored. This choice is immoral.

The second choice is to cultivate rebellion in the youth by organizing training centers promoting urban war with the goal of overthrowing American society. This goal is unrealistic in the sense that American Blacks do not have the resources, the will and the organization to effectively wage a violent insurrection given American militarism. Nonetheless, we must heed Sidney Willhelm's incisive warning in his now classic *Who Needs The Negro?*:

> The life situation of Black Americans deteriorates with the passing of each year . . . Technological efficiency makes possible the full realization of the nation's anti-Negro beliefs. The arrival of automation eliminates the need for Black labor, and racist values call for the Negro's removal from the American scene . . . What is the point, demands White America, in tolerating an unwanted racial minority when their is no economic necessity for acceptance. With machines now replacing human labor, who needs the Negro? (Willhelm 1971).

Our final choice is to promote conflict professional-managers while continuing the Black tradition of protest and resistance.

It means supporting Black youth through organizing our communities to educate them in black history, the nature of capitalism, sexism, ageism and racism. We must also teach effective child-rearing practices in our communities through grass-roots education. Above all, we must allow society to take its course. This means that we should expect the inherent contradictions in any fraudulent social system to correct themselves. We must be prepared to seize the moments to free ourselves and our children when those opportunities present themselves.

References

Banfield, E. 1970. *The Unheavenly City*. Boston: Little, Brown.

Bell, D. 1973. *The Coming of Post-Industrial Society*. New York: Basic Books.

Bendix, R. 1962. *Max Weber: An Intellectual Portrait*. New York: Doubleday.

Blackwell, J. E. 1985. *The Black Community*. New York: Harper and Row.

Blumer, H. 1969. *Symbolic Interaction: Perspective and Method*. Englewood Cliffs: Prentice Hall.

Bonacich, E. 1976. "Advanced Capitalism and Black/White Race Relations in the United States: A Split Labor Market Interpretation." *American Sociological Review*. 41, 34-51.

Bowles, S. and H. Gintis. 1972. "IQ in the United States Class Structure." *Social Policy*. 3, 4-5.

Bowser, B. 1981. "Race Relations in the 1980s: The Case of the U.S." *Journal of Black Studies*. 15, 307-324.

Brown, C. 1965. *Manchild in the Promised Land*. New York: New American Library.

Chodorow, N. 1978. *The Reproduction of Mothering: Psycho-Analysis and the Sociology of Gender*. Berkeley: University of California Press.

Eisenstein, Z. (ed.) 1979. *Capitalist Patriarchy and The Case for Socialist Feminism*. New York: Monthly Review Press.

Ellison, R. 1972. *Invisible Man*. New York: Vintage Trade Books.

Hegel, G. W. F. 1955. *Lectures on the History of Philosophy*. Vol. 1. New York: The Humanities Press.

Horowitz, I. L. 1961. *Radicalism and the Revolt Against Reason: The Social Theories of Georges Sorel*. Carbondale: Southern Illinois University Press.

Jencks, C. (ed.) 1972. *Inequality*. New York: Harper and Row.

Jones, K. 1986. "The Black Male in Jeopardy." *The Crisis*. 93:3, 16-29.

Kuhn, M. 1964. "Major Trends in Symbolic Interaction Theory in the Past Twenty-five Years." *The Sociological Quarterly*. 5.

Malinowski, B. 1948. *Magic, Science and Religion*. Glencoe,IL: Free Press.

Marable, M. 1983. "Growing With My Sisters," in *How Capitalism Underdeveloped Black America*. Boston: South End Press.

Matza, D. 1971. "Poverty and Disrepute," in R.K. Merton and R. Nisbet, (eds.) Contemporary Social Problems. New York: Harcourt, Brace and World.

Matza, D. 1969. *Becoming Deviant.* Englewood Cliffs: Prentice Hall.
McGhee, J. 1984. *Running the Gauntlet: Black Men in America.* New York: Urban League.
Moynihan, D. P. 1965. *The Negro Family: The Case for National Action.* Washington, DC: U.S. Government Printing Office.
New York Times, "Blacks in America: A Statistical Profile," August 28, 1983.
Nisbet, R. 1970. *The Social Bond.* New York: Alfred A. Knopf.
Pinkney, A. 1984. *The Myth of Black Progress.* Cambridge: Cambridge University Press.
Pitts, J. 1982. "The Afro-American Experience," in Anthony and Rosalind Dworkin (eds.) *The Minority Report.* New York: Holt, Rinehart and Winston.
Poulantzas, N. 1975. *Classes in Contemporary Capitalism.* London: NLB.
Rubin, G. 1976. "The Traffic in Women: Notes on the Political Economy of Sex," in Rayna Reiter (ed.) *Towards an Anthropology of Women.* New York: Monthly Review Press.
Sheldon, W. 1949. *Varieties of Delinquent Youth: An Introduction to Constitutional Psychiatry.* New York: Harper and Row.
Silberman, C. 1980. *Criminal Violence, Criminal Justice.* New York: Vintage.
Staples, R. 1984. "American Racism and High Crime Rates: The Inextricable Connection." *The Western Journal of Black Studies.* 8:2, 62-72.
Staples, R. 1982. *Black Masculinity.* San Francisco: Black Scholar Press.
Statistical Abstract of the United States. 1985. Washington, DC: U.S. Government Printing Office.
Statistical Abstracts of the United States. 1982-1983. Washington, D.C: U.S. Government Printing Office.
Swinton, D. H. 1983. "The Economic Status of the Black Population", in *The State of Black America.* New York: National Urban League, Inc.
Willhelm, S. M. 1971. *Who Needs the Negro?* New York: Anchor Books.
Wilson, J. Q. and R. J. Hernstein. 1985. *Crime and Human Nature.* New York: Simon and Schuster.
Wright, R. 1966. *Native Son.* New York: Harper and Row.
Young, M. 1961. *The Rise of the Meritocracy.* Baltimore: Penguin.

Section Two:

FAMILIES AND COMMUNITIES—PARENTING

FAMILIES DO NOT HAVE AND REAR CHILDREN in some abstract reality nor is it done based on isolated moral values. Real life conditions affect the context of family formation, birth and rearing of young people. Grace Massey looks at teen parents. They could be anyone's daughter and son, but under the circumstances they are also parents. Joyce King and Carolyn Mitchell give us a glimpse of the struggle Black mothers have in rearing their sons. Because of how Black people are viewed in the larger society, Black mothers' struggles are not identical to the struggles of White mothers. Differences in history and life conditions matter. And finally, Loften Mitchell speaks from experience—from biography. He has lived through and witnessed the changes in Black parenting. What we especially miss today is the tradition of community co-rearing. It made a difference in the 1930s. It could make a difference today.

Chapter 5

The Flip Side of Teen Mothers: A Look at Teen Fathers

Grace Massey

THE DATA COLLECTION FOR THIS PAPER represents a collaborative effort among three programs that provide services to teen parents. The focus of this essay is on teen mothers' perceptions of their babies' fathers. But first, a brief overview of Oakland, California is in order. Teen pregnancy is in epidemic proportions in the city's lower-income Black communities. As it is in other American cities. The city has a population of approximately 360,000 people. According to the 1980 Census, over 60% of this population is made up of ethnic minorities, 47% of whom are Black. If anything the percentages of Blacks and other minorities have increased over the past decade. Although growing in many positive directions, Oakland embodies many problems associated with "inner cities": low income, high crime rates, White flight to neighboring suburbs, schools with test scores below the national levels and increasing drug and substance abuse. The average Black income is $11,385 and one quarter of these families have incomes below the poverty level (Census 1986). The official city-wide unemployment rate is close to 10%. However, the rate for Black teens is closer to 40%.

Regarding teenage pregnancy, 54% of all adolescent births in the county of Alameda occur in Oakland—over 500 babies in 1987 and the number is growing. Of the city's adolescent births, approximately 73% are to young Black teenagers.

The problems associated with teen mothers have been well documented: 30% higher maternal mortality and infant mortality rates, 20% higher rates of miscarriage, 36%

higher rates of premature birth (Alan Guttmacher Institute 1981). This does not mention the psychological and social ramifications both to the individuals involved and the larger community.

The issues surrounding adolescence are compounded by motherhood. However, due to limited resources and opportunities available to the Black underclass, their lives are unfolding within a uniquely oppressive environment. A noted Black psychiatrist, Chester Pierce (1969) compares this situation of continuing, subliminal stressful conditions conditioning the lives of Black families in America to the isolation and stress of Eskimos in the Artic—an extreme, exotic environment. He views Blacks as living in a mundane, extreme environment; that is, an environment where racism and subtle oppression are ubiquitous, constant, continuing and mundane. This, he suggested, presents many psychosocial difficulties and stresses for Blacks in general. Black teen mothers are faced with coping in this mundane extreme stress created by racism, while combating the negative stigmas and consequences of adolescent motherhood.

Black teen fathers, too, are faced with a tremendous burden—they are Black, they are adolescents, they are male and they are all unprepared fathers. Noel Cazenave (1981) describes all Black men in this country as being put in a "double bind." He suggests that we, both men and women, Black and White, have generally embraced the notion that the man should be the provider in families; he should be the one to "bring home the bacon," provide the economic base. However, the reality is that many Black men through miseducation, lack of skills and job opportunities cannot enact this provider role. Thus the double bind of being expected to "prove" their manhood through providing the primary economic support of their families and the lack of means to play this role puts "manhood" for Black men at risk.

Cazenave then goes on to discuss how Black men creatively adapt to this situation, mainly by engaging in "macho" roles—the tough guy through sexual conquests and dominating behaviors. Young boys in lower-class communities see these behaviors and emulate them, often without the contrast of more positive role models to serve as buffers and interpreters of the environment. For example, sexual behavior is considered a cornerstone of masculinity and young boys frequently choose early sexual behavior to prove this masculinity. Past research in the area of onset of sexual interaction also indicates Black boys engage in sexual activity earlier as a result of other blockages in the opportunity structure in our society (Broderick 1965; Staples 1985).

The absence of traditional "rites of passage" into puberty with community direction and support, coupled with the ongoing media blitz on the joys of sexuality, entice young Black boys and girls to engage in sex without thought to future consequences. These consequences manifest themselves as early parenthood. Data from a program providing services to teen mothers is one way to examine these issues.

Data Collection

Fifty teen mothers, including eight mothers-to-be, completed a two-page questionnaire about their education, living and job status, and the fathers of their babies. The questionnaire also covered issues regarding the relationship each respondent has with the baby's father, her own current needs and her perception of the role played by the baby's father. The questionnaires were administered one-on-one or in small groups with a staff member. In addition to the questionnaire, focus groups about the issues on the questionnaire were held with three groups of respondents. All respondents were involved in at least one program focusing on teen mothers. The sample represents young mothers who are more connected with services than many other teen mothers who are not. They may be less isolated, and perhaps more motivated to reach out for help.

Findings

Demographics

The questionnaire respondents (N=50) ranged in age between 14 and 21 with the majority (74%) being 15-17 year old. At the birth of their babies, the mothers age ranged between 12-19 years old with 90% being 17 and younger. The fathers were older with an age range from 13 years old to 27 at the birth of their children. However, the majority (60%) of the fathers were 17-19 years old. Thus, the fathers generally were a couple of years older than the teen mothers.

Most teen mothers and fathers lived with their mothers at the time of their babies births—68% of teen mothers and 54% of the teen fathers. When living with fathers and other relatives is included, the number living within a kinship network increased to 86% for both teen fathers and mothers. Thus the strong kinship patterns and the extended family that have traditionally characterized Black families is still the norm for our sample.

Regarding education, 4% of our responding teen mothers had graduated from high school at the time of their babies' births. Twenty-eight percent of the fathers were high school graduates. On the other hand, 12% of the mothers and 32% of the fathers had dropped out, seven (14%) of these fathers dropped out by the time they were 18. The remainder were still in junior or senior high school at the time of the babies' births.

Table 1
Parent's School Status at Time of Baby's Birth

	Mothers		Fathers	
	(N)	(%)	(N)	(%)
High School Graduate	2	4	14	28
Still in School	42	84	20	40
Dropout	6	12	16	32
Total	50	100	50	100

Although there were eight respondents who did not know their babies' fathers' employment situation at the time of their baby's birth, approximately one-third of the fathers were unemployed (33%), one-third worked part-time (24%) or full-time (7%) and onethird (36%) were still in school without employment (see table 2). Thus the vast majority of these teen fathers were not prepared financially to support their babies, although a third (32%) of the respondents indicated that the fathers were looking for jobs at the time of their babies' births. Consequently, thirty of the forty-two teen mothers (71%), excluding the pregnant teens (N=8), were receiving Aid For Dependent Children (AFDC) to support their children. Of the remaining twelve mothers, eleven were supported by their families and one by the baby's father.

Table 2
Father's Employment Status at the Time of Baby's Birth

	N	%
Unemployed	14	33
Unemployed, in School	15	36
Part-time	10	24
Full-time	3	7
Total	42	100

Fathers' Participation

When we look at the teen mothers' perception of father involvement, we find that fathers do participate on varying levels with their babies. Twenty-four (57%) of the teen mothers reported that the fathers were with them at the hospital during birth and thirty-one (74%) stated that the fathers visited them in the hospital after the birth.

Approximately, two-thirds (67%) of the teen mothers

state that the fathers visit their babies regularly and that they presently have good relations with the fathers (65%). This may be a sampling artifact since our sample involves very young children with the majority of the babies (76%) under 3 years old. Ewer and Gibbs (1975) found that the relationship between adolescent Black mothers and the fathers of their babies change character between conception and nine months of birth. Typically, the couple sees less and less of one another. In this sample, group discussions with the mothers support these findings that many teen fathers tend to become less involved as their children get older and the couples go their separate ways.

However, these are good indications that these young fathers are generally not denying paternity even though they are not able to take full financial responsibility for the babies. Quite the contrary, 58% of our mothers report receiving some marginal financial support from the fathers, 41% report receiving help with baby-sitting, and 84% report having good relationships with the father's family.

Contextual Issues

In an attempt to get a general picture of the fathers, we inquired not only about their demographics and participation with the babies, but also about their involvement with the so-called "street culture." Sexual conquest was combined with being violent and tough in Cazenave's depiction of Black men who were caught in the "double bind." Due to the sensitive nature of such issues, we thought there might be hesitancy in reporting physical violence and drug involvement by our teen mothers. However, four (8%) of our sample did respond that their babies' fathers got physically violent and abusive with them. Three did not respond to this question. Nine respondents (18%) stated that the fathers used drugs, seven (14%) stated that the fathers sold drugs, and eleven (22%) stated that the fathers lived with people who sell or use drugs. Self-reports indicate that only two of our mothers stated they use drugs and now live with people who use or sell drugs.

In a 1978 survey of 421 teen boys, 72% indicated that they had not used any form of contraception in their last sexual encounter (Finkel and Finkel 1978). Our data are consistent with these findings. Slightly over 70% of the respondents state the fathers do not use contraceptives. However, over half (52%) state they, the mothers, now use contraceptives. Repeat pregnancies are common occurrences with these teen mothers. The discussions indicate that the fathers do not want to use birth control and do not want them to get abortions. This is consistent with Hendricks' data on unmarried Black adolescent fathers. He reports that, although there may be a willingness to share contraceptive responsibility, the majority of the fathers surveyed were opposed to abortions (Hendricks 1982). Vadies and Hale (1977) also found "a strong sentiment against abortion" on the part of the Black teens. There is also a strong belief on the part of Black males that contraceptive responsibility should be placed with the female. These sentiments, coupled with the vast amount of misinformation teens have about various birth control methods ensure future pregnancies. For example, in one group discussion the following statements were made:

- "Pills make you get cancer."
- "Diaphragms can get knocked around; they move and don't work."
- "Pills don't work; you get pregnant on them so why use them?"
- "My boyfriend thinks condoms are a waste of time and he can't feel it if he uses one."

It was surprising to get positive results from the mothers' subjective ratings of the fathers because of several facts: the mothers are on welfare; the young men have dropped out of school, are unemployed and may be involved with drugs. The following findings are from our mothers' more subjective responses on a listing of descriptors to the question, "Overall, how would you rate your baby's father on ____?" A five-point response scale from excellent to very poor was used. Excellent and good were combined to yield the following:

- 52% felt their babies' fathers were good or excellent fathers.
- 60% felt their babies' fathers were good or excellent friends to them.
- 42% felt their babies' fathers were good or excellent providers.
- 46% felt their babies' fathers were good or excellent role models.
- 46% responded their babies' fathers rated good or
- excellent as responsible persons.
- 54% responded their babies' fathers rated good or
- excellent as being loving and affectionate;
- 38% rated their babies' fathers good or excellent workers.
- 40% rated their babies' fathers good or excellent students.

These subjective ratings almost seem inconsistent with the more specific demographic data presented previously. However, if we look closely at the context of these subjective ratings, we find the concept of "relativity" at work. In 1947, Gardner Murphy in his analysis of personality states that choice of referents "becomes a wish fulfilling, purposeful mechanism [by which] the individual enhances and defends the self by an appropriate choice of those with whom to identify" (Murphy 1947,). Most of our respondents live in environments where many girls become pregnant and have babies. Many of the fathers do not give any support. So when they get ten or twenty dollars a week, they respond that fathers are "good" providers—good compared to the referent group of fathers that pay nothing. This also possibly allows them to defend their own behavior for actually having sex and children by young men who cannot provide adequate support. Many studies in urban school settings report this same relativity process at work for students who get very poor grades but believe they are average students (Ogbu 1974; St. John 1971; Massey 1975).

Typology of Fathers

After lengthy individual and group discussions with the teen mothers, a typology of fathers emerged:

- Type 1 depicted the teen father who felt very confused about the news of pending paternity. He was going through the typical adolescent search for identity and this news was viewed with great ambivalence. He knew he wasn't prepared. He felt guilty and ashamed but also responsible. He accepted his paternity and tried to lend support but often was not even in the position of supporting himself. He was typically still in school.
- Type 2 father reacted quite differently. Although he, too, could not support a child, he was extremely proud of the fact that he was going to be a father. He would typically plead with the pregnant teen not to even consider an abortion. A child represented a symbol of manhood, a source of pride. In some cases he had one or more children and boasted of his virility. When convenient, he would participate with his child and/or the mother.
- Type 3 represented the father who avoided all the responsibility of his baby. He would go as far as to say the baby wasn't his. Other typical accusations focused on the mother (i.e., "She could have had an abortion"; "she didn't have to say yes"; or "She should have used birth control").
- Type 4 fathers were those young men who really took full legal and financial responsibility for their children. Some were with the teen mother and baby and provided a full-time father figure. Others sent money for support and responded to the needs as they arose even though they were no longer involved with the mother. These fathers were generally older and employed.

The preceding father types are not fixed positions. Based on group discussions, mothers indicate fathers can move from one type to another just as Schulz describes in his depiction of boyfriends (Schulz 1986). Other fathers may embody characteristics of more than one of these types at the same time.

Discussion/Summary

These data were collected to get a perspective on young Black fathers, to look at the "flip side" of the coin on teenage pregnancy. Unfortunately, like many research endeavors, the accessibility of any given sample increases their likelihood of being studied. However, due to both time and fiscal constraints, the perspectives of only the more accessible teen mothers is captured in these data. This interjection is not made to invalidate nor apologize for the data; quite the contrary, the mothers' responses are very informative and provide a lot of insight. However, future research and work with fathers is critical as indicated by the following summary of findings:

1. The babies' fathers are more likely to be older teens or in their early twenties.
2. Teen parents generally live with their own parent(s) or with relatives.
3. One-third of the fathers had dropped out of school by the time they were 18 years old.
4. Teen mothers and teen fathers are not prepared for parenthood. It was not planned nor actively avoided.
5. Young fathers do participate in the lives of their babies by visiting the baby, baby-sitting and when possible, by providing modest financial help.
6. Contraceptives are not being used by large numbers of sexually active teens.
7. Teen mothers believe their babies' fathers are positive figures despite their lack of ability to fully support their children.
8. When describing their own situation, mothers frequently use other teen parents in their environment as their primary reference group when subjectively rating the role of fathers.
9. Teen fathers are not all just alike. They engage in a wide

variety of behaviors regarding their paternity status, some of which are constructive and others detrimental.

Many of these findings validate previous findings and hypotheses regarding teen parenthood. However, neither an academic, research, nor moralistic approach will begin to solve the multiple problems encountered by our teen parents. A thorough understanding that teen pregnancy, both from the mothers' and fathers' sides of the coin, is merely a symptom of much larger structural, socioeconomic and political problems is mandatory in any attempt to produce constructive change.

Due to the interconnectedness of the problem, any solution will be also interdependent. The fragmented approach of giving only child care, or only summer jobs, or only training programs will not be sufficient. Young men as well as young women must be included in successful prevention programs. Our youth, boys and girls, have to be lured away from the "live just for now" orientation and made to really believe they have a positive, worthwhile stake in their future and a firm commitment to our collective future as a race.

References

Alan Guttmacher Institute. 1981. "Teenage Pregnancy: The Problem That Hasn't Gone Away." New York: Planned Parenthood Federation of America.

Broderick, C.B. 1965. "Social Heterosexual Development Among Urban Negroes and Whites." *Journal of Marriage and the Family*. 27.

Cazenave, N. 1981. "Black Men in America, The Quest for Manhood" in H. McAdoo (ed.) *Black Families*. Beverly Hills: Sage.

Ewer, P. and J.O. Gibbs. 1975. "Relationship with Putative Fathers and Use of Contraception in a Population of Black Ghetto Adolescent Mothers." *Public Health Reports*. 90 (September):5.

Finkel, M. and B. Finkel. 1978. "Male Adolescent Contraceptive Utilization." *Adolescence*. 13:51.

Hendericks, L. 1982. "Unmarried Black Adolescent Fathers' Attitudes Toward Abortion, Contraception and Sexuality: A Preliminary Report." *Journal of Adolescent Health Care.* 2,3.

Massey, G.C. 1975. *Self-Concept, Personal Control and Social Context Among Students in Inner-City High Schools.* Dissertation, Stanford University.

Murphy, G. 1947. *Personality.* New York: Harper and Row.

Ogbu, J. 1974. *The Next Generation: An Ethnography of Education in an Urban Neighborhood. New York:* Academic Press.

Pierce, C. 1969. "The Effects of Racism," paper presented at American Medical Association Fifteenth Annual Conference of State Mental Health Representatives, Chicago, IL.

Schulz, David. 1986. "The Role of the Boyfriend in Lower-Class Negro Life," in R. Staples (ed.) *The Black Family: Essays and Studies.* Belmont,CA: Wadsworth.

St. John, N.H. 1971. "The Elementary Classroom as a Frog Pond: Self-Concept, Sense of Control and Social Context." *Social Forces* 49 (June):4.

Staples, R. 1985. "Changes in Black Family Structure: The Conflict Between Family Ideology and Structural Conditions." *Journal of Marriage and The Family.* 47.

Vadies, E. and D. Hale. 1977. "Attitudes of Adolescent Males Toward Abortion, Contraception and Sexuality." *Social Work in Health Care.* 3 (Winter):2.

Chapter 6

Black Mothers to Sons: Juxtaposing African-American Literature with Social Practice

Joyce King and Carolyn Mitchell

BLACK MOTHER-TO-SON RELATIONSHIPS figure prominently in African-American literature where they are typically portrayed as dramatic and distressing aspects of Black life (Wade-Gayles 1984). By contrast, social science literature on Black families has paid little scholarly attention to Black mother-to-son relationships. This scholarship has, however, created intense controversy regarding the presumed strengths or pathology of Black families as socializing agents—especially when the focus has been on negative effects of putatively absent Black fathers (Billingsley 1986; Blau 1981; Hill 1972). With a possible exception of studies by Allen (1985) and Clark (1983), the way Black mothers raise sons has been neglected in recent research on Black parenting (Slaughter and Epps 1987; Franklin and Boyd-Franklin 1985). By providing insights into Black mother-to-son parenting from two sources, African-American literature and a semi-structured group interview, this essay calls attention to the need for scholarship to correct this imbalance.

The purpose of this study is to explore the relationship between Black mothers and sons as revealed in selections from African-American literature and to explore the relevance of the literature to lived experience. This pursuit is grounded in questions about the ability of art to mirror experience and, therefore, to teach us something about ourselves. We feel this is especially important for African-Americans since dominant culture literature says so little about the reality of our existence (Williams 1988). In addition, linking the disciplines of literature and social science serves the further purpose of suggesting new ways in which literature might be used in teaching, counseling and parenting. The qualitative research strategy which combines literary and social analysis also suggests new ways to ground social inquiry in the perspectives and experiences of the participants (Bruyn 1966).

We recognize that we are charting new ground in attempting this merger between the disciplines because neither literary nor social science analysis, from a mainstream Eurocentric perspective, adequately characterizes Black life or recognizes the vital contribution of the other discipline to a fuller understanding of the Black Experience. We are joining others in the search for a relevant methodology in the human sciences that authenticates and seeks to understand the Black Experience and identifies oppressive social forces which negate it (Asante 1987; Lindsay 1975; Wa Thiong'o 1987; Wynter 1984). Therefore, we have chosen to use literary and social analysis in a deliberate and dialectical fashion to investigate and illuminate Black cultural practice from an Afrocentric perspective that focuses on significant themes, situations and events in Black mother-to-son relationships.

Method—An Afrocentric Way of Knowing: The Group Conversation Method

To explore the relationship between literature and Black life, we developed a culturally relevant qualitative "group conversation" method.* The group conversation method is

---

* Joyce King revised the group conversation method developed by Dubois and Li (1971) to "reduce social tension" and adapted this strategy to help participants identify shared experiences and to facilitate the discussion of highly personal or deeply felt emotional issues. This is part of the Afrocentric way of knowing.

a way of knowing and apprehending the reality of Black life. African-American literature is used to initiate a group conversation and critical reflection about participants' shared experiences, in this case raising sons. The researchers, who forego detachment for interdependence with the participants, share perspectives about the common experience of raising sons. For the researchers who participate fully, this reciprocal, reflexive group conversation is a way of knowing the Black Experience. As the participants and researchers reflect on the literature and their personal and shared experiences, thoughts and emotions, they become co-researchers in the inquiry process. For the participants, including the researchers, the group conversation is a way of apprehending or becoming more critically aware of the collective Black Experience through reflexive examination of their own reality.

This Afrocentric methodology reflects certain principles of the philosophy and culture of the Black Experience: it is communal, holistic and spiritual. For example, this methodology recreates the simultaneous, holistic affirmation of Black individuality and collectivity, two opposing tendencies in the Eurocentric perspective but which find harmonious expression in Black art (Nobles 1980; Stuckey 1987). By using African-American literature as a focal point to examine Black life, art resumes its role as interpreter of the collective Black experience and artistic expression assumes the traditional function of art "for life's sake" in African culture (Pasteur and Toldson 1982; Richards 1985). In addition, this method relies on storytelling and "testifyin'", traditional oral communicative art forms that serve important educative and spiritual functions in Black life and family socialization (Smitherman 1986; Hurston 1985; Morgan 1980).

This oral as opposed to written data collection strategy is also potentially empowering because it is consistent with and evokes the communality and spirituality of Black life. An active principle which unifies African-American and traditional African culture is that the "spoken word" has "power . . . to bring things into being" (Drewal and Drewal 1983). In the group conversation this transcendent "power of the spoken word," the essence of communal Black spirituality, evokes the "ancient things" that "remain in our ears." Speaking and listening to each other's stories generate knowledge of the collective Black condition and the self-insight needed to understand and respond effectively to the "Challenge of Blackness" (Bennett 1972). This challenge involves surviving with our "souls intact" in a society that is often hostile to Blackness and Black people (Praeger 1982). It is an inquiry process that recreates the shared experience of Blackness and affirms the communality and spirituality of the Black Experience. It can also enhance participants' selfknowledge by identifying the social origins of their shared emotions and experiences and by providing a context and process for critically examining their experiences.

In short, this Afrocentric group conversation method elicits reciprocal dialogue and creates the conditions for the researchers to learn with the participants about what "we" do and to reflect on why "we" do it in a manner that is akin to Douglas' (1985) "creative interviewing" strategy in which the interviewer engages participants in a "mutual search for self-understanding" (1985). In addition to gaining understanding about participants' experiences and social conditions, the group conversation enables participants to reflect on how things might be changed. In fact, this Afrocentric method is passionately and openly committed to understanding social reality in order to change it. It shares this debt to Marxist philosophy with other post-positivist research strategies: "reflexive critical inquiry" (Comstock 1982; Fay 1975); non-elitist "emancipatory praxis" (Freire 1970; Goulet 1971; Hamnett 1984; Lather 1986; Lindsay 1975; Markovic 1974) and calls for "passionate scholarship" in feminist social science (Belenky 1986; Du Bois 1983; McDade 1984; Welch 1985).

The Participants

We conducted the group conversation or semi-structured interview with five other Black mothers, some of whom were friends or neighbors. The mothers have worked in various occupations including domestic and janitorial service, nursing, child care, teaching, and administration in the nonprofit sector. Two mothers who were self-employed in the service sector owned their own businesses. The participants were between age 39 and 69 when the group met in April 1987. Two mothers (besides the researchers) between the ages of 39 and 46 have advanced college degrees. Of the other three mothers (between the ages of 55 and 69), the eldest attended but did not complete elementary school and two completed post-high school vocational training. In the interest of anonymity, all the names have been changed, and the age and employment status of individuals are not included. The mothers are identified as:

Annie:	two sons, 42 and 29 (and a grown daughter)
Elinore:	four sons, 24, 23, 21, 19 (and a grown daughter)
Dorothy:	one son, 14 (and a younger daughter)
Georgia:	one son, 19 (and a younger daughter)
June:	one grandson, 19 (her daughter's son)
Nadine:	one son, 20
Zelma:	two sons, 24 and 20.

At the time of the study three sons had just left home for their first year of college. Six were working; one was unemployed; one was psychologically disabled; another was struggling with a drug addiction. All the mothers had been married, although only two were married at the time of the study.

The Research Questions

The issue of survival has not been explored in other investigations of Black parenting. In a recent study of mothers and sons published after this project was started, Forcey (1987) identifies survival as a central concern of Black mothers of sons but fails to analyze or interpret its significance. Drawing from mother-to-son relationships portrayed in African American novels and poetry and our own experiences as mothers of sons, we (the researchers) examined the issue of survival and identified two questions for discussion:

(1) What have you done to protect your son(s) from society's hostile forces? (2) What have you taught your son(s) of honesty, loyalty, compassion, faith and responsibility?*

During the group conversation which lasted four hours we discussed and compared personal experiences with vignettes in African-American literature. In addition to the stories we shared about raising sons, comparisons were drawn between the life experiences and the literary selections which were read aloud before we discussed each question. This dialogue permitted participants to relate personal experiences to the collective Black experience as depicted in fiction and poetry and to reflect on the extent to which the literature mirrors black life. Since we did not interview the mothers individually before the group met, we have no way of gauging the extent to which one mother's responses (i.e., the stories she chose to recount) may have been influenced by what others said. The conversation was structured so that the participants took turns talking about events and family stories in response to the questions.

The Analyses

We used standard content analysis procedures to identify patterns in the responses to the questions we discussed and to select representative passages from the fifty-page transcript of the group conversation to illustrate the events, situations and actions the mothers recounted. We also tape-recorded several more hours of our analytical discussion about the group conversation. During this collaborative analysis and discussion of the data, we (the researchers) compared the participants' responses to the literature to clarify and refine the concepts and organize the data for presentation. We also discussed the literature analyses,

* Because of limited space three of the four original research questions and the pertinent conversations are discussed in this chapter. The authors present the study in full in a forthcoming book.

which are presented below before the group conversation data is discussed. We now turn to this juxtaposition of the literature and our experiences raising sons.

I

The literature: Three mothers demonstrate the pain and paradox of dilemma as choice, or the rock and the hard place, as they prepare their sons to survive in a hostile environment.

African-American literature presents two extremes of Black mother-to-son parenting: mothers who whip their sons brutally "for their own good" and mothers who love their sons to selfdestruction through self-sacrifice and over-indulgence. Richard Wright's (1945) semi-autobiography, *Black Boy,* is a brilliant commentary on a mother who loves her son to destruction. Wright vividly portrays the tragedy of a mother-to-son relationship which destroys the very qualities that make a child into a potentially creative and useful citizen. Wright tells how his mother beat him senseless for playing with broomstraws as if they were matches, setting the house on fire, threatening the lives of the family, and by implication, the community. Hers is neither a "rational" appeal nor an acknowledgment of Richard's active mind and restless, adolescent body. She is concerned about his lack of conformity and, understandably, the family's safety. She says, tellingly, "You almost scared us to death," and then proceeds to beat him practically to death. The mother-son relationship is tarnished by delirium and by nightmare. At this moment in the narrative, Wright focuses on his own physical and psychological pain—not on his mother's reasons for her furious punishment. Wright says:

> I was lashed so hard and long that I lost consciousness. I was beaten out of my senses and later I found myself in bed, screaming, determined to run away, tussling with my mother and father who were trying to keep me still . . . Whenever I tried to sleep I would

> see huge wobbly white bags, like the full udders of cows suspended from the ceiling above me. Later, as I grew worse, I could see the bags in the daytime with my eyes open and I was gripped by the fear that they were going to fall and drench me with some horrible liquid . . . Time finally bore me away from the dangerous bags and I got well. But for a long time I was chastened whenever I remembered that my mother had come close to killing me (Wright 1945,13).

One is forced to explore the underlying factors in the lives of the parents and in a society that could cause a mother to react in such an extreme way. Perhaps mothers feel that a Black man-child duly "chastened" or broken at home will pose less of a threat to a society already primed to destroy him. The tragedy is that she may also curb the restless inquisitiveness that informs an active and evolving young mind, because inquisitiveness and intellect are not qualities that the dominant society prizes in a Black man-child. Richard is later taught another hard lesson after the family moves to Memphis when he learns that he must assume responsibility as man of the house because his father has not been home for several days. On his way home from the store, he must thread his way through a gang of Black youth who knock him down, take his groceries and money and send him fleeing for home empty-handed. Wright describes his mother's reaction:

> "Take this money, this note, and this stick," she said. "Go to the store and buy those groceries. If those boys bother you, then fight." I was baffled. My mother was telling me to fight, a thing that I had never done before . . . "Please, let me wait until tomorrow," I begged. "No," she said, "go now! If you come back into this house without those groceries, I'll whip you!" She slammed the door and I heard the key turn in the lock . . . I had the choice of being beaten at home or away from home . . . If I were beaten at home, there was absolutely nothing I could do about it; but if I were beaten in the streets, I had a chance to

> fight and defend myself. I walked slowly down the sidewalk, coming closer to the gang of boys . . . (ibid., 24-25).

Again, Richard Wright faces a life-threatening situation, and again his mother is the hostile force, but this time she appropriates his obedience in order to make him stand up for himself. This is a vital stage in young Richard's rite of passage into understanding, but the mother's position as one poised to do as much violence to him as the gang of street rowdies is problematic for several reasons. She must use violence to teach him violence in the form of self-defense. The sense of adventure that she crushed when he explored the fire, she now, paradoxically, calls upon to send him forth into the hostile world. The further paradox is that this hostility comes from his own Black brothers and the danger emanates from those who should be his support system. Wright's initiation into responsibility is accompanied by Black-on-Black violence and frustration. In the absence of the father, the mother forces him into the potential violence of self-defense, negating the traditional view of the mother as pacifist and nurturer. But a youngster who can stand up for himself in the community will, even as he knows his limitations, also stand up for himself in the larger world and will fulfill his responsibility to help the family.

The second model of mother-to-son relationships we identified in the literature is the overprotective mother who imposes herself as a buffer between her son and the hostile world of both intraracial and interracial violence. She seeks to shield her son—seen as more precious than anyone or anything else in the world—from legitimate correction from others and rarely corrects him herself. She overindulges him in every respect. The result is a human being stripped of personhood, a man-child emasculated, that is, without self-esteem and dignity.

Mattie Michael, the matriarch in Gloria Naylor's 1983 novel, The Women of Brewster Place, is guilty of just such a relationship with her son. Mattie Michael works herself mercilessly through the years to give her son, Basil, everything he wishes. In addition, she intercedes for him in every dispute, whether he is wrong or right. When Basil is arrested on charges of manslaughter, Mattie puts up her house for bail so that her son will not have to spend time in jail. As the day for his hearing approaches, Basil grows more and more irritable; he is whiny and petulant; he is mindful only of his own comfort and is afraid that he will ultimately wind up in jail. Naylor writes:

> Whatever was lacking within him that made it impossible to confront the difficulties of life could not be supplied with words. She saw it now. There was a void in his being that had been padded and cushioned over the years.

Mattie rationalizes Basil's actions:

> After all, he was under a great deal of pressure, and it wasn't fair that he bear it alone. Was it so wrong that he seemed to need her constant support? Had he not been trained to expect it? And he had been trying so hard those last two weeks; she couldn't let him down now (Naylor 1983, 52-53).

Mattie understands the harshness of the community and the world beyond, but she did Basil no favor to shield him so completely from it. Basil has never been whipped and has never known a day of discomfort, and he is unequipped to lead a responsible life. He skips bail and Mattie loses her home. She must move to the poorest section of town—the ghetto known as Brewster Place. She and Mrs. Wright are opposing ends of a mother-to-son spectrum, which precludes what is considered a normal, healthy relationship with one's son.

John O. Killens (1954) affords us another look at the mother-to-son spectrum in his novel, *Youngblood.* The story of Joe and Laurie Lee Youngblood and their two children unfolds in rural Georgia racism and poverty before World War I. The novel centers on the dignity, self-esteem, racial pride, and courage the parents pass on to their son and daughter. Joe Youngblood is crucial to the story but it is

Laurie Lee who is most often seen. She is the tender, natural balance between the extremes of Mrs. Wright and Mattie Michael. Joe Youngblood is whipped by a system that works him like a mule, then kills him in cold blood for refusing to take a short paycheck, but his son Robby is whipped literally in two episodes. His mother is the perpetrator of the violence.

Robby goes to the store to buy baking powder so that his mother can make him a special treat. He meets his best buddy, Gus, and they enter the store together. Several idle White men looking for diversion decide to have it at the expense of Rob and Gus, whom they force to don boxing gloves and fight one another. When Robby is late returning, Mrs. Youngblood goes to look for him and finds him fighting Gus. The degradation of two Black boys fighting each other for the pleasure of White men is more than she can bear and she intends to whip Robby when she gets him home. She sends her daughter for a switch; she orders Robby to strip naked and lie on the floor. However, her love for him stops her. Killens writes:

> He looked so helpless and pitiful and innocent and picked-upon as he lay down on the floor, and angry as Laurie was, she didn't want to fight him. She wanted to love him, because she really did love him. They were making her fight him. . . She looked down at him and she wanted to strike him all about his face, beat the pitiful look from his eyes and the resemblance for her that seemed more striking than ever before, and she drew back her arm, but her heart filled up . . . and her love came down, and she dropped the switch, and she picked up the boy (Killens 1954, 75).

Intuitively, Laurie Lee seems to understand that whipping Robby after he has already been whipped by the White men would strip him of dignity. A component crucial to his ability to function with an intact self would be destroyed. The mothering strategies are totally different, but Laurie Lee, unlike Mattie Michael, knows that a man is better dead than living without self-respect and self-esteem. This is a supreme moment of psychological reality, for his resemblance to her is familial and also reflects her own powerlessness in the face of White brutality.

The second episode we examined finds Laurie Lee facing another "dilemma as choice," or caught between the "rock and the hard place." Robby has been caught by the police fighting white boys who were trying to rape his sister. The police intend to punish Robby even though the other boys were guilty. Killens forces us to look at the old reality that a Black man has nothing (not even his sister's honor) that he can legally defend against white injustice. Laurie hopes that she will have no problem getting Robby out of jail; instead, she has the "option" to whip Robby in front of White policemen or see him sent to the reformatory. Killens writes of Robby's reaction as his mother approaches him:

> The boy looked up into his mother's harassed face, his eyes asking questions. He didn't know his mother acting this way. Laurie was a different person, a total stranger who wore Mama's face. Don't be a bully, she always said. Don't pick a fight, but don't be a coward either. You can't run away from life, she always said. You're as good as any white person alive and much better than a whole heap of them. But this was his mother, the person he trusted above everybody, loved a thousand times more than anything or anybody in the world, and without a word . . . he began to unbutton his jacket . . . (*ibid.*, 170-171).

Robby's thoughts at this point are a crucial part of our thesis—that the African-American mother is caught in a dilemma—for Laurie Lee's reasoned way of shaping Robby's emerging manhood up to this point seems to give the lie to the violence of Richard Wright's mother and the leniency of Basil's mother. But Killens reminds us of the fact that no method of black mothering is immune from the capriciousness of racism. The police force Laurie to beat Robby brutally because they want to hear him cry for mercy; they want her to strip him of the pride and dignity she has instilled in him. The more he is silent, the more they force her to apply the whip. Killens describes the scene:

> WHACK! The whip bit into his flesh like an angry rattlesnake cutting the welts open; blood seeped out and spread over his back . . . His eyes were wide now, pleading for her to stop . . . There was a mechanical motion about her now, as if she didn't know what she was doing. She might have been whipping the trunk of a dead tree (*ibid.*, 172).

Killens continues:

> Robby began to whimper like a puppy suffering slow and deliberate torture. It seemed she was somewhere far, far away, as she heard him, beaten to the floor and kicking like a dying animal. "Don't whip me anymore, Mama! I do anything you say!" (*ibid.*, 172-173).

The beating ends. Robby is reduced to an animal; his mother, too, is now an animal. This family is forever scarred by the intransigence and inhumanity of racism. Moreover, Laurie is bent by a profound sense of guilt, having been the instrument of Robby's emasculation. This guilt originates in the contradictory roles a Black mother is forced to play in a racist society: being a nurturer and protector involves the dilemma of transcending society's hostile forces sometimes successfully, sometimes not.

Mrs. Wright and Mattie Michael are also caught in this contradiction, as were the mothers with whom we talked.

The Conversation: What have you done to protect your son(s) from society's hostile forces?

Before addressing the extremes presented by African-American literature, we began the conversation by sharing memories of when we were most proud and most disappointed in our sons. We used this approach to break the ice among ourselves, to soften the pain of sharing our dilemmas, hopes and failures, and to identify where we stood in relationship to a hostile society.

Several mothers described situations that threatened their

sons' Black self-identity when they were very young. Dorothy told a story about what her son confronted at school when he was six. The first grade teacher, a White woman, told her all-Black class that Malcolm X's birthday, an official school holiday, "should not be celebrated because he went to prison." Dorothy's son decided that the teacher was wrong and told his mother what he thought about Malcolm: "Since Malcolm improved himself when he was in prison, I think we should celebrate his birthday for a whole week!" Dorothy was relieved to hear him say that he "learned all about Malcolm" in the Black-run program he was attending after school. It was this experience that had prepared him to reject this kind of mainstream miseducation.

One of the most destructive dilemmas resulting from the miseducation and racism in schools is that our sons have been often forced to choose between group solidarity and individual "success." Annie's youngest son was nine when he confronted it. Black children in her neighborhood were bussed across town to desegregate a White school in the late 1960s. Annie said she reluctantly agreed when he asked to ride his bike to school to avoid the stigma of being labeled as one of the "bus kids." Black children from the neighborhood who rode the school bus were stigmatized, kept in a group and had no opportunity to participate in extracurricular activities. Riding his bike to school gave him a chance to join the crossing guard squad, an achievement he took great pride in. Paradoxically, participating in the life of the school cut him off from his Black peers at a time when peers usually become very important. We can only speculate about the effects of this experience on Annie's young son's racial identity and his relations with the other Black "bus kids" from his neighborhood.

While some might view such a separation as the inevitable price of achievement, the connection between this aspect of Black identity development and education has become more apparent as Blacks have gained greater opportunities to choose where they will live and whether they will send their children to "integrated" schools (Morgan 1985; Sharp 1988). Still, there are hostile forces in the Black community, too. Elinore decided to stay in the Black community and keep her four sons in school there. But they were often harassed by their peers because teachers made invidious distinctions between her sons and the other Black students. As an active parent advocate, Elinore struggled to protect them from a poor education and from this divisiveness generated by teachers who conveyed the idea that her sons were "better" than the other children because Elinore had taught them to resolve their problems without fighting.

Nadine recalled a situation related to her son's identity. When he was ten years old he stood up to the taunts of Black children in the neighborhood who teased him about coming "from Africa" where they said there were "no houses or roads." They had just returned to California after living in Africa (with his father) since he was a toddler. Nadine said he was "essentially an African kid who [even] talked with an accent." When he began to make friends with the other black children, they taunted him. "At first he ran inside screaming," Nadine said. Then she told us how he defended his African identity and claimed his "place" among these new friends by teaching them the first of many positive lessons about Africa and their own heritage. "He went back outside and proudly told them that Africa was a place with fine houses that were better than the houses here and that his father's driver took him to school everyday."

Zelma told the group about the time White youths from the neighborhood near the school where she worked harassed her sons when they came to her office one day. The older boy, who was about twelve at the time, was in charge of taking care of his younger brother. Zelma was amazed by his insight as he pointed out the contradiction of being called "nigger" on a college campus—"where people are supposed to be educated—and on Good Friday, too!" Zelma said he had begun to understand the difference between the reality and mythology of education and religion and she was glad about that.

These stories of our proud memories of our young sons as self-possessed, insightful, and capable of coping with hostility contrast sharply with the fear we developed for their safety as they grew older. Like the fictional mothers just described, we have tried to protect them from the economic and psychological violence this society wages against Black people as they interact with its institutions and in the Black community. Annie, Nadine and Zelma talked about how their sons experienced society's hostile forces as an assault on their Black self-identities, and in particular, how being perceived negatively stigmatized them. The sons of Annie and Zelma were accosted by Whites; Nadine's son was accosted by intraracial hostility and ignorance about Africa. In each instance their innate identity as Blacks was called into question. However, some of our strategies represent the middle ground between the extremes of Mrs. Wright/Mattie Michaels and Laurie Lee Youngblood. For example, Georgia's strategy for protecting her son included finding the "right school" and moving into the "right neighborhood."

If the racism in the White community has been less overt, teaching sons how to cope with its manifestations in the Black community is no less challenging and some mothers feel guilty about overprotecting their sons and about "loving them too much." When June was raising her grandson, she kept him home from junior high school many days to avoid problems with other students and teachers and he came very close to not graduating. Both June and Annie, the two eldest mothers, regretted loving their sons too much and "giving them too much." Although June and Annie raised their sons in two different eras—two decades apart—they described similar pressures. Annie "couldn't say 'no'" to her"handsome" son when he was in high school (twenty years ago); she said the result was an overextended credit card which she "should have thrown away."

> I was caught . . . between this finance thing (with what you can do supplying all the things for these handsome boys and men) the finance [needs] just seemed to me no end. And then I suffered with the guilt of working all the time . . . and not putting up the fight to say no.

Annie and June both felt "the guilt" of "work, work, work all the time" and not "being there." Just as Annie "could not handle being tough and standing up and saying harsh words" when it came to family finances, June regretted giving her grandson "too many material things":

> I gave (him) too much love; I loved him and I should have been with him when I was working. But I was giving him material things. I gave him everything he wanted. There was nothing he wanted that he didn't have. And I guess I didn't want to believe that it wasn't benefiting him . . . This is very wrong; now I see it.

Elinore told the group that she raised her sons in a very "hard-nosed" way as far as material things were concerned. Yet, she wondered if she had not "overprotected them when they were little by always going up to the school to straighten things out." And after they grew up, she says she continued to overprotect them by not letting go when she should have:

> I found it really hard to let them go; (it was) really hard not to try to control their lives, to make their lives right, to make everything work for them. It's hard to say no. You have to put them out of your house. You have to tell them, I'm going to evict you. And I've had to do those things.

In summary, Mattie Michael's story suggests that giving a son too much or doing too much for him does not develop the strength of character and force of personality a Black youth needs to cope with life's difficulties and society's "mini-violences." But how does a mother who is strong and self-sufficient enough to secure the family's economic survival in a racist and sexist society raise a son to become strong and resilient in his own right? This question concerns the values and virtues mothers teach to mediate the forces that are hostile to Black male development and survival. It is to the question of how mothers help sons develop the character, personality and integrity a Black man-child needs to transcend these forces that we turned next, first by examining the literature and then in the conversation about social practice.

II

The Literature: Two mothers, through word and deed, teach their sons the qualities necessary to build good character.

For African-American sons, building chracater—the experience of growth into honesty, faith, responsibility, compassion, loyalty—is not a harmonious, modulated, paced experience, but one fraught with tension played out against a backdrop of poverty, extremity, pain and ubiquitous racism. Again, African-American literature suggests that it is the mother who is the link to, the filter through which knowledge comes and the rite of passage is initiated. Langston Hughes' poem, "Mother to Son (1972)," and Ernest Gaines' short story, "The Sky Is Gray (1972)," seem appropriate examples of the dilemma a Black mother faces in her attempt to mold the character of her son in a nation that pays lip service to good character, but rules out all actual examples of it that are not predicated on wealth and privilege. In other words, in America, wealth, privilege, and prestige are synonymous with good character. One sees how the "dilemma as choice" again becomes operative in a Black mother's relationship with her son and what she teaches him. Langston Hughes writes in "Mother to Son":

> Well,son, I'll tell you:
> Life for me ain't been no crystal stair.
> It's had tacks in it,
> And splinters,
> And boards torn up,
> And places with no carpet on the floor—
> Bare.
> But all the time

I'se been a-climbin' on,
And reachin' landin's,
And turnin' corners,
And sometimes goin' in the dark
Where there ain't been no light.
So boy, don't you turn back.
Don't you set down on the steps
'Cause you finds it's kinder hard.
Don't you fall now—
For I'se still goin', honey,
I'se still climbin',
And life for me ain't been no crystal stair.

In this poem the mother teaches by example and by word. She is a woman of faith, honesty, compassion and responsibility. Hughes' strategy in the poem is subtle. Nowhere is there any overt mention of religion or faith, yet the reality of both is implied in each line. The poem evokes images and memories of work-worn women we have all known who defy limits. The image of her "a-climbin' on, / And reachin' landin's, / And turnin' corners / And sometimes goin' in the dark / Where there ain't been no light" is an example of her spiritual and physical endurance. The refrain, "Life for me ain't been no crystal stair," appears at the beginning and end of the poem, bracketing the lesson of pain and perseverance the mother is teaching her son and symbolizing the linear, upward mobility on which the dominant society thrives. The image of the crystal stair is Langston Hughes' way of characterizing the hierarchy, wealth, privilege, prestige of the American Dream.

The mother in the poem initiates her son into paradox, into the "dilemma as choice" for she suggests that life is hard whichever way you cut it—standing still or moving on. She acknowledges that for her, "Life ain't been no crystal stair." But she admonishes him not to "turn back" or "set down on the steps"—not to lose ground or become immobilized by life's difficulties (because by implication, the "system" will have won) but to opt for perseverance, to keep on climbing, defying the obstacles. In a beautiful irony, the mother "crystalizes" in her words of encouragement and advice the essence of her life. She says, in effect, "All I have to give you are my deeds, my words and my faith." We have no image of the son to whom she speaks, but our hope is that he is attuned to hear what has been told and insightful enough to see what has been described.

The mother in Ernest Gaines' story, "The Sky Is Gray," like the mother in the poem, teaches by word and example, which in her case also includes corporal punishment. The story is about an eight year-old boy who tries to brave out a toothache but finally admits to his pain and journeys with his mother into the segregated town to see the dentist. The deprivation of this rural Louisiana family is the backdrop for the young boy's coming of age. His father has gone to war, leaving the mother as the sole support of the family. The tension in the story is between the young boy and his over-worked, strong-willed, but loving mother.

We learn simultaneously about the boy and his mother through his thoughts.

> I look at my mama and I know what she's thinking. I been with Mama so much, just me and her I know what she's thinking all the time. Right now it's home—Auntie and them. She's thinking if they got enough wood—if she left enough there to keep them warm till we get back . . . She always worry like that when she leaves the house. She don't worry too much if she leave me there with the smaller ones, 'cause she know I'm go'n look after them and look after Auntie and everything else. I'm the oldest and she say I'm the man . . . I love my mama and I want to put my arm round her and tell her but I'm not supposed to do that. She say that's weakness and that's cry baby stuff, and she don't want no cry baby round her (Gaines 1972, 782).

The regard the young boy feels for his mother almost overwhelms the reader, who is drawn immediately into the warmth and compassion that holds these characters in loving tension. The mother's tendency to worry about the family is the example by which the boy gauges his own maturity and understanding of her and of himself. With a few simple words, the mother initiates him into manhood. The reader shares his pride when he thinks, " I'm the oldest and she say I'm the man."

In another episode the young narrator is asked to kill red birds he has trapped for the family meal. He can't do it and his mother whips him.

> "Get him out of there," she say.
> I reached in for him and he kept on hopping to the back. Then I reached in farther, and he pecked me on the hand.
> "I can't, Mama," I say.
> She slapped me again . . . "Give it here," she say, and jerked the fork out of my hand . . .
> I heard the fork go in his neck, and I heard it go in the ground. She brought him out and helt him right up in front of me.
> "That's one," she say. She shook him off and gived me the fork. "Get the other one."
> "I can't, Mama," I say. "I'll do anything, but don't make me do that."
> She went to the corner of the fence and broke the biggest switch over there she could find. I knelt 'side the trap, crying . . .
> But she hit me and hit me and hit me.
> I'm still young—I ain't no more than eight; but I know now; I know why I had to do it . . . Suppose she had to go away? That's why I had to do it. Suppose she had to go away like daddy went away? Then who was go'n look after us? They had to be somebody left to carry on (Gaines 1972, 784-785).

In a sense, the mother is faced with teaching the boy, James, that he might have to do unpleasant and seemingly inhumane things in order to be the man of the family. One laments the beating she gives him but sees it through their mutual love described earlier in the story. Moreover, his Auntie is an intermediary, for she tempers the mother's determination and explains to James why his mother whips him the way she does. "Auntie" and a family friend help him understand that he will be the provider one day, that he will have to carry on. He says, "I didn't know it then, but I know it now. Auntie and Monsieur Bayonne talked to me and made me see" (Gaines, 783). The talking is weighed against the whipping; his understanding comes about because of his love for his mother, which makes it possible for him to hear her and to demonstrate the maturity she demands.

"Dilemmas as choice" force the African-American mother to teach some values, which should ideally be transmitted in a positive manner, in a seemingly inhumane and negative way. The literature we have examined so far suggests that the harshness of the social environment sometimes requires that life's loving lessons be taught harshly. Yet, the values mothers in these literary works try to instill can actually give sons an alternative interpretation of life's hard lessons that strengthens and develops their character. As examples from the conversation will show, mothers try to help sons develop the ability to balance faith and compassion with the strength necessity demands.

The Conversation: What have you taught your son(s) of honesty, loyalty, compassion, faith and responsibility?)

The mothers readily agreed that the values we identified in these two selections are our values. Indeed, honesty, loyalty, compassion, faith and responsibility are important standards by which we judge our sons' behavior and assess our effectiveness as mothers, especially when our sons fail to demonstrate them. As the events described below illustrate, these values represent a bond of trust between mother and son. When this trust is violated, we are not only disappointed but we worry and grieve that the lapse indicates a flaw or serious shortcoming in our sons' characters. Conversely, when these values guide their behavior, our pride in our sons and our self-identity as Black mothers are affirmed.

After his first year of college Nadine's son didn't renew his financial aid application in time to receive a scholarship for the next year. She was so angry and hurt that she cried as she told us the story. She wondered aloud: "How could he be so irresponsible? How could he let me down like that?" Fortunately, she knew someone in the administration who pulled some strings and got his scholarship reinstated. But she wondered whether she had already done so many things for him that he had not yet learned what his own responsibility should be.

Several events related to our sons' self-responsibility and character development were troublesome because we had previously discussed the very issues causing the problems. For example, when Dorothy's son began junior high school, he wanted to participate in a fund-raiser that involved buying and selling other students as "slaves" for a day. They had agreed the year before that he would not participate in a similar activity. Although she understood his need to be "accepted," she felt betrayed by his enthusiasm—he said it would be "neat to make a profit." For Dorothy his participation in "Slave Day" would violate the spirit of compassion and loyalty to his heritage she thought he had internalized. Zelma reassessed her son's character and questioned his honesty and integrity after he promised to stop drinking but then showed up so drunk one night after a high school game that he passed out on the doorstep and she could not get him into the house by herself.

After listening to these stories, Georgia said:

> Like the rest of you, I've got a financial aid story, an arrest story, a drunk story, a run-up-all-my-charge-accounts story, an "I-don't-know-whether-I'm-black-or-white story," but my biggest disappointment in my son was when the hospital called me to come to get him because he had a motorcycle accident coming back from the beach—[on a school day].

It was "Senior Cut Day"—he was a junior—but he cut school with his friends. Georgia said his behavior was "a breach of trust." The fact that he had cut school, was driving without a license, and had endangered not only his physical safety but his future, was traumatic for her. She said his injuries were the only thing that kept her from "beating him to within an inch of his life" because they had just discussed this kind of thing:

> And it was like we had just gone through all of this the week before—about why he didn't have any transportation. His license was revoked because he didn't renew his moped registration . . . I realize kids do this sort of thing, but what it did was magnify in my own mind how much I don't know about the kinds of decisions he makes and the things that he does.

Georgia realized she would never have known that her son was making these choices had it not been for the fact that he was seriously injured.

Elinore reminded us that she and her husband had raised four sons. She cautioned us not to expect our sons to "understand" everything we are trying to teach them until they are older and have experienced some things, perhaps not even until they have their own children. Then she told us a very funny story about a chicken one of her sons had raised. "When it came time to kill it," she said, "he couldn't do it." Elinore told him how to kill the chicken but he tried to "rope" it instead. Luckily, unlike the situation in Ernest Gaines' story, the family wasn't depending on this "bird" for their survival.

We wondered then, how do we get our sons to be both compassionate and tough when they need to be? Dorothy said, "We want them to care, to be kind and gentle, but then there are times when they have to be strong and tough. And where do they get that from? How can they learn to judge when to be one way or the other?" Here is Elinore's reply:

> Well, they have to get it from experience. When I was growing up a chicken didn't look like a pet to me, it looked like something to eat. So now, our kids don't deal with that. So our sons have to get it from the way we handle tough situations . . . And when they get older they'll realize what you've been talking about . . . Then you'll be glad you stuck it out, that you were hard-nosed about things, because there's no

way they can relate to it until they're older.

Elinore's comments emphasize how important it is that Black mothers persevere in their role as character-builders. Like the mothers in Hughes' poem and Gaines' story, it is necessary to demonstrate through word and deed the values we want to teach our sons even though they may not hear or see what we are saying. Given the "endangered status" of young Black males today, any lapse in the behavior we expect of them is frightening because the values we try to instill are essential for their survival (Hare 1987). As the dialogue continued, it was evident that teaching honesty, loyalty, compassion, faith, and responsiblity to the family and community were most important to the mothers. In addition, the mothers were concerned about linking these traits to lessons about family secrets and background and family lore.

Discussion

Several questions and concerns guided this inquiry. One question is whether Black mothers consciously experience motherto-son relationships like those portrayed in African-American literature. In other words, does this literature mirror Black life? Although the characters and fictional events differ in historical time and geographical location from the situations described in the group conversation, many experiences of the fictional mothers and the participants in this inquiry are nonetheless comparable. Contrary to stereotyped, one-dimensional images of the domineering "matriarch" and the emasculating "strong Black woman" in some fiction and social science literature, the group conversation reveals the complexity of Black life and the diversity of mother-to-son relationships.

Illuminating the social and psychological context of Black mother-to-son relationships is another concern of this inquiry. The study reveals certain "dilemmas as choice" that confront Black mothers raising sons. These dilemmas or contradictions often threaten their sons' development and ultimately, their survival. Violence presents one such contradiction. While the society morally condemns violence, the economic and cultural violence it wages against black people produces a social and psychological context of routine frustration, anger and rage in which violence becomes commonplace. Necessity forces mothers to use violence, in turn, to protect their sons or to teach them to be violent in self-defense. Consistent with the demands of survival and a cultural ethos that values harmony (Asante 1987), the mothers offer a uniquely Black perspective on Black anger, calling it a "terrible strength" that can be harnessed through mutual love.

Another contradiction the study identifies is that the mothers, who are already three times victimized by race, class and gender oppression, often feel deeply guilty—after the fact—about parenting. We (the researchers) concluded that this guilt arises because Black mothers send sons into a system that is irrational and dangerous. Although the mothers in this study have intervened to protect our sons, particularly in school, we often feel like "you're damned if you do and damned if you don't." While some mothers have tried to protect their sons by shielding them from societal or community hostility and others have given in to their sons' demands for material things, structural inequality and societal racism prevents Black parents from saying to their sons, as the Dogon people of Mali do, "Become who you are" (Erny 1968). So, to some extent, parenting appears to be a no-win situation.

The mothers talked about another kind of contradiction or dilemma: trying to instill values to mediate the materialistic, individualistic ideology of the dominant society. Traditional Black collective values can strengthen Black youth and protect them from the self-deceptive, illusory success competitive individualism offers. These values and expectations can reinforce family and racial identity and give our sons an alternative interpretation of Black life and social reality. Indeed, the mothers discussed how important it is for Black youth to maintain a positive Black identity. On the other hand, we (the researchers) are aware that some social scientists and educators insist that Black cultural identity and individuality are inherently conflictual (Praeger 1982). This study suggests, however, that such an interpretation of "the conflict between cultural allegiance and opportunity" (Rousseve 1987) is not useful for protecting Black youth from racism or for preparing for it.

Not surprisingly, we discovered that neither class background nor education insulated the mothers in our study from racism nor gave any of us an advantage to judge our parenting as superior to what other mothers have or have not done. This is not to imply that all parenting strategies we discussed are equally effective or desirable. In fact, each of the mothers in our study has her own way of dealing with how she has fallen short of her own ideal. In spite of the guilt and other contradictions this study reveals, this analysis of African-American literature and the social practice of the mothers suggests some tentative parenting strategies for raising sons: It is important to teach our sons to be honest, loyal, compassionate and to demonstrate reciprocity, mutuality and deference in family and community relationships. Further study is needed in different family contexts to determine if parenting that incorporates these values, along with an emphasis on the continuity of the family from one generation to the next, helps young people develop the strength to transcend anger, hopelessness and society's hostility.

The Afrocentric methodology this interdisciplinary inquiry uses to combine literary and social analysis brought to life fictional images of mother-to-son relationships that were affirmed by a diverse group of Black mothers. The method offers researchers and participants a way to know more about Black life and provides opportunities for much-needed community dialogue to regenerate the communal Black experience. The reciprocal group conversation resembles the convocations of our ancestors, who "would assemble to determine the cause and the remedy . . . when they had a problem" (Drewal and Drewal 1983). Some unanticipated effects of this group conversation which exemplify traditional elements of African-American culture are: relieving stress through humorous storytelling; gaining strength by recollecting painful memories and testifying together; affirming hope and belief in ourselves by truth-telling about our own shortcomings, a healthy expression of self-acceptance; and honoring the active role family ancestors play in the lives of the living (Pasteur and Toldson 1982; Richards 1985; Stuckey 1987).

In conclusion, African-American literature is a valuable resource that can be used to teach parents and educators about the realities of Black life and to dispel stereotypes of Black people and families. In literature, as in Black life, the stereotype of the matriarch proves to be false. Instead, this study reveals the extraordinary struggle of mothers who are attempting to teach their sons to survive and transcend the limitations society places on Black men and women. The "dilemmas as choice" we identify arise because we live in a society where Black mothers will never shape sons who will be accepted by the status quo. We need to recreate community support for parents engaged in what has always been and still is a political, economic and cultural struggle to ensure Black male survival and development in this society. Their particular vulnerability makes this an urgent necessity; this Afrocentric approach to social science inquiry is a beginning step in the reconstruction of our society.

References

Allen, W. 1985. "Race, Income and Family Dynamics: A Study of Adolescent Male Socialization Processes and Outcomes," in M. Spencer et al. (eds.) *Beginnings: The Social and Affective Development of Black Children.* Hillsdale, NJ: Lawrence Erlbaum.

Asante, M. K. 1987. *The Afrocentric Idea.* Philadelphia: Temple University Press.

Belenky, M. et al. 1986. *Women's Ways of Knowing: The Development of Self, Voice and Mind.* New York: Basic Books.

Bennett, L. 1972. *The Challenge of Blackness.* Chicago: Johnson Publishing Co.

Billingsley, A. 1968. *Black Families In White America.* Englewood Cliffs, NJ: Prentice Hall.

Blau, Z. 1981. *Black Children/White Children: Competence, Socialization and Social Structure.* New York: Free Press.

Bruyn, S.T. 1966. *The Human Perspective In Sociology: The Methodological Participant Observation.* Englewood Cliffs, NJ: Prentice Hall.

Clark, R. 1983. *Family Life and School Achievement: Why Poor Black Children Succeed or Fail.* Chicago: University of Chicago Press.

Comstock, D. 1982. "A Method for Critical Research," in Bredo and Feinberg, 1982, *op. cit.*, 370-390.

Douglas, J. 1985. *Creative Interviewing.* Beverly Hills: Sage.

Drewal, H. and M. T. Drewal. 1983. *Gelede: Art and Female Power Among The Yoruba.* Bloomington: Indiana University Press.

Du Bois, B. 1983. "Passionate Scholarship: Notes on Values, Knowing and Method in Social Science," in G. Bowles and R. Klein (eds.) *Theories of Women's Studies.* London: Routledge and Kegan Paul.

Du Bois, R. and M. Li. 1971. *Reducing Social Tension And Conflict: The Group Conversation Method.* New York: Association Press.

Erny, P. 1968. *Childhood and Cosmos: The Social Psychology of the Black African Child.* Rockville, MD: Media Intellects Corporation.

Fay, B. 1975. *Social Theory and Political Practice.* London: George Allen and Unwin.

Forcey, L.R. 1987. *Mothers of Sons: Toward An Understanding of Responsibility.* New York: Praeger.

Franklin, A. and N. Boyd-Franklin. 1985. "A Psychoeducational Perspective on Black Parenting," in H. McAdoo and J. McAdoo (eds.) *Black Children: Social, Educational and Parenting Environments.* Beverly Hills: Sage.

Freire, P. 1970. "Cultural Action for Freedom." *Harvard Educational Review:* Monograph No. 1.

Gaines, E. 1972. "The Sky Is Gray," in R. Barksdale and K. Kinnamon (eds.) *Black Writers of America: A Comprehensive Anthology.* New York: McMillan.

Gibbs, J. 1988. *Young Black and Male In America: An Endangered Species.* Dover, MA: Auburn House.

Goulet, D. 1971. "An Ethical Model for the Study of Values," *Harvard Educational Review*, 41 (2),205-227.

Hamnett, M. et al. 1984. *Ethics. Politics, and International Social Science Research: From Critique to Praxis.* Honolulu: University of Hawaii Press.

Hare, B. 1987. "Structural Inequality and The Endangered Status of Black Youth," *Journal of Negro Education.* 56(1),100-110.

Hare, B. and L. Castenell. 1985. "No Place to Run, No Place to Hide: Comparative Status and Future Prospects of Black Boys," in M. Spencer, G. Brookins and W. Allen (eds.) *Social and Affective Development of Black Children.* Hillsdale, New Jersey: Lawrence Erlbaum.

Hill, R. 1972. *The Strengths of Black Families.* New York: Emerson-Hall.

Hughes, L. 1972. "Mother to Son," in R. Barksdale and K. Kinnamon (eds.) *Black Writers of America: A Comprehensive Anthology.* New York: MacMillan.

Hurston, Z. 1935. *Mules and Men.* Bloomington: University of Indiana Press.

Killens, J. O. 1982. *Youngblood.* Athens, GA: University of Georgia Press.

Lather, P. 1986. "Research as Praxis," *Harvard Educational Review.* 56 (3), 257-277.

Lindsay, L. 1975. *Methodology and Change.* Kingston, Jamaica: University of the West Indies.

Markovic, M. 1974. *From Affluence to Praxis: Philosophy and Social Criticism.* Ann Arbor: University of Michigan Press.

McDade, L. 1984. "The Interweavings of Theory and Practice: Finding the Threads for a Feminist Ethnography," *North Dakota Quarterly.* 52 (1),91-109.

Morgan, K. 1980. *Children of Strangers: The Stories of a Black Family.* Philadelphia: Temple University Press.

Morgan, T. 1985. "The World Ahead: Black Parents Prepare Their Children for Pride and Prejudice, *The New York Times Magazine* (October 27), 32-36.

Naylor, G. 1983. *The Women of Brewster Place.* New York: Penguin Books.

Nobles, W. 1980. "African Philosophy: Foundations for Black Psychology," in R. Jones (ed.) *Black Psychology.* New York: Harper and Row.

Pasteur, A. and Toldson, I. 1982. *Roots of Soul: The Psychology of Black Expressiveness.* Garden City, NY: Anchor Press/Doubleday.

Praeger, J. 1982. "American Racial Ideology as Collective Representation," *Ethnic and Racial Studies.* 5 (1),99-119.

Richards, D. 1985. "The Implications of African-American Spirituality," in M.K. Asante and K.W. Asante (eds). *African Culture: The Rhythms of Unity. Westport,* CT: Greenwood Press.

Rousseve, R. J. 1987. "A Black American Youth Torn Between Cultures." *The Humanist.* 47 (2),5-8.

Sharp, S. 1988. "Growing Up Integrated: Did Momma Do the Right Thing?" *Crisis.* (March), 8-14.
Slaughter, D. and E. Epps. 1987. "The Home Environment and Academic Achievement of Black American Children and Youth," *The Journal of Negro Education.* 56 (l), 3-20.
Smitherman, G. 1986. *Talkin' and Testifyin': The Language of Black America.* Detroit, MI: Wayne State University Press.
Stuckey, S. 1987. *Slave Culture: Nationalist Theory and The Foundations of Black America.* New York: Oxford University Press.
Wa Thiong'o, N. 1987. *Decolonizing the Mind: The Politics of Language in African Literature.* London: James Currey, Ltd.
Wade, Gayles. 1984. *A Crystal Stair.* New York: Pilgrium Press.
Welch, S. 1985. *Communities of Resistance and Solidarity.* New York: Orbis Books.
Williams, J. A. 1988. "Prior Restraints," *The Nation.* 246 (16),574-577.
Wright, R. 1945. *Black Boy: A Record of Childhood and Youth.* New York: Harper and Row. (A Perennial Classic, 1966).
Wynter, S. 1984. "The Ceremony Must Be Found," *Boundary/2* 12(3)/13(1),19-61.

Chapter 7

We Are the Children of Everybody: Community Co-Parenting—A Biographic Note

Loften Mitchell

I

Memories soar, encased in the silver lining of a dark
cloud,
Sharply etched against a sky of blue.
Memories-edited, filtered, seen through tinted glasses,
And what was then is what is now,
And then—then
The cloud bursts and fogs the glasses
And reality rains down
Torrents of unhappy endings
And endless pain . . .

In the Harlem of the early 1930s, vicious White thugs terrorized the area from 124th Street to 125th Street on St. Nicholas Avenue. This gang, known as the Hancocks, attacked Black people, young and old, and beat them mercilessly. Black blood flowed in that area which was a long way from the Howard Beach of the 1980s. Racism then was like racism now. It flourished.

125th Street, Harlem's main business district, was a no-man's-land for Black people. Black employment in stores was virtually nonexistent. The same was true of the telephone company and the utilities company. In fact, civil treatment for Black customers was virtually nonexistent. Two things brought change: the Reverend Adam Clayton Powell, Jr. led a series of demonstrations in front of the utilities and telephone companies. The Harlem riot of the mid-1930s forced local businesses to change their hiring policies. Restaurants—like Child's and Schrafft's—also "got religion," especially after actor Canada Lee started a lawsuit.

It was not a lawsuit that ended the Hancocks' reign of terror. The gang attacked a youngster from my block and beat him into a bloody mess. The gang then beat an elderly neighbor, nearly killing him. That was the moment of decision. Many of us fought back, individually. Now we decided to act collectively.

We sent our track star into Hancock territory. He taunted the gang, then turned and ran. The gang members pursued him right into our block. We were waiting. We hit that gang with every rock we had found in Morningside Park. The Hancocks retreated and we followed them. We had lead pipes covered by paper bags. We beat their heads from 119th Street to 124th Street.

By the time we reached 124th Street scores of Blacks had joined us. Before this battle ended, nearly one hundred Black men walked into an Eighth Avenue bar where the owner broke glasses after he served Blacks. The one hundred Black men demanded the owner to break one hundred glasses. He did, but he never broke another glass. This was more than vengeance. We children of Harlem were the children of everyone. An attack on an elderly person was unheard of. People were attacking your parents when they attacked an adult.

We were the children of everyone.

We were born soon after the end of World War I—less than three generations after the end of chattel slavery in America. After 246 years of slavery, most of our ancestors were freed with only the rags on their backs. Neither they nor their parents had been able to acquire wealth, build factories nor leave vast fortunes to their children and grandchildren. Instead, this nation of high-sounding pretensions and false promises launched reigns of terror against us. We were vilified in the press, the pulpit and the public forum. The cultural media attacked and insulted us, then spread lies about us.

This vilification, this terror forced us into small communities, never knowing when the next attack would occur. It forced us to jealously care for and guard neighbors and friends. And parents, relatives and friends educated us about this vicious American system. Repeatedly, we heard their advice ending with: "I am *duty bound* to tell you this!" We learned from them. And in later years we youngsters often stood around, cursing about Peola wanting to be an *Imitation of Life*. We laughed, mockingly, at the thought of Porgy riding his goat up Lenox Avenue, looking for his Bess.

We laughed, too, about *The Emperor Jones* running barefoot through the jungle, looking for *The Green Pastures* in *Abraham's Bosom*. Present-day phonies and political hacks do not face the reality we faced in the 1920s and 1930s. That reality is that when we were called on to salute the flag and recite the Pledge of Allegiance, we did that, but we added—to the dismay of many a White teacher—these lines: "With liberty and justice for some of the people." We knew even then that great books by Black writers would never be promoted the way know-nothing White writers would have their "Black books" promoted. To this day one of the greatest books ever written remains ignored by many. That book is *Black Reconstruction* (1935), written by the great William Edward Burghardt Du Bois . . . .

We were the children of everyone and I am certain that other Black communities were much like ours. This, however, is a personal memory of the years beginning in 1919 and confined to that section of New York City known as Harlem. This was the scene of my youth. It was also the scene of the Harlem renaissance. I did not know it then.

. . . To the land north of 110th Street came Southerners escaping physical lynching, West Indians escaping economic lynchings and Northern Negroes escaping from the terror they knew in lower Manhattan. They brought with them their folkways, their mores, their religiosity and their dogged determination. They brought, too, their community spirit which involved caring for neighbors and their children. They would discipline *any* child *any* place *any* time. This was double jeopardy because a child caught hell from a neighbor and more hell when he or she got home.

Harlem was difficult, but it was fun! There were churches and lodges and clubs and there was friendship on every block. There were institutions such as the Schomburg Collection where Negro history and culture were housed. There was the old Dutch Bell on Mt. Morris Park Hill and the Jumel Mansion and the 135th Street library and the Savoy Ballroom and the Renaissance Casino. And there were legitimate theatres—first the Crescent on 135th Street, then the Lincoln, the Lafayette and the Alhambra. And there were block parties and family gatherings and outings.

One of my earliest memories was visiting the 135th Street Library—the site of the Schomburg Collection. There in the sixth year of my life my father ushered me through the doorway, wrapped his arm around my waist and lifted me up to the library desk. I signed my first card. I remembered that for years. In 1950 I did the same thing with my oldest son, Thomas, at the 124th Street Library. In 1955 I repeated this with my youngest son, Melvin, at the Astor Place Library.

Home for me during the 1920s was 28-30 West 131st Street. There my parents, Willia and Ulysses Mitchell, settled with their three children: Gladys, Clayton and this writer. They managed a large elevator building. My father, a heavyset man with a robust sense of humor, was a generous, communicative human being. Often we had a lonely stranger brought home to dinner. Often we awoke in the morning to find a homeless stranger sleeping on our living room sofa. Each night my father left a package of food on our roof for some hungry person. I was told that this was a habit of his mother's, Rhoda Freeman Mitchell. Each night she left a package of food down by the mailbox of her North Carolina home for some hungry, lonely traveler who might happen by.

My mother was a slim woman with copper-colored hair and greyish-green eyes. She was communicative, brilliant and knowledgeable—a doer, devoted to family and friends. She believed passionately in education. She took herself and my father off to night school to complete the education they had been denied in their youth.

Two maternal uncles—Hosea and Richard Spaulding—lived with us during the 1920s. The Mitchell children started off with two "extra" parents. I liked them. They were loving, strong and determined.

Uncle Hosea, a large, brilliant man left his rural home during the first decade of the twentieth century, following ideas of progress. He wandered to Florida, then joined the Navy and made his way to New York City. There he wrote to my parents, singing the praises of the city. My father's sister, Anna, had moved there, too—and soon my parents were there.

On his twenty-first birthday my uncle Richard came north.

This agile, energetic man adjusted rapidly to the city. He worked hard and he played hard. He was also a stern taskmaster. If I sat in a chair he wanted, he simply put his hand on the back of the chair and that meant "move." And I moved.

I don't believe I liked it, but I certainly said nothing about it. Discipline, religion and respect for elders were all intertwined and part of life. No one dared address an adult by his or her first name. No one thought of doing so. And it was "Yes, sir," and "Yes, ma'am." This was also an age when you held doors for people, removed your hat in the elevator and offered grown-ups your seat on the subway. I do not recall a single schoolmate calling a teacher by his or her first name. I had to start teaching at age fifty to hear that!

In the backyard of our Harlem home, brother Clayton and I made wagons from baby-carriage wheels and scootermobiles from old roller skates. We played stickball and boxball in the streets. Relatives and friends often umpired those games without being invited to do so. Personally, I liked that—especially after I hit a screaming liner that the opposing team called "Foul!" My father's voice roared from the block: "That wasn't no foul ball!" Silence followed and I raced around the bases, happily.

Yes. We were the children of everyone. Our neighbor and family physician, Dr. Charles Petioni, was an authority on the West Indies, race, art and literature as well as medicine. Mr. Charles Woolcott owned a grocery store across the street from our building. Often he told us stories of his West Indian background. On 131st Street near Fifth Avenue stood Mr. Hochstein's grocery store. Here one could hear endless stories of Jewish life. The Hochsteins were loved by our community. They also had trustworthy scales. Customers from Harry's, a nearby butcher shop, streamed into Mr. Hochstein's store to weigh their packages on trustworthy scales. It was said that Harry was "heavy with the thumb."

There were other early influences. Mr. Tony, an Italian, owned a vegetable store on the corner of Lenox Avenue and 131st Street. He readily supplied stories of life in Italy. Across from him was Mr. Wong's Chinese Hand Laundry. He willingly supplied Chinese history and culture.

None of these people resembled the portraits of their groups shown on movie screens. This fact lingered with me down through the years . . . .

On June 30, 1928, I went into the bedroom of my parents and found a beautiful brown baby in my mother's arms. This was Louis Duval Mitchell. Sister Gladys' face broke into a big smile. Brother Clayton was happy because he would no longer be called the baby in the family. I remember smiling and thinking that now I would join the many parents I knew and dearly loved. This was the ninth year of my life.

> Those were my salad days,
> Green like the grass growing in the backyard of
> my Harlem home of summer
> When the sun kissed the leaves of the sycamore tree—
> Greener now than they were then,
> But, green—so very green.

Variety, the show business newspaper carried a 1929 headline: "Wall Street Lays an Egg!" The stock market, our legalized gambling center, had crashed. The Great Depression engulfed America.

Panic raged. Tears flooded the nation as economic depression clawed the souls, minds and bodies of all who lived during that era. The scars from the clawing remain with us today, making us frightened in the midst of abundance and unimaginative in the face of homelessness and hunger. Joblessness reigned during the 1930s. Once-proud men stood on 125th Street with signs on their coat lapels, reading: "Unemployed. Please buy apples." But few people had money to buy even an apple.

Families who could not pay their rent saw their furnishings put out on the sidewalks. Poverty forced many families to move constantly. Homes for these families became dark, dank, shifting rows of tenements, totally lacking in permanency and security. Homeless people wandered across the nation, eating from garbage cans if they found any filled. Once-proud workers lived in "Hoovervilles"—the name given to the collection of shacks they erected in vacant lots along river fronts. And Black women "shaped up" on the Bronx slave market—which means they stood around, waiting for white women to approach them and offer a day's domestic work at twenty-five cents per hour. Meanwhile, in Washington, President Herbert Hoover declared prosperity was just around the corner, that soon there'd be a chicken in every pot and two cars in every garage. Well, prosperity may have been around the corner, but it was going the other way. Chickens were dying of starvation before they were big enough to be put into a pot. And very few people owned garages and no one had money to buy one car, let alone two.

My father gave up his job on 131st Street just before the Depression struck. He had ideas of progress, but those difficult year denied them. By 1931 we had moved to 154th Street, 129th Street and 126th Street. During this period I won second prize in a city-wide essay contest on Fire Prevention. And, with the total support of my parents, I decided to become a writer. I always wondered what I would have said if, during hard times, a son of mine had made that decision.

During that time I once again learned that we were the children of everyone. For I was put in jail. The charge? Selling papers without a license.

I had learned from other kids that early editions of the *Daily News* and *Daily Mirror* could be purchased at the News Building for a penny a piece. These papers were then sold on the streets for a nickel each. Well, I became a newsboy. I went to East 42nd Street, bought a stack of papers, then took the subway back to Harlem and sold these on the streets. And I made at least a dollar each night which, in 1930, was a lot of money. This money went into the family till and, for a time, I knew "prosperity." I went to school during the day, then rushed downtown, saw a movie, then picked up my papers. No one bothered to tell me that newsstand owners were "feeling the pinch" of youngsters selling papers all over the city. They began to pinch us.

One night a plainclothesman approached me on 42nd Street and asked if I had a license to sell papers. He had hold of my sweater. I pulled away from him and started running as I called him a few names. And I ran into the arms of another plainclothesman. I was ushered into a patrol wagon, crowded with other youngsters. We were driven to the Children's Society on East 104th Street and Fifth Avenue. The White children were placed in rooms. We, Black children, had to sleep on cots in the hallways. We tried to joke about it, but we were all scared, scared.

It was a miserable experience. The night seemed endless, yet very short. We were awakened early for some awful food, then sent out onto a fenced-in roof, waiting to be taken to court. We met a number of White boys who had run away from home. Some of them claimed to be from well-to-do families. All of them agreed on one thing: We would be kept here for months.

We went to court. Anxiety charged through a jam-packed courtroom where my parents sat with a crowd of other parents—Black parents, White parents, Hispanic and Asian. The Judge called us all before him. Children and parents held their breaths. The Judge told us we had been selling papers without licenses, that we couldn't do that. He warned us not to do that again and threw our cases out of court. Pandemonium prevailed. Through my tears I saw parents hugging their children, then hugging other parents. At that moment in time people from all groups did what they should have done at all times. They had united in the saving of their children.

It took me a while to understand what had happened.

Few people had telephones in those days so the police had to visit our homes and notify our parents of our whereabouts. At my house my brother Clayton cried out: "I wish it had been me!" I am told that my parents marched off to the local police station, then on to the home of the local political leader. I had to smile as I multiplied this image. Irish parents, Jewish parents, Hispanic parents and Asian parents marched to the homes of their leaders. And their leaders marched to the home of the Judge. The Judge knew what he had to do. And he did it.

There were dividends in being the children of everyone. Fifty-three years passed before I walked inside that building where I had been jailed. When I walked inside again, time had replaced the boy of eleven with a man in his sixties. On the lower floor of that building was a performance of *Mama, I Want to Sing*. On the upper floor Rosetta LeNoire and her Amas Repertory Theatre were showing my play, *Miss Waters to You*—later called *Miss Ethel Waters*. I was pleased with the show and with the members of the audience. But, somehow amidst all that excitement, old memories raced back—memories of being jailed and being released because I was one of the children of everyone.

After I became an ex-newsboy, I started writing scripts for Brother Clayton and other neighborhood children. We performed them in the backyard of our 127th Street home. And we charged other children a penny each to see our work. Some church people heard about this and promptly invited us to do shows in their churches. And they paid us. In fact, I earned more than I had as a newsboy.

A major development followed. My father was employed to assist in managing a large building, 86 West 119th Street, on the corner of Lenox Avenue. Black people were moving across 125th Street, spreading toward 110th Street. Here we met the Hispanic community and many White groups. Our classes were filled with members of all groups as they had been in upper Harlem. The teachers were all White—as they had been in upper Harlem. I remember only two Black teachers during grade school—a Mrs. Porter at Public School 89 and Mr. Cooper at Public School 157.

There were none in my junior high, Public School 184.

At DeWitt Clinton High School I had only one. She was novelist Jessie Faust Harris—and she was beautiful. I am certain there must have been other Black teachers, but I never met them.

The building my father was employed at evoked memories of our former home on 131st Street. We had there, professionals and "blue collar" workers. My aunt Anna lived there with her husband Louis Valbuena. Judge James Watson also lived there with his family. The great Thomas "Fats" Waller and other celebrities frequently visited friends who lived there.

Across the street was another apartment building, 95 West 119th Street. There lived political leader Frank R. Crosswaith, Sr. and his family. His sons—Frank, Jr., Paul and Norris—spearheaded a boy's club, the Panthers. They invited me to join and I did. When they learned I was interested in writing, they told me their mother, Mrs. Alma E. Crosswaith, was producing a play. They invited me to participate. They didn't have to ask me twice—especially since I was offered the leading role.

The Panthers Club came under the umbrella of an organization known as Pioneer Youth. One of the leaders of the latter group was a man named Walter Ludwig. Pioneer Youth had various groups throughout the city. Members were invited to its summer camp and to activities sponsored at the Church of All Nations on the Lower East Side. Pioneer Youth also sent social workers into the field to lead its clubs. Three of them worked with the Panthers—first writer Andrew M. Burris, then social worker Glenn Carrington and later, artist Zell Ingram. These were brilliant dedicated men.

They directed the Panthers Club members into unknown areas. We were the sons of professionals, politicians, civil service workers and so-called blue-collar workers. Our parents were of southern, West Indian, Puerto Rican and White American origins. Our minds were on playing stickball, boxball, football and other games. Over a period of time we found our leaders bringing to our meetings writers and artists—people like Langston Hughes and Countee Cullen. This, of course, led us to reading their works, holding discussions of their works and exploring areas outside our experiences. We saw plays and movies together. We became acquainted with each other's parents, siblings and relatives. Many of us—as of this writing—remain in touch with each other.

The Panthers met at the People's Educational Forum, 2005 Seventh Avenue, at 120th Street. This large hall had the offices of Frank Crosswaith, Sr. It was also the headquarters of the local Socialist Party. On the walls were posters and pictures. One had a white hand shaking a black hand with the caption: "Black and White Unite." One sign said: "Help fight Hitler" and another said: "Stop lynching."

Here Mrs. Crosswaith produced and directed *The Maid of the Silver Slipper*—a play about Cinderella. Frederick Pollard, another member of the Panthers, was in the cast. I did not realize that I was collecting more "extra" parents. The success of Mrs. Crosswaith's production inspired many of us. Fred Pollard and I promptly began to write, produce and direct our own shows at the Forum, using a fine young singer named Charles Granger in those works. Our production methods were, to put it gently, unorthodox. We pooled nickels and dimes, made a deal with the Forum to share our profits, secured a production date, then had tickets printed.

Here again was the advantage of being the children of everyone: We not only had a ready-made audience, but ticket sales people as well. They were all relatives and friends of our youthful cast members and they were aggressive sales people. They brought us large audiences—at fifteen cents per ticket. Many of their patrons followed my work through the years.

In 1935 we presented our last work at the Forum. It was my play, *The Lightning,* billed as "stark tragedy in a prologue, three acts, and an epilogue." It was, like our other plays, horrible. By 1936 some of our club members had joined John Bunn's Progressive Dramatizers, which met at Salem Methodist Church. We rehearsed plays directly above the gymnasium where Sugar Ray Robinson, Danny Cox and Buddy Moore took boxing lessons.

After high school graduation in 1937 several of us drifted from the Progressive Dramatizers and started the Pioneer Drama group. A pianist named Catherine Richardson joined us in launching three one-act plays, presented at the 129th Street Elks Auditorium on January 16, 1938. My lifelong friend, Albert Grant, joined our group. There followed three other productions by this group. During this period I met Muriel Rahn and her husband, Dick Campbell, professional theatre artists. They had organized the Rose McClendon Players and I was invited to join and receive professional theatrical training.

I did join and Muriel and Dick became "extra parents." Not only was I learning theatre, I was also taking advantage of them. I read every play I could get my hands on, then appeared at their door, uninvited, unannounced, but never unwanted. They reviewed these plays with me, analyzed them and discussed with me areas of theatre I had never known. Groups of us had previously gone to see Broadway shows with club leaders Andrew Burris and Glenn Carrington and had long discussions with them. They—like the Campbells—were brilliant, but Dick and Muriel had worked professionally for many years and they knew every foot of the stage.

Nineteen thirty-eight and 1939 brought a flurry of activity. I worked with the Rose McClendon Players (my own drama group) had one line in a Broadway failure, and I worked at menial jobs. And I went to ball games, dances at the Savoy and the Renaissance Ballrooms and other places, partied and played stickball, baseball, football—and I had a ball! Often I have said that I am possibly the only "Cat" from Harlem who cannot sing, dance or play basketball, but—that did not stop me from making attempts. And I got in my Sunday strolling. The importance of that to me came back in later year when I wrote a column for the *Amsterdam News* about strolling. This article subsequently became a part of my play, *Tell Pharaoh.*

II

Within the happy heart lies a troubled soul -
Truth strikes at unguarded hours
During a restless sleep or awakening,
While laughing, singing or dancing,

Or guzzling drinks -
Unrelenting truth bobs its head
And demands a time of reckoning . . .

Truth slashed at me and I had to face that truth. I had my name in the local newspapers, but my pocketbook was not keeping up with my publicity. I had studied playwriting at City College, but I saw no significant advancement in terms of my work. I had to face the truth that I needed additional learning and other skills to enter the writing profession. I was vexed with my own limitations and I had to face this directly.

I discussed this with my mother and my father. He was recovering from a stroke. I discussed my concern with my sister Gladys and my brother Clayton. They agreed with my conclusion which was to go to college. By this time I had another brother, Melvin, who was then six years old. Gladys and Clayton said they would look after the family. I worried. This would mean they would have me dropping another load on their shoulders, but they insisted that they knew what they were doing.

I went out and discussed this with my "extra" parents. Muriel Rahn and Dick Campbell absolutely agreed with my parents and my siblings. So did Glenn Carrington and Andrew Burris. Mr. Burris contacted Professor William H. Kindle of Talladega College in my behalf. I received a scholarship to that Alabama college in September, 1939, and I packed my bags.

It was a time of movement. I had to get around to see all of my "extra" parents. That list had gotten longer and longer over the years. The Stoute family and the Grants lived nearby, but others—like Uncle Hosea, Aunt Lillian, Uncle Richard and Aunt Betty lived uptown. I must have worn out my shoes getting around to people, but I dared not leave town without saying goodbye.

On a warm Tuesday afternoon I left my home in lower Harlem and walked to the bus station on 137th Street and Seventh Avenue. I was making my first trip into the Southland, traveling more than a thousand miles from 125th Street.

From September, 1939 until May, 1943 I did my undergraduate work. I met adults who made lasting contributions to my life—both on and off campus. Present-day poet and teacher, James C. Morris, was a native of Talladega. He and his wife, Gladys Reynolds Morris took this writer out into the community where we were welcomed warmly. This was the rural South, a "dry county" where I learned to drink home brew and corn liquor, where the people of the community barbecued ribs for me, made collard greens for me—and homemade pies which they sent up on campus for me.

I graduated in May 1943 and returned to New York. My father became ill in July and he died that September, leaving a void that remains with me until this day. I faced then the responsibility of helping Gladys and Clayton support my mother and two younger brothers. I worked full-time at night and attended Columbia University Graduate School. And I complained about being pained and I moaned and groaned. Still I had fun.

Inglorious days and glorious days! Talladega friends and Harlem friends made their way to our house on 113th Street. A good friend from college, Gloria Angela Harris, was then living and working in Chester, Pennsylvania. She would jump on a train and visit without notice. Sometimes she brought her brothers, William and Rod, and other times she brought her beautiful mother, Odessa Harris, who joined my "extra" parents group. Often Gloria came alone and we saw every show on Broadway. We also visited every cabaret in and out of Harlem. She was an actress—then and now—and she married and became Gloria Daniel.

Glad times and sad times! Uncle Sam decided he needed me in World War II. I found myself in the Jim Crow Navy because, when I was called by Selective Service I passed the physical examination and was asked, "What branch? Army, Navy or Marine Corps?" I said "You mean that as bad off as I feel, I can get in the Marine Corps?" I was told that I was in excellent condition and, when I chose the Army, I was told I had been put down for the Marines. While I was recovering from shock, I was sent over to the Navy quarters. The Negro Marine quota was filled at the time, and that left me in the

Navy. I did not cry. Sometimes discrimination works in your favor.

And so I went into the Jim Crow Navy and shipped out of Great Lakes, which is just outside Chicago. This was later to prove significant to me. Something happened to me then that I did not fully understand. The truth was that I was suddenly facing life without my parents and "extra" parents for the very first time. There was no supervision, no advice from "above." I had to make decisions on my own because my shipmates were all in my age group and younger. So were my superior officers. I was suddenly among the children of no one. The post-World War II period underscored this. Death came to many of the adults I had known. Those who remained now saw me as an adult and they spoke of yesterdays. I had to figure things out for myself.

There followed Columbia Graduate School, more shows, work for the City of New York Department of Welfare, marriage to actress Helen Marsh and two children. The marriage brought two in-laws, Viola and Ray Marsh, but other than that I noted that vanishing generation on "top of me." It was actor Frederick O'Neal who told me, bluntly "Whether we like it or not, that generation on top of us is dying, and we ourselves are dying!"

The pace of life accelerated and memories of younger days receded. I worked for the Department of Welfare from 1947 until I won a Guggenheim Award in 1958. When I returned to work in 1959 I was assigned to the Day Center Program for Older People. This unique program, spearheaded by gerontologist Harry Levine, involved community organizations that provided space for a day center while the Department of Welfare staffed those centers. There were twenty-five such centers when Mr. Levine invited me to join his staff. For this writer it was a "dream" assignment. I had to prepare Mr. Levine's weekly radio program, write press releases, go on outings with groups from various centers, then write about them.

One of these centers was the Red Shield Day Center, located on 124th Street in Harlem. The program there was jointly sponsored by the Salvation Army and the Department of Welfare. Don't you know the Salvation Army asked the Department to send a Black man to that center? Coincidentally, I had grown tired of the bureaucracy of the Department's central office. Every two-for-a-nickel executive wanted me to do some special writing about his or her division. Levine and I conferred and I was sent to the Red Shield Day Center where all I had to do was produce the radio shows, write publicity releases and go out into the streets of my Harlem and sing the praises of the Day Center Program. This center was exactly eleven blocks from my family home. If you think I cried about this assignment, you don't know me very well.

It was a remarkable experience. To this center came Harlemites who had turned sixty. Many of them knew me and members of my family. These were brilliant people who had lived the Black Experience and I made notes on our many conversations.

To this day I remember each and every one of them. But, most of all, I remember Mother Brown, then 106 years old. I had met her casually on a number of occasions. Sometimes I stood on the streets, watching her as she walked along, her cane tapping the sidewalk, rhythmically, announcing her presence, announcing her presence. She was a small, thin, grey-haired woman who walked with a limp. When she appeared she seemed to grow before your eyes. Teenagers who stood on corners, cursing, suddenly stopped and tipped their hats to her. Winos hid their bottles when they saw her walk by. And the community's leading personalities greeted her with the utmost respect. Mother Brown's activities were legendary. On Sundays she served as chief usher at Friendship Baptist Church. On Mondays she delivered flowers to hospitalized parishioners. On Tuesdays she appeared at the Red Shield Day Center where she participated in the drama group. On Wednesdays she performed household chores and on Thursdays she was again at the Center. Her Fridays were spent doing housework and on Saturdays she met with church groups to prepare for Sunday service. In addition, she cared for a backyard garden during the spring and summer.

She remained mentally alert, blunt, determined, deeply religious and amazingly independent. Once I pointed out that she might need some type of housekeeping service and that any number of community agencies could supply this service. She looked directly into my face and said:

> "No, thank you."
> "Oh, it won't cost you a penny," I said.
> "Ain't worried about no cost," she said. "Thank you just the same."
> "Now, look," I said. "Maybe I didn't make myself clear."
> She said "Young man, I know every word you said. You said that 'cause of my age I can get somebody to do my washing and cleaning and shopping. And I said no, 'cause Alice Brown ain't having nobody to do her work for her." I was puzzled. Mother Brown said: "That's what's kept me on this earth so long. That and God. All this exercise I get—picking up things and using my mind—that keeps me going. Ain't good for a body to sit up on the Stool-of-Do-Nothing. Laziness has put more folks in the ground than you can keep count of. Some mornings I lay in bed and the devil tells me, 'You too tired to get up and go. You oughta just lay there a bit longer.' Well, I push him away and I get up and go."

Life with Mother Brown remained a series of amazing events. On the day of her 108th birthday I arranged an afternoon press party. When I arrived at my office that morning the elevator had broken down. My staff and I trudged to the fifth floor office, blowing hard. We flopped into chairs, worn out. Then—we hear the tap, tap, tap of a cane. Mother Brown had walked up the five flights: she stepped into my office, took two deep breaths, then sat down to talk with me.

Fortunately, the elevator was repaired before the time of the press party.

She couldn't stay out of controversy. At the Salvation Army camp during the summer of 1964, the authorities sought the identity of the group that was leading Mother Brown up into the hills each morning. The result of that probe showed that Mother Brown was the ringleader of that group. She took the group into the hills each morning to witness God's work and to offer prayers.

One cloudy afternoon I met her on 124th Street, bound for home. "It's going to rain," I said, solicitously. "Don't you want someone to walk with you?" "I got someone to walk with me," she said, positively, starting to walk away. "Who?" I asked. "Jesus!" she flung back over her shoulder. And she turned the corner, her cane emphatically tapping the concrete.

Yes, I remember Mother Brown. The early nineteen sixties ushered in the most difficult period I have known in all my years. Wild tragedy engulfed me and pushed me into a swirling sea. I struggled to stay afloat and stay alive. I wondered about my career and, indeed, my life. And sometimes my behavior was absolutely bizarre.

It was during this time that I collaborated in writing the Broadway musical, *Ballad for Bimshire*. That genial, brilliant composer Irving Burgie had invited me to work with him. Well, one night one of his associates said something innocuous to me and my Harlem disposition flared. I cursed him from the day he was born until the day he was going to die. He mentioned that he knew things were difficult for me and he was sympathetic. Well, that only made me curse more than ever.

The next day I sat in my office, feeling contrite, embarrassed and full of self-hatred. Mother Brown came into the office. She sensed something was bothering me. She prodded me into tell her what had happened. When I completed my story, I dropped my head in shame. Mother Brown got out of her chair and placed the palm of her hand on the back of my head.

"Lord, help this child," she prayed. "Lord, help me to help him. If you let me walk this earth all this time, it musta been for some reason. This is a real Christian-hearted child, and if he lost his temper and called that man a dirty name, the man must be one. Lord, forgive this child and help him to forgive himself—and ease the pain in his heart."

She walked out of the office. I wiped away my tears, but the memory of this moment has lingered with me down through the years.

Muriel Rahn Campbell and father-in-law Ray Marsh died during the early 1960s. Scores of others—including Langston Hughes—followed. Mother Brown died in 1969 and my mother on New Year's Day in 1971. In late January 1971 I accepted an offer to teach Theatre and Afro-American Studies at the State University of New York at Binghamton—an offer made to me because of the encouragement of civil rights leader Floyd McKissick, choreographer-dancer Percival Borde, sculptor Ed Wilson and Professor Basil Ince, then Chairman of the Afro-American Studies Department.

And so I went up to Binghamton which was nearly two hundred miles from New York City. This was indeed a long, long way from 125th Street. And truth came out and glared at me.

I was alone. There were no parents and no "extra parents." For the first time I learned the term "surrogate parents." A student told me, "Prof, every student in my dormitory—Black and White—looks upon you as a surrogate father." I trembled. I was not prepared to face this. It meant acquiring inhibitions I had not had: no more telling people off and getting ready to fight! No more temper tantrums nor throwing punches! No more drinking in public! I had to face what my parents and "extra" parents had faced. That was a terrifying responsibility and called for a measure of patience I had never known.

What then am I looking at today? One truth is my total indebtedness to those who have contributed so very much to my life. Another is that—despite my revolutionary nature—I hope we can "stroll towards what we call the mainstream" with our past virtues strolling with us. In short, for me, many of the old ways need to be applied today. This is not going to be easy. Black people, their relatives and friends, now live in faraway places, not just around the corner. Neighbors dare not censure the children of others. We are silent in the midst of powerful forces who maintain their power through lies, disillusionment, ignorance, miseducation, drugs and despair—while the rich get richer and the poor catch hell!

We who were the children of everyone cannot retire from living. We must rally again to defeat the thugs who once terrorized the St. Nicholas Avenue area between 124th and 125th Street. This rallying demands, among other things, not only lead pipes, but positive thinking, organization, discipline, and the unrelenting belief of our ancestors.

Section Three:

EDUCATION FOR SURVIVAL AND SUCCESS

EDUCATION IS NOW THE FRONT LINE for Black survival, liberation or continued oppression. The focus of the following articles is on success. What does it take to be not just academically "successful," but successful in passing on and living the values and traditions that have made Black survival and resistance possible for past generations. Benjamin Bowser and Herbert Perkins with a team of investigators interviewed a group of academically successful young people. They told us what it takes. Robert and Mindy Fullilove outlined an absolutely crucial health and educational challenge that we cannot afford to see as someone else's problem: AIDS. Lawford Goddard presents the concept of developing a community education program which will teach values. And Omonike and Muata Weusi-Puryear present an alternative approach to education which contains elements of parenting which others may consider.

Chapter 8

Success Against the Odds: Young Black Men Tell What It Takes

Benjamin P. Bowser and Herbert Perkins

WHILE THERE ARE MANY ASPECTS of a young person's life which can be judged as a success or failure, their educational achievement is decisive. Success in school is a prerequisite for maximizing life chances and for taking advantage of new opportunities. Ironically, the single most difficult piece of information to find is what goes on in the lives of academically successful Black and Hispanic adolescents? How do they beat the odds? The importance of this information is obvious. If we can find out what successful Black and Hispanic students do and have in common, then we have some idea of what can be done to intervene into the circumstances of the majority who are not succeeding (Ogbu 1987).

The Interviews

There is research underway that looks directly at the lives of successful Black students. The primary focus is on the role that parents play in their academic success (Weiss 1969; Clark 1983). At different times since 1960 the schools, community, peers and parents have been identified as primary factors in academic success and failure. Researchers have more often found the family to be the most important factor (Moynihan 1965; Coleman 1966; Jencks 1972). Because of this history, the authors developed a series of questions to be used by focus group leaders to probe student relations with parents, relatives, teachers, peers, other people and organizations within their community.

The students who participated in our focus groups consisted of forty Black and Hispanic high school sophomores through seniors. Roughly half of the students were males and most of the males were Black. The students were evenly divided across the three academic years. They had 3.0 plus grade point averages in college preparatory tracks and were the top minority academic achievers in three integrated suburban high schools in California. What made this group of students interesting to us is that it cut across virtually all categories. Most had attended segregated junior high schools. They were doing well in integrated suburban high schools where the academic programs were very competitive and demanding. Virtually all of these students came from working-class households and half had single parents. Their parents worked, for example, as nurses, bus drivers, mechanics, stock clerks, physical education instructors, part-time ministers and hospital attendants. Only three students had parents who were professionals—a lawyer, teacher and engineer. Also their community reflected what will be the more common circumstance for Blacks and Hispanics in the next century. They are mostly from working-class households living in suburban racial ghettos.

Several years ago their high school district realized that they had very few academically successful minority students. The district principals decided that the first step was to identify the few who were doing well and encourage their efforts. They developed a district program where any minority student in their schools who achieved a 3.0 plus grade point average (GPA) was to be rewarded and encouraged with field trips, recognition and opportunities to meet, interact and encourage one another. These students represented a unique opportunity to derive insight on what makes for academic success for working-class minority students in suburban integrated schools. These students were brought to the California State University at Hayward campus and spent an afternoon divided into six focus groups, led by student service staff and faculty. We asked the students to tell us in taped discussions: What did they do to perform well in school; who in their family, school, community and peer groups played important roles; what were the barriers; was race a factor; and how would they account for their peers' lack of success?

The students were assured that their individual identities would be kept confidential. With the formalities over, they lit up and had a lot to say. No one had asked them these questions before, so they were eager to respond. In no session did the focus group leader dominate the discussion. The students responded to the questions with amazing candor and detail. While we had a special interest in what the young Black men had to say, it was very clear right from the beginning of the sessions that the students' experiences and insights cut across gender and ethnicity. The following is what they told us based on a review of the tape recordings of each session.

Students' Reflections on Academic Success

Relations with Family

Past and current research suggests that there is a very close relation between student academic success and parents. Early in each focus group a number of students said that their parents were important as sources of encouragement. These students reported that their parents always had time for them, would help them with their homework, clearly rewarded success, punished failure and were generally "on their case." One student had a mother who corrected her papers and a father who tutored her in mathematics. But when we probed this response and got all of the students in the discussion, a far more complex picture of relations with parents emerged. Most of the students had a different situation. After the groups became more comfortable, several "acknowledgers" as well as most who had remained quiet said that their immediate parents were really not their main source of support. The key persons, who they named as their main sources of family support for high academic achievement, consisted of grandparents or, more often, older brothers or sisters. While parents may or may not have been "on their case" and were pleased that the student was doing well, it was actually some other member of the family who helped the student to define his long-term career goals and who turned him on to high academic achievement.

> My older sister really got me going. She is in the Navy, is doing well and has told me many times what I need to do to be successful. I have admired her and have always listened to her.

Ironically, most of the people who were reported as the main source of family motivation were not successful in school. Many of our high achievers as elementary and junior high school students had watched their parents struggle with older siblings. These older brothers and sisters had made all sorts of mistakes, primary of which was failure in school. The outcomes in troubled lives, purposelessness, underemployment and unemployment are now very apparent within each family. It turns out that the experiences of these older brothers and sisters serve as a powerful source of motivation to take some other route. The students said repeatedly that they would do anything not to end up like their older siblings who were models of the consequences of underachievement. In many cases, these older sibling became directly involved in making certain that their younger brother or sister did not end up as they did. One student who was the sixth and youngest boy in his family reported:

> All five of my older brothers did not do well in school and have been in some form of trouble at one time or another. One day they got together and sat me down in the middle of them and told me that they wanted me to do better and that I had to get A's and B's in school. No matter what they're doing, they all check my report card. If it's good, they really make me feel great. If it's bad, they'll kick my ass.

Another student said, "All I have to do is look at how my parents ended up unhappy and fighting all the time and I know I have to do well in school—I work harder and harder." Other students reported that what got them achieving was an older sister's struggle to graduate from high school as a single parent, defiance aided by an older brother against parents who don't believe "I can do it," and a brother's trouble in college because he was not well prepared. What all of these high achieving students had in common is that there was somebody outside of school in their immediate OR extended family who was "on their case" and who more often served as a direct example of what happens to those who do not achieve.

Relations with School

It is overly simplistic to assume that home motivation, regardless of its source, translates directly into high academic achievement. Work which focuses exclusively on family and academic achievement makes such an assumption by default. In reality, schools can either take advantage of or frustrate homebased motivation to achieve. It is also necessary to look at the related influence of schools on individual academic achievement. Otherwise, schools appear to be culturally neutral and totally objective entities—an impossibility. Our high achievers come to school with very strong motivation from home to do well. But it is also clear from the focus groups that family motivation is not all that it takes to maintain a 3.0 plus grade point average in college preparatory courses.

What was said in all of the focus groups was that someone at school took a personal interest in each student's work. There was at least one teacher who held each student in high regard and who told them repeatedly that they could do well. The students reported that these "mentor" teachers then worked with them.

The "mentor" teachers were important to the initial translation of personal and home derived motivation into actual high grades. Several students reported having a series of supportive teachers who showed them that they could do good work—repeatedly. Others had only one teacher now and then who took a special interest in them. In addition to a "mentor" teacher all of the high achievers had counselors. The fewer supportive teachers they had, the more important were these counselors. Even with a series of supportive teachers, caring counselors were essential to monitoring, encouraging and getting students into good classroom experiences.

Active counselors were also reported to be essential in their role as in-school advocates and for coaching students through classes with unsupportive teachers who could have easily broken their motivation and early successes.

Several focus group leaders explored with their students the nature of the relation the students reported having with "mentor" teachers and counselors. Amazingly the responses were consistent across each focus groups. The students reported that the people in school who were supportive treated them more like friends or close relatives than like students. It was very important that the formal student-teacher and student-counselor relation be reduced to a more personal one-on-one relation.

> Mrs. X treats us like her son. She is excited about me, shares with me her feelings, makes me feel special and a part of her life. I even have her home telephone number.

The students reported that it was easier and even fun to study with a teacher who really cared and "did not talk down to you." Teachers who would stop them in the hall while they were with other students and ask how they were and how were things going were well regarded. One student said that he really did not believe that he could do superior work until he realized that two of his teachers were willing to stay after school to work with him on science and math problems. But besides being personal and supportive, these significant school persons held high expectations and did not hesitate to monitor each students progress, in which case, the students' relations with their "mentor" teachers and counselors became additional motivation to do well. Poor grades and lack of effort would have violated these positive personal relations and would have hurt and disappointed their mentors.

In contrast, teachers who insisted on being impersonal, who showed no signs of caring and had no time or interest in the student, drew angry, hurt comments. "Mr. Y would see me on the street and wouldn't even say 'hello' and, if you ask him a question in class, he would tell you 'go look it up—I already talked about that in class.'" Especially hurtful were teachers who were clearly very positive toward their White students, but were very impersonal with minority students in the same class.

One of the more fascinating elements in the students' discussion about school was when they began to realize that they really could be high achievers. The first time they attained their 3.0 plus in high school was not the point at which they realized that their achievement was special. The seniors had had at least two years of high grades and had no doubts about accepting and identifying with their achievement. The seniors told us that their earlier confidence was closer to what the sophomores reported. The less experienced achievers said that, while they knew that they were doing well, they still did not think that what they had done was exceptional or important—even after making the dean's list several times and being part of a program for high achieving minority students! One student had a 3.9 GPA at the end of his freshman year and seriously considered dropping out for a temporary labor job. He knew that a 3.9 was a high average, but he had no sense of its meaning in his own life or what he could attain by maintaining that average. Another student had so thoroughly identified with the stereotype that minority students do poorly in school that she assumed that her 3.6 was simply not good enough.

High initial attainment in itself was not sufficient to be a source of motivation for continued effort nor did it mark special status. One of the Black males with high grades was also a top athlete. Like the others, he did not think of his academic achievements as important. At first, his only concern about his grades was that they be high enough for him to continue playing ball. The turning point for him and the others came with some public declaration that their academic achievement was "special." The athlete did not fully realize that he was also an exceptional student until the city newspaper sent a reporter and photographer to his home. They took pictures and did a story with a focus on him as an athlete who was also a top student. Another student was called to the principal's office. He thought that he was in some sort of trouble. Instead, the principal gave him an award for his academic achievement.

The other students indicated that the minority scholar's annual awards and recognition banquet was the turning point for them. At this banquet each student received an academic award with their peers and parents present. A number of students had part-time jobs after school—they were assisted in placement by their school counselors. People on their jobs were aware of their academic achievements and also encouraged them. The students were asked by the people they worked with if they ever considered going to particular colleges and universities. The students had always assumed that these schools were beyond their means and abilities. They were asked if they knew about various fields of study in college. Again they either had no knowledge or simply never associated themselves with the fields. On some of these jobs there were college students who offered to help them with their homework and told them to consider going to their university—they could get in. These events impressed on them that what they were doing was important and was not to be taken for granted. But it was equally important that the point be made to their parents, friends and peers. After public acknowledgment, each student had a new identity to live up to and a sense that the opportunities before them were real.

Finally, if you ever thought that high academic performance was largely due to proper study skills, what these young people reported was shocking. They violated every rule for efficient and effective study. They studied with their radios on. They studied lying down. They studied in between classes and on the run. They studied when they were tired. They studied for examinations the night before or just an hour before. Occasionally, they did not study at all! Only a couple of students reported studying consistently several hours per night. Out of the entire group only two students studied together and at the library. Ironically, they all knew how they were supposed to study, but the proper way was simply not how they did it. With regard to study habits, they seemed to have only two points in common: They all did some sort of studying and they were all diligent about completing homework assignments on time. But they may have had an additional and very subtle point in common. Several students mentioned that they paid very close attention to what went on in each class and practiced recalling what they learned right after classes. I suspect that there is a close relation between their relations with teachers and how well they retained information. Being personally close to teachers makes recall easier, while the formal social distance common to the teacher-student relation makes retention and recall more difficult.

Relations with Community

Virtually all of these high achievers lived in low income, working-class suburban communities which are segregated by race and by economic class. The students were asked if there were other nonfamily members in their community who contributed to their academic achievement. The most common response was emphatically "none." In exploring their community experiences we found a rough and tragic terrain. The students saw academic achievement as a way out of depressed and dangerous environments. One student said, "You do whatever you can to get out of X."

Others commented that their community was varied by income and people and was not all negative. Everyone's concern was that others, especially their White peers at school, held consistently negative stereotypes about their communities and all of the people who lived there. People who lived in X community were considered to be "stupid, lazy and criminal." This stereotype was a formidable barrier to how others treated the students. Only one student said that his community motivated him. He wanted to get an education so that he could return to help turn it around. Another student realized that education was the only way out after having worked during a summer on a survey project. The households he interviewed that had the least education were the poorest and the most troubled.

Virtually all of these high achievers conveyed a sense of walking a fine line in their community lives. The subject that got them all especially animated was drug trafficking in their communities. This was the most threatening aspect of their community life. They could live with poverty and the stereotyping, but drug trafficking was another matter. They had family members involved as sellers and users. Neighbors and friends also used and sold "crack." This is what the "crowd" did and there was considerable peer pressure on them to also get involved. One student said "you can't act like they [drug sellers and users] don't exist. They are family, neighbors and friends. You got to live with them." But the fine line is that "you have to not be a part of them while they are all around you." Another student said "I stay by myself away from the crowd and spend as much time as possible outside of the community." The consensus was that you either do well in school or you do drugs. There was literally no other option. Focusing on school was banking on the future because in the present those who sold drugs clearly had the money, cars, clothes and high regard of the "crowd."

We asked about church and other institutions in their community. Were community institutions viewed as supportive of their high achievement? The responses were mostly negative. One church was mentioned where the pastor acknowledged student academic achievement in the congregation. He always asked, "How are you doing in school?" and never forgot to tell them "to keep up the good work." But most of the other churches the students attended only gave lip service to the need for students to do well in school. Individual student achievements were not recognized or acknowledged. There is no place in the format or tradition of the Catholic masses for this sort of acknowledgment. And as one student put it, his church was so down on young people that they wouldn't know how to recognize him even if they knew of his work. Two female students, whose families were Pentecostal and Jehovah's Witnesses respectively, told stories of how their churches actually opposed their focus on school. The time they spend at school would be better spent at church and it was not good to become too much a part of "the world." Only three students talked of being a part of youth groups in their communities. A number of organizations for young people existed some years ago, but not any more—"there is no money for them and people are now scared of the dope."

Relations with Peers

"It helps to have someone to talk to and work with." But more typically these students did not have peers whom they were really close to. They had many acquaintances but few close friends. Even participation in the three schools' minority scholars program did not change their relative isolation. There were enough differences among these students that they rarely got together outside of program activities. They were also spread across three high schools and several communities. The lack of close friends highlighted the need for open and warm friendships with teachers and counselors. The students gave a variety of explanations for their situation. One of the Black males said "When the kids I used to hang with found out that I was doing well [in school], they didn't want to hang with me no more." Most of the students reported that very few of the young people they spent their time with were doing well in school. When the achievers were together with their friends, they simply did not talk about school. In some cases, friends who were doing poorly were pleased to have a partner who was "smart" and encouraged their achieving friend to continue doing well.

Friends were mostly of the same sex and race. But occasionally support and motivation came from unanticipated places. Several female students spoke of their boyfriends as being very supportive of their achievement—especially friends in colleges who were a year or two older. One male student said, "I wanted to be friends with a girl who was a good student. But she don't want to be bothered with me when my grades were bad. When your grades are good, you can go out with a lot more girls." Most White students expected the minority students to do poorly and were often openly hostile to those who managed to be exceptions. Several of our achievers had experiences similar to a student who said, "When the White students in my classes found out that I was getting As, they stopped talking to me. At first they thought I was there for their entertainment—to talk about sports. Several said to me that Blacks aren't suppose to get As—especially those from my community." Another student said, "When I answer questions correctly in class, the White students turn and look at me in amazement."

Not all of the White students constantly mirrored prejudice. One student told of an incident in one of his classes when an examination was being returned. A White student asked, what grade did he get? Before he could answer another White student said laughingly, "He probably got a D." The comment hurt and the Black student resented it, but he and the White student who made the comment are now good friends. Another student told the group that, if it had not been for a White friend from junior high school, he would not have enrolled in college preparatory courses.

His White friend kept after him to get into the right classes—he had no idea that a decision in the eighth grade would make a difference.

As part of the focus group questions, each facilitator asked the student to tell us why they felt other "bright" Blacks and Hispanics did poorly in school. The achievers began discussing other students who were smart and did better work than they did in junior high school. Their explanations ranged across school, peers, family and community. They pointed out that if there was no one in the family who actively cared, the young person was finished. A student not on the college track by the ninth grade was also finished—"Nobody is going to go back to take the right courses." They called for more guidance counselors and wondered why, the very year their district high schools were integrated, the guidance departments were cut out? They also pointed out that the low achievers were unwilling to give up their friends for school. Other comments were that their peers did not believe in themselves—just as our scholars had not. The low achievers thought that they could not do any better because deep down they really believed that Blacks and Hispanics are dumb—precisely what many White teachers and students believe. So there was no point in committing themselves to studies. The worst part of what they reported was that alienation from school fed directly into alienation in the community. There were no opportunities for a young person to simply make mistakes, sort out their lives and mature. The drug scene was there waiting with open arms.

The Significance of Race

We asked the students, had they experienced racism and, if so, did it have any effect on their academic performance? Most replied that they had no direct experience with racism. What they meant was that they had not experienced blatant and obvious discrimination like that which existed in the South during Jim Crow segregation. Instead, what they experienced were actions directed at them personally that kept them guessing whether it was or was not racist. Not really knowing was worse than the acts. There were key teachers in the college preparatory track who seemed friendly toward their White students, but were cold and matter-of-fact with Black and Hispanic students. One student with a B average in the class got a D as a final grade. The teacher said it was because he did poorly on the final examination. When the student's counselor and father demanded to see the examination, the teacher claimed that it was lost. The grade was changed. Another "unfriendly" teacher wanted to give the student a failing grade for one unexcused absence. The student knew of White students in his class with unexcused absences who were not failed. It turned out that the teacher could not fail this minority student after all, because he had really not been absent.

Another student remarked, "It seems like they [unsupportive teachers] are just laying for you and looking for an excuse to mark you down. It is hard to go all semester and make no mistakes."

In listening to the focus group tapes it was interesting to note that only males reported that teachers were "laying for them." The female students also experienced covert mistreatment, but there appeared to be greater tolerance among unsupportive teachers for Black and Hispanic females being exceptional students. White students exhibited covert racism by assuming that all Black and Hispanic students were dumb and by wanting to maintain this belief even when they encountered exceptions. Sometimes underlying racial hostility would be manifested in actions. Students reported occasionally opening their lockers and finding notes stuffed in through the air holes. The contents of these anonymous notes were personally insulting, racist and derogatory. These covert acts of racism took a much greater toll in anger and personal hurt than the overt acts. "It is hard to get your mind off of it [an anonymous act of racism] and study, especially when it came from a teacher." In addition, those who held jobs pointed out that they saw racist behavior on the job. It was usually directed at Blacks and Hispanics in lower-level roles. In these cases, racism was an incentive to study in order to be better employed.

Conclusion

What we have uncovered from these interviews are insights from the lives of a group of Black and Hispanic students as to why they are successful in school. They have also given us a glimpse of the price they are paying for choosing to focus on school.

What these students provided in one intense afternoon is by no means the whole story. Black and Hispanic students from other social class and community circumstances could undoubtedly give us additional insight on what it takes to be academically successful. This small group of students went quickly beyond the demographic and statistical picture of success and got into the factors and processes that account for their achievement. Others may wish to use this information to design surveys to see just how representative the experiences are of the students who participated in our focus groups. If we learned anything from these group discussions, it was the value of involving teens in an inquiry about their lives and experiences.

There are a number of specific points which the students raised that are well worth testing and considering:

1. Both family and school involvement and encouragement are essential to student motivation to succeed. Also both sources of motivation have to be complementary.
2. A student's family should be defined more broadly so that it includes extended relations. We should note that there is a bias toward crediting parent(s) with influence even when the primary motivation comes from some other, non-parent family member.
3. Students can be motivated to succeed by family and friends who are not themselves "successful" role models.
4. An effective and motivating relation between students and their teachers and counselors begins when teachers and counselors take a personal interest in the students and work with them. Willingness to drop the formal teacher-student or counselor-student role is important.
5. Public acknowledgment and identification of an achieving student are essential to those students' realization that they are indeed doing exceptional work and can qualify for opportunities in the larger society outside of their community. Acknowledgment is also very important for encouraging continued support from a high achiever's peers and family.
6. The specific study strategies that lead to high academic achievement are primarily to study consistently, to pay close attention in class and to be diligent in turning in assignments. Specific study techniques or number of hours per-day of study are of secondary importance.

The Black and Hispanic students we interviewed are

paying a very high price in being shunned and isolated from their peers and community. They have to literally disassociate themselves from their communities and normal friendships in order to maintain their motivation to academically succeed. Also they cannot afford to make mistakes in walking the fine lines in their communities between drug trafficking and resentment over their choice or at school between racist teachers "laying for them" and White students who do not accept their competitiveness. The personal price these students are paying for their academic achievement is remarkable and ironic. It is remarkable because they have to pay such a price at all. It is ironic because all well-meaning individuals and institutions in American life profess to support and would applaud their achievement. Yet they are isolated, shunned and could not achieve without a system of special support. The problem is that for these students professions willing to have them as important players in the larger society are too far away from their day-to-day reality.

The Community Factor

The students we interviewed are doing well academically because of extraordinary efforts from their schools which have made it possible for individual teachers and counselors to take interest in each student and to work with them. Their achievement also required someone at home to convince each student to forgo the immediate world around them and to count on school and the future for a better life—another extraordinary effort. Why are these extraordinary efforts necessary in order to produce high achievers? It is very clear that if motivators at home or at school had not taken special interest and given attention to these students, we would not have had any Black and Hispanic high achievers to interview. These young people would be indistinguishable from their peers—many of whom are just as talented. The answer can be found by looking at the factor the students found least supportive and hoped to escape from: the community.

Researchers may be able to conceptually separate families from communities and then research the relation between families and academic achievement as if the community were not a factor. But the family lives of the young people we interviewed would suggest that to separate family from community is to ignore very important factors in student motivation. The community more than any other factor is a reflection of the morale, expectations and life conditions of its residents. It is also the community that serves as the immediate environment for family life. If we focus on what the students told us about their parents and older brothers and sisters, we get a glimpse of a real struggle. That struggle is not simply between family members; it is about the family living in its environment. It was through the community that older brothers and sisters got into their troubles. It was peers in the community that parents competed against in shaping their children's lives and in controlling them amidst fast money and other potentially destructive distractions.

Current research suggests that Black student academic achievement is largely due to family influences, in which case declining achievement is due to declining family support. What researchers might be really looking at is declining community morale and declining social resources mediated through the family. By overlooking community influence, one can focus on the extraordinary uphill struggles of those few families who do produce a high achiever and overcome their communities. But this is to ignore the obvious. The obvious is that if the majority are failing because of community influences, the majority can also succeed if community becomes positive and supportive. Our students' older brothers and sisters and friends are a testimony to this fact. The interviewers asked each group of students to name the one thing which could be done to produce more academically successful students like themselves. We fully expected them to focus on improvements within their schools such as expanding special programs. To our surprise the most common answer had to do with community improvement—get rid of drugs and get more jobs.

References

Alvy, K. 1987. *Black Parenting*. New York: Irvington Publishers.

Billingsley, A. 1972. "Black Families and White Social Science," in J. Ladner (ed.) *The Death of White Sociology*. New York: Vintage Books.

Clark, R. 1983. *Family Life and School Achievement*. Chicago: The University of Chicago Press.

Coleman, J., et al. 1966. *Equality of Educational Opportunity*. Washington: U.S. Office of Education.

Gibbs, J. (ed.) 1988. *Young Black and Male in America*. Dover, MA: Auburn Publishing.

Jencks, C., et al. 1972. *Inequality*. New York: Basic Books.

McAdoo, H. and J. McAdoo (eds.) 1985. *Black Children*. Beverly Hills: Sage.

Moynihan, D. 1965. *The Negro Family*. Washington: Office of Policy Planning and Research, U.S. Dept. of Labor.

Ogbu, J. 1987. *Minority Education and Caste*. New York: Academic Press.

Sniderman, P. and P. Tetluck. 1986. "Symbolic Racism: Problems of Motive Attribution in Political Analysis." *Journal of Social Issues*. 42:2, 129-150.

Weiss, J. 1969. "The Identification and Measurement of Home Environment Factors Related to Achievement Motivation and Self-Esteem." Ph.D. Dissertation: University of Chicago.

Chapter 9

You Can Teach Wisdom: Ways to Motivate Black Male Adolescents

Lawford L. Goddard

> When I was a child, I spoke as a child,
> I understood as a child, I thought as a child;
> but when I became a man, I put away childish things
> (First Epistle of Paul the Apostle to the Corinthians, Chapter 13, verse 11).

> And it came to pass that Kunta Kinte, oldest son of Omoro Kinte, grandson of Kairaba Kunta Kinte, must be led to the Jujujo [manhood training village]. There he would be turned over to the "Kintango"—the man in charge of manhood training (Excerpted from *Roots* by Alex Haley).

WHEN SAINT PAUL WROTE THIS EPISTLE there appeared to be a clear distinction between what it meant to be a child and what it meant to be a man in his society. Similarly when Kunta Kinte reached the age of puberty, the elders gathered up all the young men in the village and took them into the "secret place" where they undertook a training program that educated them into the secrets and responsibilities of manhood. In former times there was a clearly defined path to adulthood that was recognizable by the society and its members. Today the distinction between childhood and adulthood is still explicit. However, what is missing or left unstated is the process that moves one from the state of childhood to the status of man. There are no clearly defined rites of passage to differentiate the progression to adulthood.

Adolescence

Adolescence is generally considered a period of transition bridging the gap between the child and adult world. This perception of the stage of adolescence has been primarily defined by Euro-American child development specialists who have argued that adolescence represents the period of breaking away from the family of origin and the creation of a separate and distinct individual identity. For example Erikson (1956) suggests that adolescence is a normal phase of development that necessarily includes increased conflict that will eventually contribute to the formation of the adolescent's separate identity. Havighurst (1972) indicates that the developmental task of the adolescent is the struggle to achieve an identity that is unique and separate from his parents. He goes on further to suggest that there are critical teachable moments which are important for developmental tasks and if a particular developmental task is not learned at the appropriate time, later learning is difficult, if not impossible. In the Piaget notion of child development at the end of "the operational period" around 16 years, a youngster should be capable of abstract thinking and mature problem-solving. The basic building block for the development of independence from family and interdependence with other adults in the society should have developed (Piaget 1952).

Adolescence is often a period of confusion as significant physiological and social changes take place. The transition to adulthood includes concern for managing new responsibilities. In addition, it represents a period of individual social and emotional growth. When all of these changes are combined it imposes a great deal of stress and confusion that is likely to delay the ability of the person to mature and develop into an effective member of the society. The general perception is that adolescence is a period during which the child learns to be an adult. In this process he comes to acquire some definition of his social being—that is, who he is, what he will be. In his being he is laying the framework for who and what he will become as a man. But despite these general theories about the period of adolescence, society has not provided either a clear explication of the processes that an individual must undergo or a systematic, cumulative body of knowledge and skills that an individual must master during this period.

The past two decades have witnessed significant and far-reaching changes that have direct implications for the understanding of the period of adolescence. As the median age of Americans goes up, the period of adolescence has lengthened. This is a result of the increased standard of living and the lower rates of mortality. Today, the normal pattern of educational development is high school, college, and even postgraduate training before an individual enters the labor market and/or acquires the status of adulthood. That is, the adolescent/young adult throughout the educational process is not yet considered an adult. One of the formal rites of passage to adulthood in modern society is the entry into the labor market. Since this entry is being delayed longer and longer, the period of transition is consequently lengthened.

For the African-American population, the transition to adulthood is particularly critical given the extreme environmental stresses imposed upon the Black community. During this process of adolescent growth and development the Black man-child faces the most difficult ecological conditions impacting upon any social group in society.

Condition of Black Males

A review of socioeconomic data reveals that Black men in America are an endangered species. On almost every indicator of socioeconomic well-being the Black male lags far behind women and Whites in this country. For example, the Black male has a lower life expectancy than any other sex and ethnic group. The Black male mortality rate of 1,020 per 100,000 in 1983 was 50% higher than that for White males (698 per 100,000), almost double that of Black females (590 per 100,000), and two and a half times that for

White females (393 per 100,000). The incidence of cirrhosis of the liver for Black males under 35 years is twelve times higher than in any comparable group. In 1983 the death rate for cirrhosis of the liver for Black males was 23 per 100,000, almost twice that of White males, with 13 per 100,000; twice that of Black females, with 11 per 100,000; and four times that of White females with 6 per 100,000. The death rate for heart disease for Black males was 308 per 100,000, the highest rate for all sex and ethnic groups.

Violence, victimization and crime are increasingly becoming part of the everyday experiences of Black males. The Black male has a 1 in 21 chance of being murdered in his lifetime (i.e., by age 65) compared to a 1 in 104 chance for the Black female, a 1 in 131 chance for the White male, and a 1 in 369 chance for the White female. Homicide is the leading cause of death among Black males 15-24, and one out of every three deaths (38.5%) of Black males 20-24 was due to homicide. The male homicide rate of 54 per 100,000 males was seven times that for White males, five times that for Black females and eighteen times that for White females. Although Black males comprise only 6% of the total population of America they account for 34% of all the murder victims.

Similarly the incarceration data indicate the level of victimization of Black men. Although the Black population represents 12% of the total population, it accounts for 46% of the prison population. Of the Black prison population Black males account for 89%; 54% of the Black males in prison were below 29 years (U.S. Bureau of the Census 1988).

In terms of the opportunities for participation in the mainstream economic activities the data indicate that Black males are increasingly becoming a marginal group. Labor force participation for Black males fell from 83% in 1960 to 75% in 1983. At the same time the unemployment ratio for Black males has remained constant at double that for White males and currently stands at 20%. The implication of these data is that large numbers of Black males are not participating in the formal economic structure of American society. Unemployment among Black male adolescents was 49.6%

in 1983 (U.S. Bureau of Labor 1985). Educational data indicate that Black students, in general, are scoring consistently below the national average across all grade levels and all subjects and are not being prepared for entry into college. In addition the data also indicate that Black male students drop out, or are pushed out, of the school system at higher rates than other sex and ethnic groups.

Environmental Context

If we are to promote the positive growth of the Black man-child, then we must develop a pathway of development through which he must pass in order to attain the status of "man" in the community. The Black community simply cannot afford to allow its youth a period of total and absolute confusion when they are supposedly "finding" themselves. The critical ecological forces impinging on the Black family are such that Black parents have the added task of protecting their children from a hostile environment that is not conducive to a "laissez-faire" pattern of parenting. Parenting the Black man-child is fraught with additional problems and concerns in a society that denies his very identity and legitimacy and in an environment that has a diminished capacity to recognize the sanctity of human life. In our model of development we must recognize the special and exceptional needs of the Black man-child if we are to effectively turn around current trends toward self-destruction.

Living in the urban environment is an extremely stressful situation for the Black adolescent. In addition to the difficulties of inadequate employment opportunities for teens, the urban environment is characterized by high levels of noise and environmental pollutants, lack of open space and limited recreational facilities (Goddard 1985). Pierce (1970) has stated that Blacks, and particularly adolescents, are constantly bombarded by "micro-aggressions." Much like cases of combat psychosis, these experiences hinder young people's attempts to realize the basic functional imperatives required for normal adjustment in society. This constant bombardment, Pierce contends, produces a condition of status dislocation wherein the individual cannot fully function in society and seeks escape mechanisms to enable him to survive. Pierce (1974) has also indicated that life in a mundane but stressful environment characterized by the urban ghetto requires accessible escape mechanisms in order for any humans to minimally survive. The interaction and mutually reinforcing effects of racism and stress conditions disposes many to opt for addictive escapism.

Substance abuse has emerged as a leading form of escapism and as a major economic and health problem. It is a critical factor in the erosion and deterioration of family life as evidenced by the increase in crime, family violence and the growing rate of violent deaths among Blacks. More significant than this is the emergence of a drug culture that threatens to destroy the very fabric of the Black community. The rules by which one lives and the value system guiding one's behavior in the drug life-style emphasize selfishness, individualism, violence, hostility and impulsivity. In addition, those in the drug culture have persistent habits of dishonesty, irresponsibility and callousness without signs of remorse, personal responsibility or interest in change. These behavior patterns reflect the most devastating of psychiatric characters: the psychopath. With the emergence and apparent permanence of the drug culture as a dominant environmental influence on the lives of Black families and children, we are witnessing a shift in black cultural orientation. The subsequent cultural shift is a most powerful danger which Black children and families must daily confront.

What Needs to be Done

In order for the transformation between adolescence and adulthood to result in responsible community members, families have to plan and guide the process at an early age. They must make a conscious and deliberate attempt to alter the negative images that are imposed upon the Black man-child and to develop strategies to break the cycle of apathy, despair and hopelessness.

Cultural Realignment

A solution to the problems of adolescence for Black families is not to be found solely in the efforts of individual families. Rather, the solution to these problems must lie in Black cultural realignment as well as an economic revitalization of the Black community. The Black community needs to develop its own family policies and agendas. From our vantage point it is clear that only those community practices and programs which are consistent with the black cultural orientation can be expected to succeed. Culturally consistent programming would provide a spiritual base, a sense of connection and a value system that is based on an intrinsic black cultural orientation. It is imperative that we provide our young males with a solid value orientation if we expect to develop mature, responsible Black adults.

Staples (1974) has indicated that the Black community possesses a unique value system that is expressed through spontaneity, adaptability, and that these values have been handed down from generation to generation. Hill (1972) has also pointed out that the traditional strengths of the Black family include a strong work orientation, strong family bonds, strong achievement orientation and a strong religious orientation. Nobles (1974) and Staples (1974) have further suggested that Black culture provides Blacks with a value system that enables them to survive racist oppression. This culture can be defined as a process that gives Black people a general design for living and patterns for interpreting their reality (Nobles 1985). Black culture provides a sense of identification, a sense of belonging and a sense of legitimation. Within the Black community the individual has a place in the society; he has a sense of identity, he belongs to a larger group and his action is regulated and legitimized within that structure.

Akbar (1985) has suggested that in the process of restoring mental order, the individual has to become aware—that is, to possess self-knowledge. This awareness is the focal point for self-discovery, self-acceptance, self-help and ultimately self-preservation. Similarly Kagan and Knight (1979) have indicated that self-esteem in children is partially a function of the extent to which children live up to their cultural norms. Kaplan, Robbins and Martin (1983) have also found that the ability of the individual to overcome negative life events is enhanced by the nature and meaning of family support and the substitutability of supportive relationships.

Culturally Consistent Training Program

We are proposing a training program that is built upon the reclamation and reaffirmation of traditional Black cultural values as a means of altering the negative environmental factors that confront Black adolescents on a daily basis. The program is a uniquely-designed training strategy that is delivered in modular form and consists of the following:

- Values Orientation
- Capacity Building/Competency Acquisition
- Decision-making Skills
- Adolescent Behavior
- Family Dynamics
- Responsibility/Manhood Training

Values Orientation: The overall goal of this module is to provide Black youth with a grounding in the cultural values and orientation that have been historically characteristic of black people. Values form the basis of the behavior that we see manifested. The task, then, is to provide Black youth with a values orientation that emerges from their own culture and is consistent with that culture. We believe that Black youth will be able to make correct (i.e., appropriate) decisions about their self-identity and behavior to the extent that they are aware of (i.e., possess with knowledge of) their cultural orientation.

Capacity Building/Competency Acquisition: The goal of this module is to provide youth with capacity building and competency acquisition techniques that will enhance and/or promote social and functional competencies and hence improve their level of psychosocial functioning. Basic skills in interpersonal relations, assertiveness, behavioral control and motivational factors will be taught and practiced within this module. Early systematic competency acquisition and capacity building influence the youth's present self-esteem during adolescence and the development of effective adaptations to later life situations.

Decision-making Skills: The goal of this module is to develop a decision-making process that provides youth with a foundation for making decisions that are based on logical, consistent and sound information about themselves, their culture, history and community. Decisions are made on a daily basis and in a variety of contexts, all having importance for each individual's sense of well-being. In this module the youth will learn to identify and recognize their own values and to use values as a determinant of decisions. This module will provide the youth with a framework for making critical decisions about the future with a clear understanding of the consequences of those choices made.

Adolescent Behavior: The goal of this module is to explain the psychosocial nature of adolescence and to distinguish between normal, appropriate behavior and inappropriate behavior. In this module the youth will learn how to deal with anger, hostility, separation from parents, clarification of values and establishment of interpersonal relations.

Family Dynamics: The goal of this module is to explain the nature of family dynamics from the organizational purpose of the family, the social organization of the family and interpersonal relations within the family. Youth will be provided with a clear perspective of the operational dynamics of the family system and the way in which parental values and behavior affect children.

Responsibility/Manhood Training: The goal of this module is to develop within youth the appropriate behavior that is consistent with manhood and maturity. The youth will be provided with a clear perspective of the behavioral modalities of "men," the values associated with maturity and the techniques for developing responsible behavior.

The training program is targeted to youth 10-14 years and can be delivered in the school system, the church and other social and fraternal organizations; e.g., Jack 'n Jill, the Links, Youth Clubs, YMCA, etc. The goal of the training program is to provide youth with the social skills and competencies that will equip them to develop a sense of competence and confidence, a sense of maturity and responsibility and the ability to face, resist and overcome the pervading pressures to engage in self-destructive behavior. The outcome measure of the program is the development of confident and competent youth who can make critical decisions, based on a firm value foundation, regarding their own behavior.

Values: a Basis for Black Character Development

While each module is important, only the first will be explained in detail since it provides the fundamental theoretical structure for the effective functioning of the other modules in the program. The overall goal of the first module, values orientation, is to provide Black youth with a grounding in the cultural values and orientation that have been historically characteristic of the Black people.

Black cultural orientation manifests itself in two general themes. Nobles, Goddard and Cavil (1985) defined cultural themes as dynamic affirmations that reflect the individual's or group's purpose and rules for responding to reality. For Black people, the cultural themes are a sense of excellence and a sense of appropriateness. In the sense of excellence, the individuals are expected and encouraged to develop their own style while being and doing the best at what they choose to do. The sense of excellence allows for competition, strong achievement motivation and a belief in hard work. The sense of excellence requires that individuals in authority over Black youth establish standards of expectations that are realistic and achievable, and challenge the ability of the youth to perform. In addition, authority figures must establish standard criteria of what is acceptable or not and must enforce these in a compassionate, nonjudgmental fashion. The work/product of the youth is evaluated, not the innate ability of the youth. Lack of success on any individual task should not be generalized to imply a lack of ability. Within the educational context the task of the educator is to draw out of the child the innate ability he possesses and translate present failings into future successes.

In the sense of appropriateness, behavior is governed by notions of formality, deference, civility and courtesy. Individuals are expected to display the appropriate behavior for the particular social setting in which they are located. The sense of appropriateness also requires authority figures to delineate clearly-stated rules and regulations, to determine the acceptable mode of social interaction, to specify the rewards and sanctions associated with these rules and to engage in a uniform and consistent application of these standards of rewards and punishment. The lack of consistency in the enforcement of rules, and the absence of clearly-stated rules often lead to interpersonal conflict between youth and authority figures.

These cultural themes manifest themselves in traditional values that determine the "code of conduct" for Black people. In our prior work we have identified four values that are critical in any developmental and transformational program. These are: (1) restraint; (2) responsibility; (3) respect; and (4) reciprocity. Restraint is a value in which children and youth learn to appreciate self-control in their behavior. The youth should understand that his rights are always balanced against the requirements of the group to which he belongs. In the Akbar (1985) model of restoration, restraint is the basis for the development of self-discovery. Responsibility is a value that encourages individuals to share in the management of the activities of the group and to develop a sense of belonging. It is through the collective activities of all the members that the group is able to achieve its goals. Each individual has a role to play in the success of the group. Respect allows children to develop self-awareness and a willingness to acknowledge the presence and accomplishments of others. Respect for the child is first a sense of self-respect, and then respect for others. Self-respect involves the development of a positive self-esteem, a sense of competence and a sense of confidence in one's abilities.

Self-respect lays the foundation for respect of others. In

respecting others the youth learns that differences are not deviant or sick and to appreciate the feelings of others. Reciprocity is the value that allows children to realize that they are not isolated and alone. Reciprocity indicates that each is interdependent and interconnected with each other and that what happens to one affects the entire group. Reciprocity provides the child with a grounding that extends beyond his own individual being. In addition, reciprocity allows the child to see that he can determine what happens to him by what he chooses to do.

This values orientation itself forms the basis for the development of programmatic structured activities for Black youth. These developing activities are culturally consistent and are meant to be ongoing. The program builds and creates a strong and positive reference group to counter negative peer pressures that exist outside of the training activities. In a real sense the activities foster a sense of belonging, instill in its participants a sense of identification, and provide a source of legitimation for its participants. Adults cannot completely counter the effects of peer pressure. But the training services can change the nature of the peer group by creating an alternative support system for the adolescent that will fortify him against negative peer pressures and that will reflect nondestructive behavioral modalities.

Conclusion

This training program has the ability to alter the sense of negativism, hopelessness and despair that pervades Black youth. It provides Black adolescents with a sound value system that emphasizes the need for excellence in all that they do and stresses the need for a sense of appropriateness in their behavior. We believe that these youth can and will develop the kinds of personal characteristics that would result in a more successful performance in society. The values orientation provided in this training program would provide youth with a sound foundation to enable them to confront their environment in a positive manner and to resist the pressures to engage in self-destructive behavior.

Reference

Akbar, Na'im. 1985. *The Community of Self.* Tallahassee, Florida: Mind Production and Associates.

Erikson, E. H. 1956. "The Problem of Ego Identity." *Journal of American Psychoanalytic Association.* 4.

Goddard, L. L. 1985. "Contemporary Conditions Affecting the Black Family." *Southern Christian Leadership Conference National Magazine.* Feb-Mar.

Haley, Alex. 1976. *Roots.* Garden City: Doubleday.

Havighurst, R. J. 1972. *Development Task and Education.* New York: David McKay Co.

Hill, R. 1972. *The Strengths of Black Families.* New York: Emerson Hill.

Kagan, S. and G.P. Knight. 1979. "Cooperation, Competition and Self-Esteem: A Case of Cultural Relativism." *Journal of Cross-Cultural Psychology,* 10:4, 457-467.

Kaplan, H. B., C. Robbins and S.S. Martin. 1983. "Antecedents of Psychological Distress in Young Adults: Self-rejection, Deprivation of Social Support and Life Events." *Journal of Health and Social Behavior.* 24:3, 230-244.

Nobles, W. W., L.L. Goddard and W.E. Cavil. 1985. *The Km Ebit Husia: Authoritative Utterances of Exceptional Insight for the Black Family.* Oakland: Black Family Institute Publication.

Nobles, W. W. 1985. *Africanity and the Black Family: The Development of a Theoretical Model.* Oakland: Black Family Institute Publication.

Nobles, W. W. 1974. "Africanity: Its Role in Black Families." *The Black Scholar.* 5,9.

Piaget, J. 1952. *The Origin of Intelligence in Children.* New York: International Universities Press.

Pierce, C. M. 1974. "Psychiatric Problems of the Black Minority," in S. Arieti and G. Caplan (eds.) *American Handbook of Psychiatry.* (Vol. 2, 2nd ed.). New York: Basic Books.

Pierce, C. M. 1970. "Offensive Mechanisms." in F. Barbour (ed.) *The Black Seventies.* Boston: Porter Sargent Publishing Co.

Staples, R. 1974. "The Black Family Revisited: A Review and Preview." *Journal of Social and Behavioral Sciences.* 24.

U. S. Bureau of Labor Statistics. 1985. Handbook of Labor Statistics. Washington, D.C: U.S. Government Printing Office.

U. S. Bureau of the Census. 1988. U.S. Statistical Abstract. Washington, D.C: U.S. Government Printing Office.

Chapter 10

Black Men, Black Sexuality and AIDS

Robert Fullilove and Mindy Fullilove

A POPULAR PASTIME among Black leaders these days is decrying the sorry state of Black youth. Young Black men receive the brunt of this concern since the problems that are peculiar to them at this point in the 1980s are legion: Black youth account for 51% of the violent crime committed in this country; Black men have one chance in six of being arrested by the time they reach the age of 19; and Black men have a one in 22 chance of being a homicide victim (NAACP 1986).

The 1980s have also brought a new scourge, AIDS, that threatens to make these grim statistics pale by comparison. Blacks are disproportionately represented among AIDS victims (Center for Disease Control 1986). We will argue here that there is considerable evidence that as the AIDS epidemic spreads, the life-style of young, Black, heterosexual men will place the Black community at considerable risk. But we will also argue that this scourge has the potential to be a blessing in disguise, and that efforts to prevent the spread of AIDS—if they are successful—will have "spillover" effects that may remedy a significant number of problems that are confronting the Black community.

Black Men and Structural Inequality

When we consider the life-style of young, Black and heterosexual men, we have to look at the material and social boundaries that condition these young mens' behaviors. Bruce Hare (1987) has argued that "the relative academic and economic failure of Black Americans in the American social order is functional, if not intended, given racism and the differential distribution of wealth, power, and privilege in the social structure." He argues that despite this nation's commitment to democracy and equal opportunity, its people live in conditions that range from grinding poverty at one extreme to enormous wealth on the other. There is not enough to go around and since someone has to be the loser, Black people are uniquely suited to play the part. The genius of our system, Hare asserts, is that "the myth of equal opportunity serves as a smoke screen through which the losers will be led to blame themselves [for being losers], and be seen by others as getting what they deserve" (Hare 1987, 101).

There is significant evidence to support Hare's assertions. Black youngsters are born with the same innate abilities and potential as other children, but by the time they have reached the third grade, substantial differences will be observed in their academic abilities (National Science Board 1986; National Science Foundation 1986). Their academic disadvantage will increase as they progress through school, and by the end of the senior year of high school, only a small proportion will be eligible to pursue a baccalaureate degree (American Council on Education 1986). Failure to complete high school and to obtain any further academic credentials will seriously affect their position within the workforce and, typically, will consign them to inferior jobs with little future.

The schools, Hare argues, play an important role in affecting the future options that are available to students. It convinces them that what they get in life is "what they deserve." Students who earn low grades, who fail to master key academic skills, who do not progress at the same rate and with the same amount of learning as their more advanced peers invariably will conclude that their lot in life results from not being smart enough or not trying hard enough to succeed in school.

The role of schools in enforcing social stratification in this country has come under increasing scrutiny in recent years. Colclough and Beck (1986), for example, found evidence that schools play an important role in "reproducing" the economic class status of parents; that is, "through the various schooling processes . . . students are systematically allocated to adult class positions that are similar to their origins. Inequalities of social class in our society are thus reproduced and legitimated through the schooling structure and process" (Colclough and Beck 1986, 456).

The "structure and process" to which the authors refer is tracking students by ability. Students are grouped in many schools according to academic aptitude/ability, classroom behavior, or a combination of factors. Whatever the reason, tracking is typically done to ease the task of managing the classroom and, presumably, to improve the quality of teaching.

The problem, of course, is that there is considerable evidence that tracking does not help students but, rather, hinders their social, moral and intellectual development. Halinan and Sorensen (1983), for example, found evidence that tracking systems promote greater inequality in educational attainment. Rosenbaum in a comprehensive review of tracking, concludes:

> By creating separate groups which are identified as homogeneous and unequal, ability grouping and curriculum grouping create hierarchical grouping systems which classify students into different categories that receive differential esteem. These classifications tend to be difficult to alter, and particularly difficult to improve. Although the group classifications purportedly define only educational programs, they also define simultaneously the academic and social esteem students receive in the school, the way students evaluate their social status and academic competence, and their social interaction in and out of school (Rosenbaum 1980, 371).

Colclough and Beck (1986) examined data drawn from the National Longitudinal Study (NLS) to determine the degree to which students who were in a particular social class during their senior year in high school in 1972 had either moved up, moved down, or had remained in the same social class in 1979. They discovered that the overall rate of class reproduction in the sample was 64.31%—that is, better than six out of ten male students did not change social class location in the seven year period encompassed in this study.

Significantly, they found that being from a "manual class background" (i.e., coming from a household where the family breadwinner was in an occupation classified as "manual, unskilled, or nonskilled" labor) meant that a student was twice as likely to be placed in a vocational track in high school. Moreover, being placed in a vocational track resulted in an 89% chance of being in a manual class position within the workforce seven years later. Class reproduction was also more likely for nonwhite students placed in a vocational track in high schools, particularly in economically advantaged communities. Although class reproduction was not 100% among sample students, the rate at which they reproduced the economic class they occupied in high school was considerably greater than what might be expected if random factors determined where students ended up on the social ladder.

The weight of the evidence in these and other studies is clear: schools play a tremendously important role in affecting the life options available to young people, and they rarely succeed in assisting students to escape the limitations that a low socioeconomic status (SES) background can impose. Hare (1987) concludes from his examination of this research that young Black students—and most particularly Black young men—seek other, nonschool avenues for demonstrating competence when they are unable to succeed in school.

> The black youth peer culture may be regarded as a long-term failure arena primarily because even though it succeeds in providing alternative outlets for the demonstration of competence, as through street, athletic, and social activities, it offers little hope of long-term legitimate success. Rather, it carries the real dangers of drafting young people into the self-destructive worlds of drugs, crime, and sexual promiscuity (Hare 1987, 109).

AIDS and the Black Community

As Black youth peer culture leans increasingly toward drugs and sexual promiscuity, the threat of AIDS looms ever larger. According to the Center for Disease Control (CDC), as of September 1986, Blacks—who comprise roughly 10.6% of the nation's population (age ≥ 15 years)—were substantially overrepresented among AIDS victims. Specifically, Blacks were 51.4% of all intravenous drug users with the disease, 14.8% of all homosexual AIDS victims not known to be drug abusers, 35.3% of all women who contracted the disease from a bisexual male partner, 47.8% of all AIDS patients who contracted the disease from an intravenous drug using partner, and 43.7% of all AIDS victims for whom no mode of acquisition was known. Overall, at the time of CDC's October 1986 update, approximately one AIDS victim in four was Black.

The Black community has a high incidence of drug abuse (Secretary's Task Force on Black and Minority Health 1986) and sexually-transmitted diseases (San Francisco Department of Public Health)—facts that suggest that the AIDS virus has a number of entry points into the community. Thus, the disease is likely to increase its hold on the non-drug abusing, nonhomosexual Black community through the inadvertent movements of members of three risk groups: the sexual contacts of intravenous (IV) drug users with AIDS, the sexual contacts of bisexual men and the sexual contacts of homosexual men.

The most dangerous aspect of AIDS is that there is a long period during which someone who is infected with the AIDS virus is both asymptomatic and capable of infecting others. The scenario that haunts the researchers currently studying the disease is one in which a large proportion of the Black community becomes infected with AIDS through the movement of sexually active, (IV) drug users and bisexual men who have been infected with the AIDS virus.

Young people are particularly at risk in such a scenario. Many teenagers who experiment with drugs may dabble with the intravenous injection of cocaine or heroin under circumstances in which they share "dirty" needles with other users who carry the AIDS virus. Since many of these youngsters are at an age when they are both sexually active and promiscuous, the disease would have ample opportunity to gain a solid hold in the community. There is evidence that such a scenario is particularly likely to occur within the ranks of black teenagers. The incidence of venereal disease, Black teenage pregnancy and the high arrest rate of Black teenagers on drug-related charges all suggest that this particular population is both sexually active, promiscuous, and experimenting with drugs. The consequences of these behaviors, needless to say, are frightening.

The good news, however, is that the spread of the disease can be contained. If needle-sharing ceases and if safe sex practices are followed, the virus would have almost no opportunity to take hold in the community. The issue, of course, is how to educate those who are at risk to the dangers of their risk practices.

AIDS Prevention Campaigns

Calls for public education campaigns, particularly directed to minority communities, have been increasing as the AIDS threat becomes more widespread and known. There has also been widely expressed concern that campaigns directed at White gay men will not reach Blacks and Latinos. Rogers and Williams (1987), for example, observe that differences in culture and in patterns of communication exist between gays and "straights" and between Whites and nonwhites and that these differences may hinder the effectiveness of AIDS prevention campaigns that are directed solely at White gay men. Similar concerns are voiced by Mays and Cochran (1987) and by Williams (1986), each noting that the general public perception that AIDS is a disease of White gay men makes it particularly difficult for nonwhites and nongays to attend to AIDS prevention measures.

Williams, in a survey of Black homosexuals in Detroit, found little understanding of how the AIDS virus is transmitted, substantial ignorance of the threat facing homosexuals from AIDS, and a troubling lack of understanding about where information about AIDS might be found. The results of the survey confirm fears that AIDS education efforts have not penetrated to the members of the Black community that face the greatest risk of acquiring the disease.

The issue is clear: AIDS prevention messages must be developed and must be transmitted in a fashion that ensures their reception by the members of the groups at greatest risk. What is not so clear is how to develop messages that will be heard.

Teens Rap About Drugs, Sexually Transmitted Diseases, and AIDS

Peer culture has been identified as an important medium through which American teenagers acquire attitudes toward authority, adult life, sex, drug use, and school (Billy and Udry 1985; Ishiyama and Chabassol 1983; Marcos et al. 1986; Peterson and Peters 1983). The weight of evidence in these studies suggests that peer culture has a tremendous impact on actual behavior as well. In a recently concluded study conducted by one of the authors (M.F.), teen culture was the focus of an attempt to communicate messages about AIDS, drug abuse, and sexually transmitted disease (STD's).

Reasoning that the most useful means of communicating with minority teenagers was through teen-to-teen messages, a "Rap Contest" was held in which San Francisco teenagers were encouraged to compete. Sponsored by the Bayview Hunter's Point Foundation and the City Department of Public Health, teenagers were asked to write raps in which the dangers of unprotected sex, needlesharing, and drug abuse were linked to the risk of contracting AIDS. Prizes were offered for the best written and best performed raps. Preliminary rounds of the contest were held in local youth centers throughout the city, and the final round was taped and later aired on a popular local TV show aimed at Bay Area youth, "Home Turf."

Of particular interest in this contest was the degree to

which the challenge of writing a competitive rap influenced participating teens' knowledge of AIDS, sexually transmitted diseases (STD's), and drug abuse. To test the level of knowledge of participants, rappers were given pretests and posttests using the AIDS Literacy Test (ALT), a ten-item instrument designed to assess knowledge of the basic facts about AIDS.

Fifty students competed ranging in age from 7 to 21; the mean age of rappers was 15.2 years. Eighty-eight percent were male, 12 % were female. In both administrations of the ALT, rappers demonstrated substantial knowledge of the basic facts about AIDS, with pretest and posttest mean scores of 90%.

The rappers were not selected at random; thus, there were no tests of statistical significance using these data. Nonetheless, comparisons of rappers by age and sex revealed no noteworthy differences in pretest and posttest performance on the ALT or in responses to key questions on the test (e.g., "Can AIDS be passed through casual sex?" and "Only homosexuals get AIDS." [true or false]). The results suggest that these teens were highly informed about AIDS before their raps were written, and presumably, that they understand the nature of the risks posed by such behaviors as needle-sharing and unprotected sexual intercourse.

What is more useful than the test results is an analysis of the raps themselves. Raps, which were judged for content as well as the performer's style and delivery, demonstrated a vivid concern with AIDS: as one young author wrote, "AIDS Is Destroying Society." Raps are reproduced here exactly as they were presented in the author's original contest submission. They had vivid images of AIDS as a new, deadly disease but one which could be prevented, as in these lines:

> Before you lay down for a love connection
> you better make sure you have protection
> If you wind up with the thing they call AIDS
> It just may leave you laying in your grave.

The rappers focused on the damage that drugs were doing, both directly and as a mode of AIDS transmission. In

"Drugs are on the Rise," the rapper commented,

> Drugs in your bank account will leave a big dent
> After your your money is spent
> youl just resent,
> Feel as IF you Just lost your best friend, so In order to mend Youl go and get some more again, But the only thing your doing is Living In Peril, First class ticket to hell as your referel, The best way out is Just to avoid or youl get No sleep, Never eatWorry be PArANoid. You could loose close, home, gold, even pounds,so leave drugs alone thats all Im trying to announce.

The rappers depicted the plight of the addict with a combination of understanding and impatience: "Stop using drugs and use your head, before you O.D. and wind up dead."

The rappers uniformly urged sex with protection—condoms and limiting the number of partners—but none expressed disapproval of premarital sex. Marcus, regarding STD's and AIDS, rapped:

> I'm here to talk about the S in STD
> because the S stands for sexually.
> And to the right of S the T is committed,
> for the simple reason T is transmitted.
> So if I may please, especially with ease, freeze,
> and tell you that the D stands for disease.
> So you better watch out if you know what I mean,
> don't date a floosey, be choosey and you'll stay clean.

The raps tell us a good deal more than just the health education message they carry: they tell us a about the culture of the authors. Few, if any, of the raps are written in standard English, which suggests that the authors, as a group, are 1) native speakers of Black English, rather than standard English, and 2) unevenly educated in standard English. These findings are not surprising. Dillard's careful work on Black English in 1972 documented its importance as a unique dialect, in common use among Black people throughout the United States.

If, as the raps suggest, our rappers are uncomfortable and unskilled in standard English, their fate (and the fate of many of their peers) will be uncertain in the highly technological world of the 1990s. The odds are that they are involved in a subculture that will be greatly isolated from the mainstream of economic life in the U.S. This is not at all to suggest that speaking Black English is the cause of their isolation, rather, that it marks of the degree to which that isolation is expressed in their speech and their mode of expression. It does suggest, however, that our Black English speaking rappers and their peers may not be open to messages that are presented in standard English. "Sex, drugs and rock and roll," as the expression goes, constitute components of the world that these youngsters will experience now and in the future.

AIDS and The Black Community: At the Crossroads

At a community meeting in Newark, New Jersey, 20 years ago, the subject of genocide was discussed. A local leader, hearing the word used with increasing frequency, muttered audibly, "Hell, the way to wage genocide against the Black man is simple: make f—king fatal." As the facts about AIDS become increasingly well known, and as its impact on the Black community is understood, Blacks frequently ask, "Could AIDS be a plot—an attempt to destroy the community?"

The question, we have tried to suggest here, is not without merit. AIDS will strike the community via routes where Blacks demonstrate particular vulnerability: drug addiction and sexual promiscuity. As we have noted, high rates of sexually transmitted disease, teenage pregnancy and drug addiction suggest that many young Blacks pursue a life-style that makes them particularly vulnerable to the disease. We have also suggested that their commitment to this life-style is, in part, a function of the structure of the nation's social and economic institutions. Unable to function adequately within the schools, Blacks—particularly young Black men—

seek avenues outside the schools and apart from the world of work to demonstrate their legitimacy and their worth. Structural inequality and AIDS appear to be the perfect formula, therefore, for genocide.

The AIDS epidemic places the Black community at the crossroads. Whatever the source of the epidemic, it confronts a significant number of community members with a simple, brutal choice: *change your life-style or die.* Black men are clearly the significant actors here. Recent studies (May and Anderson 1987) suggest that transmission of the AIDS virus via sexual intercourse is fifteen to twenty times more likely to occur from men to women than from women to men. Men are far more likely, in other words, to be the agents of AIDS transmission, and the imperative to change life-styles and sexual practices falls on them far more heavily than on Black women.

Our interactions with Black community mental health workers, however, suggest that it is Black women, rather than Black men, who may hold the key to the community's salvation. We wanted to "take the pulse" of the community concerning AIDS and to learn how well (and to what degree) messages about AIDS, safe sex, and abstention from drug abuse were being received by members of the Black community in San Francisco. Specifically, we asked these workers to tell us (1) do people know about AIDS? and (2) do you (the mental health worker) have the sense that life-styles—particularly around dating and sexual relations—have undergone any noticeable change?

We interviewed ten workers (five women and five men) who work for the Bayview Hunter's Point Foundation in San Francisco. The vast majority of those interviewed suggested that although there is a great deal of misinformation about AIDS in the Black community, there is a clearly perceived fear of the disease that has intruded into the interactions between Black men and women. Couples were perceived as more likely to engage in safe sex practices—specifically cited was a perceived increase in the use of condoms and, significantly, women were more likely to demand that their lovers use condoms. Black men were described as "worrying more about steppin' out on their wives" and more committed to "stayin' close to home." Both men and women interviewees suggested that women were being more assertive in insisting that safe sex practices be followed. Black women's fear of the disease was forcing them out of their traditionally passive role in sexual relationships and into a stance that would reduce their risk of contracting the disease. High rates of illegitimacy in the Black community (McGhee 1984) suggest that in the past Black women have been unsuccessful in practicing birth control or in getting their partners to take precautions. These current responses—if accurate—signal potentially far-ranging developments for Black sexuality.

Although these are anecdotal data that rely heavily on personal (and therefore biased) observations, they hint at fascinating possibilities. Is it possible that Black women's fear of AIDS will transform the nature of sexual relations (and ultimately interpersonal relationships) between Black men and women? Will Black women be able to channel the Black man's presumed "massive" sex drive into more responsible sexual practices and specifically, into greater use of condoms?

Were this transformation to occur, its impact would not stop with AIDS. Reductions in high STD rates and in illegitimate pregnancies would be two impressive, far-reaching changes in the life of the Black community. It is also conceivable that these changes would affect the degree to which Black couples engage in monogamous relationships and ultimately reverse the alarming trend in recent years to single-parent, female-headed households.

Accordingly, many educators (Hare 1987) posit that two-parent households may have a more dramatic, positive impact on the education of Black students than any single educational innovation that is introduced into the schools.

This all suggests one simple but dramatic message: The threat of AIDS could signal the salvation of the Black community. The threat of the disease is so severe for Blacks because it strikes at the community through its most passionately maintained vices. But what we Blacks have been unable to do "for the good of the community" may now have to be done because reform is, literally, a matter of life and death.

Ultimately, AIDS appears to be an agent of natural selection (or artificial selection, if conspiracy theorists are to be believed). It will be many years before an AIDS vaccine is perfected and the only salvation from the disease is prevention. Prevention for the Black community involves an act of will—a commitment to see the evils that we inflict upon ourselves and to do something immediately about them. When the disease has run its course, it will have claimed many innocent victims: children, unsuspecting wives and lovers, and the ignorant. It is not clear that "the fittest" will survive this epidemic, but it is clear that the cautious and the responsible have an undeniable edge.

References

American Council on Education. 1986. *Minorities in American Higher Education*. Washington, DC: ACE, Office of Minority Concerns.

Billy, J.O. and R.J. Udry. 1985. "Patterns of Adolescent Friendship and Effects on Sexual Behavior." *Social Psychology Quarterly*. 48, 27-41.

Centers for Disease Control. 1988. "AIDS Weekly Surveillance Report–U.S. AIDS Program." August 1.

Colclough, G. and E.M. Beck. 1986. "The American Educational Structure and the Reproduction of Social Class." *Sociological Inquiry*. Fall, 456-476.

Dillard, J.L. 1973. *Black English*. New York City: Vintage.

Halinan, M.T. and A.B. Sorensen. 1983. "The Formation and Stability of Instructional Groups." *Sociological Review*. 48, 438-451.

Hare, B.L. 1987. "Structural Inequality and the Endangered Status of Black Youth." *Journal of Negro Education*. 56, 110-110.

Ishiyama, F.I. and D.J. Chabassol. 1983. "Adolescent Fear of Social Consequences of Academic Success as a Function of Age and Sex." *Journal of Youth and Adolescence*. 14, 37-46.

Marcos, A.C., et al. 1986. "A Test of the Positive Association Theory of Adolescent Drug Use." *Social Forces*. 65, 135-161.

May, R.M. and R.M. Anderson. 1987. "Transmission Dynamics of HIV Infection." *Nature*. 326, 137-142.

Mays, V.M. and S.D. Cochran. 1987. "Acquired Immune Deficiency Syndrome and Black Americans: Special Psychosocial Issues." *Public Health Reports*. 2, 224-231.

McGhee, J.D. 1984. "A Profile of the Black, Single Female-Headed Household." *The State of Black America 1984*. New York: Urban League.

NAACP. 1986. "Black Youth and Crime." *Crisis*. March.

National Science Board, Task Committee on Undergraduate Science and Engineering Education. 1986. *Undergraduate Mathematics, Science and Engineering Training*. Washington, D.C.

National Science Foundation. 1986. *Women and Minorities in Science and Engineering*. Washington, D.C.

Peterson, G.W. and E.F. Peters. 1983. "Adolescents' Construction of Social Reality: The Impact of Television and Peers." *Journal of Youth in Society*. 15, 65-85.

Rogers, M.F. and W.W. Williams. 1987. "AIDS in Blacks and Hispanics: Implications for Prevention." *Issues in Science and Technology*. Spring, 89-94.

Rosenbaum, J.E. 1980. "Social Implications of Educational Grouping," in D. Berlinger (ed.) *Review of Research in Education*. New York, 361-404.

Secretary's Task Force on Black and Minority Health. 1985. *Report*. Washington: U.S. Department of Health and Human Services.

Williams, L.S. 1986. "AIDS Risk Reduction: A Community Health Education Intervention for Minority High-Risk Group Members." *Health Education Quarterly*. 13, 407-421.

Chapter 11

Returning Formal Education to the Family: Experiencing the Alternative

Omonike Weusi-Puryear
and Muata Weusi-Puryear

WE STARTED OUR PARENTAL ADVENTURE by choosing natural childbirth, followed by breast-feeding, with a deep concern for our children's health care. We avoided the negative aspects of our surroundings and turned toward the positive aspects of our African heritage. The decision to teach our children at home came as a normal development of our parental style. In contrast, we saw our peers, in reaction to the public and private school environment, spend more effort to unteach and reteach their children than it would have taken them to do the entire job themselves. We concluded that we could do a better job of educating our children than any local public or private school system could do.

As parents, we were concerned for our children's physical well-being, their emotional, social, and intellectual development. In traditional African culture the extended family and community taught children the social, intellectual, and work skills that were needed to perpetuate the culture. This model seemed to us to be a sound one. The problem for us, however, was how to raise African-American children who would perpetuate the ideals of our family while living in a country dominated by a different culture.

It seemed unrealistic to expect the dominant culture to teach the values we prized. For example, the dominant culture favors competition over cooperation as the general way in which people should interact. We, however, value the dynamics of cooperation, especially within the family.

Without discussion, we independently concluded that "cultural transmission" was as important a concern in education as "the three R's." We envisioned that the new Weusi-Puryears would be proud Black people capable of receiving the cultural baton, carrying it forward, and then passing it on to the next generation.

In January 1977 we agreed upon the following guidelines for our children's education. Education should produce young people who:

1. understand, accept, and practice the Nguzo Saba
2. accept the African concept of family
3. have knowledge and pride in the history of Black people, their family, and themselves
4. understand their physical, cultural, political, and social environment
5. understand the world's development (physical, cultural, political, biological, and social)
6. exhibit good communication skills (i.e. can read, write, speak, listen, observe, and act effectively)
7. have arithmetical and algebraic skills and knowledge of science and scientific methods
8. have knowledge and appreciation of folk arts, appreciation, and have skill in African arts
9. have practical skills in farming, animal husbandry, carpentry, plumbing, domestic science, weaving, camping, hunting, fishing, and preventive medicine
10. have reached a healthy level of physical development and have demonstrable skills in the martial arts
11. have acceptable social graces (including respect for elders)
12. have knowledge about nutrition and have the ability to apply nutritional information on a day to day basis

Schooling was sometimes very informal, but became more formal as the children grew older. There were no dress codes; in the beginning, instruction was conducted at the breakfast table in pajamas. School was an integral part of the parent/child interaction. It was continuous: it started with each son's naming day ceremony and continued without breaks until his manhood ceremony. There were no summer vacations from schooling, but the seasonal changes did result in major activity changes. Soccer lessons, music lessons, Tai Chi lessons, tennis lessons, swimming lessons, among others, were conducted by nonparent teachers but were considered a part of growing up (learning to be an adult).

One of the advantages we had was that we started from scratch. We were in control before a peer group could establish negative norms. We did not have to unteach—that is, change attitudes or correct statements learned in another educational system. Our children played most with the children of our (culturally) Black friends.

The success of teaching our children at home can be attributed to planning, organizing, scheduling, and following the plan/schedule as consistently as common sense allowed. We tried to always to keep in mind our philosophy (or the reasons why we were teaching our children at home) and an appreciation for each child's individuality. Our success is also due to in part our decision to forgo the luxuries of a two-income household so Omonike could apply her teaching/management skills full-time to the education of our children.

A typical school day started with breakfast at 7:00 am. The family sat at the table with a wholesome meal of hot, whole grains and fruit or vegetables and homemade wholegrain bread. Breakfast was a time to "chat" before school started.

The boys cleared the table after breakfast, transforming it into the teacher's assignment desk. Each child in turn met with Omonike to go over the assignments he had done the previous day. Meanwhile, his brothers worked on assignments in the classroom, a room specifically set aside for school work. Later the children developed a degree of independence and could successfully anticipate assignments. This gave them a sense of control that aided in their enthusiasm for education. At mid-morning there was usually a break for a snack. Lunch was at noon followed by recreation. Sometime between 1:00 p.m. and 3:00 p.m. each child had from sixty to ninety minutes to lead a discussion of his written work and/or to do some oral reading.

The local public libraries became important adjuncts to the home education process. When the boys were too young to catch the bus to the library, we chauffeured them two or three times per month. We brought home dozens of books at a time. We censored their reading. We would pick some "must read" books. They would pick many "would like to read" books. Before we went to the checkout desk, a parent would give a "yes" or "no" judgment to each of the "would like to read" pile. Books about Black people, social studies, science, science fiction, literature, crafts, cookbooks, riddles, and magic usually got a "yes" judgment. By the time they could catch the bus by themselves, adult censorship was no longer needed.

Public television programs were a vital part of the curriculum. "Sesame Street," "3-2-1 Contact," "Reading Rainbow," "Square One," "Cover to Cover," "Vegetable Soup," "Newton's Apple" were among the "educational" programs they watched. Other programs received the same censorship that their choice of library books received. When they were young, the television set was placed on a special shelf that was hung from the ceiling, so only an adult could control it. Sex, violence, and most cartoons shows were censored.

Because of Muata's work (educational computer software), we always had either a computer or a remote computer terminal in the house. The boys early learned to use computer programs and enjoyed learning how to program in the LOGO and BASIC languages.

The recreational facilities of our city and county—tennis, swimming, and parks—were used to provide the physical aspects of their education. Vacations were also a part of the learning process. A geography lesson caused the family to tour the U.S.A. by train to various Black American historical sites. The trip also gave us a chance to show the children the extent of our family in the U.S.A.

We felt the boys needed positive social interaction with their peers. Therefore, Omonike helped organize a family support group that had activities for adults and children.

The group, along with the children, met once a month and usually planned several outings for the children and several family activities. Children's activities included a chess workshop, roller skating parties, a computer workshop, and camping trips. There were many family picnics. Museum visits, nature preserves, book readings by noted Black writers and concerts were among the enrichment activities for our sons.

We were fortunate to be living in a state in which the laws allowed for private tutoring as an alternative to public education. We expected (and were prepared for) state inspections of our activities. We keep good records but were never called upon to justify what we did. Often we used surplus texts and educational materials from public schools. We can imagine how much more difficult it would have been if we had been in constant battle with local school authorities.

Section Four:

DEVELOPMENT OF CULTURAL IDENTITY

THE EDUCATOR AND LINGUIST Faye McNair-Knox has studied Black teen language and observes that parents need not wonder what is going on with Black teens. It is not a mystery. What we need to know is right before us—in their language, if we will listen. Ironically, the language of Black teens is part of our African heritage and they are the standard-bearers. Then Tee Sweet describes young Black men who have rejected their culture as a price of occupational success. She points out specifically what in their backgrounds disposed them to reject their race and themselves. The counselor Ronald Hudson looks at the social context that compels Black men and women to question the need for a Black identity. He challenges the myth that you cannot be "Black" and succeed. The psychoanalysts James Moss links the psychology of oppression with the social circumstances of powerlessness. He does this with a compelling analytic model. Finally, Daphne Muse, editor of The Children's Advocate magazine, points to one of the most effective ways to address the issues of cultural identity and empowerment—through reading. She also presents an exciting bibliography specifically for young male readers.

Chapter 12

Tapping into Teen Talk: Parenting Strategies for Bridging the Intergenerational Communication Gap

Faye C. McNair-Knox

THE INTERGENERATIONAL COMMUNICATION GAP is a universal parenting concern that has been a dominant theme of conflicts and other crises associated with parent-teen relationships in American families. The problems are significant enough to have become a common topic of American family folklore and various other popular cultural expressions. One of the more well-known portrayals is the song "Kids" from the musical, *Bye Bye Birdie* (Adams and Strouse 1960), which captures the spirit of perennial parenting frustrations:

> Kids! I don't know what's wrong with these kids today.
> Kids! Who can understand anything they say?
> Kids! They are disobedient, disrespectful oafs.
> Noisy, crazy, sloppy, lazy loafers—and while we're on the subject,
> Kids! You can talk and talk till your face is blue.
> Kids! But they still do just what they want to do.
> Why can't they be like we were, perfect in every way?
> Oh what's the matter with kids today?

But parent-teen relationship frustrations are not the exclusive domain of adults. Indeed, teens also have an indicting set of complaints which adds another dimension to communication problems. The popular rap song "Parents Just Don't Understand" (D.J. Jazzy Jeff and the Fresh Prince 1988), provides the following representative summary of the teen viewpoint:

> You know parents are the same, no matter time or place.
> They don't understand that us kids are going to make some mistakes.
> So to you, all the kids, all across the land,
> Take it from me, parents just don't understand.

For contemporary African-American families, the intergenerational communication gap involves a broader range of issues than those more lightheartedly depicted above. So much so that many consider the challenges to effective parenting to be anything but a laughing matter. Specifically, African-American parent-teen relationships are complicated by an overlay of factors associated with the disproportionately low socioeconomic status of their families and community environments. For example, in the National Urban League's annual series, *The State of Black America,* the factors repeatedly cited during the 1980s include, but are not limited to, poverty, crime, drug abuse, teen pregnancy, single-parenthood, educational underachievement and high drop-out rates, and youth unemployment and under-employment. Additionally, the educational and linguistic literature of the last thirty years extensively discusses language divergence as another major factor associated with the low-income status of African-Americans (Baratz 1969, 1973; Cullinan 1974; De Stefano 1972; Fasold and Wolfram 1970; Hoover, et al. 1988; Labov 1974, 1987; Laffey and Shuy 1973; McNair-Knox 1985; Politzer 1973; Smitherman 1977; Spears 1987; Stewart 1970; Vaughn-Cooke 1987; R.L. Williams 1975).

While these factors may pose significant and perhaps insurmountable challenges to the success of parenting efforts, that of language divergence is particularly germane to a discussion of the communication gap within African-American families. It encompasses a multifaceted array of problems that may create a barrier to mutual understanding and cooperation in parent-teen relationships. To a certain extent, the gap may result from the common parental perception of teen language incomprehensibility described in the lyrics of the song "Kids": "Kids! Who can understand anything they say?" However, on a broader level, the gap also involves inappropriate parental treatment of structural and sociopolitical phenomena pertaining to African-American language divergence from the variety of English prescribed as the standard for mainstream American society.

This paper will discuss selected aspects of teen language divergence phenomena and ways in which they may interfere with effective intergenerational communication. Its major assumptions are based on language data from sociolinguistic interviews with African-American female teenagers conducted as part of the East Palo Alto Neighborhood Study (EPANS). EPANS is an ongoing research project investigating intra-ethnic and inter-ethnic variation in urban vernacular English among residents of East Palo Alto, a predominantly African-American and low income city located 30 miles south of San Francisco, California (Rickford 1986). While the interview data presented are from female teenagers, males can be expected to reflect the same behaviors and language usage. The discussion will also include suggestions for parenting strategies designed to improve communication which emphasize respecting teen language as a viable medium of expression and a valuable source of feedback on teen development concerns.

On the Nature and Origin of African-American English: Do "To Be or Not to Be" Still Be the Question?

Since the early 1960s, a "flood of research" (Rickford 1985) has been conducted investigating English variation within the AfricanA-merican speech community. As a result, AfricanA-merican English (AAE) has been extensively documented as a medium of communication. This research has established a generally accepted definition of AAE as a well-formed, and valid linguistic system that adequately serves the communicative needs of its speakers (Baratz 1969; Fasold and Wolfram 1970; Harber and Beatty 1978; Labov 1972; Shuy 1971; Simons 1976; Smitherman 1977; Wolford 1979; Wolfram 1970). Along with establishing the communicative validity of AAE, a consensus has developed in the literature on AAE's intra-system variation. It is a continuum of varieties ranging from those which overlap completely with Mainstream American English (MAE) to others which differ to the extent of being categorized as "unique" (Nichols 1981) or "quasi-foreign" (Stewart 1970) languages. Labov proposes:

> "Black English" might best be used for the whole range of language forms used by Black people in the United States: a very large range indeed, extending from the Creole grammar of Gullah spoken in the Sea Islands of South Carolina to the most formal and accomplished literary style (Labov 1972, xiii).

Another researcher adds the contention that intra-system variation occurs " . . . according to such variables as geography, social class, age, sex, amount of education, etc . . . In sum, differences emerge as a function of the social situation in which the language is produced" (Taylor 1975, 34).

In describing the parameters of AAE as a total linguistic system, explanations are offered for its distinctiveness from MAE (Mainstream American English). For some authors, the differences between AAE and MAE are a function of the African language heritage of African-Americans (Williams 1975; DeFrantz 1979). For a second group of researchers, the distinctiveness of AAE is attributed to the American experiences of African-Americans (Johnson 1971; Mitchell-Kernan 1972). A third view recognizes the influence of both African and indigenous American factors combined with historical patterns of geographic isolation and the use of language as part of survival strategies. Smitherman states:

> In a nutshell: Black Dialect is an Africanized form of English reflecting Black America's linguistic-cultural African heritage and the conditions of servitude, oppression and life in America. Black language is Euro-American speech with an Afro-American meaning, nuance, tone and gesture . . . It has allowed Blacks to create a culture of survival in an alien land . . . (1977,2-3).

The debate on the causes of AAE-MAE differences are of secondary importance in the literature when compared to the attention given to the variety of AAE associated with the speech of low income African-Americans in general, and youth in particular. This variety, referred to as African-American Vernacular English (AAVE), has also been extensively analyzed and described. AAVE is what is commonly called Black Vernacular English or Ebonics. Labov offers a widely used definition: "By the . . . vernacular we mean the relatively informal dialect spoken by the majority of Black youth in most parts of the United States today, especially in the inner city areas . . . It is also spoken in most rural areas and used in the casual, intimate speech of many adults . . . " (1972, xiii).

Descriptions of AAVE also emphasize its legitimacy and suggest a common core of structural features (phonology, morphology, and syntax) very different from corresponding MAE characteristics (Abrahams 1970; Bailey 1970; Burling 1973; DeFrantz 1979; DiGiulio 1973; Dillard 1972; Fasold and Wolfram 1970; Labov 1969; Labov et al. 1968; Mitchell-Kernan 1972; Politzer and Bartley, 1969a, 1969b; Rhodes 1970; Taylor 1969; Turner 1949; Toliver-Weddington 1979; Weltz 1974; Wolfram 1970). The following chart provides a representative, but by no means exhaustive, description of the grammar (Lourie 1978,92):

Black English Vernacular Features and Examples

Phonological Contrasts

Forwarding of stress	–police, fessor
Weakening of final contrasts	–seed=seat=see, rowed=row, run=rum=rung
Consonant-cluster simplification	–lass=last, roped=rope, its=is specific=pacific
/ / becomes /t/ or /f/	–thin=tin, Ruth=roof
/th/ becomes /d/ or /v/	–then=den, clothe=clove
Absence of postvocalic /r/, /l/	–guard=god, par=pa, four=foe, help=hep, toll=toe
Certain vowel contrasts collapse	–tin=ten, fear=fair, sure=shore, pride=proud=prod, boil=ball

Grammatical Contrasts

Nouns and pronouns:

Nonstandard noun plurals	–two pound, foots, mens, desses
Absence of possessive marker	–William mother, they mother

Verbs:

Variable absence of auxiliary and copula	–She thinking, you happy
Uninflected present tense	She go
Phonological rules weaken past tense marker	–She talk in class yesterday
Habitual (invariant) "be"	–She be working
Completive "done"	–She done forgot
Remote time "been"	–I been know it

Negation:

Ain't	–Jan ain't working/worked/work
Negative concord	–Can't nobody write no poetry

Clause structure:

Double subject	–Lynn she sick
Existential "it"	–It wasn't nothing to do
Absence of relative pronoun in subject position	–There's a horse goes by here
Conjunctive "which"	–I went to Utah, which Sue lives there
Inverted word order in question	–I asked her could I go; Why she took it?

Other publications detail AAVE paralinguistic and nonverbal features and point out that many are global in nature and distribution, i.e. applicable to the speech community as a whole irrespective of socioeconomic status. They identify distinctive suprasegmental patterns, kinetic behaviors, and oral expressive styles (Abrahams 1970; Dalby 1972; Johnson 1971; Kochman 1972; Mitchell-Kernan 1972; Smith 1974; Smitherman 1977; Whatley 1981). Suprasegmental traits include elongation of words or raising pitch level for emphasis, use of a wide range of vocal effects from falsetto to false bass to growl, unexpected slowing or speeding of delivery, and emphasizing syllables or words (Abrahams 1970,27). In another study the author provides an extensive treatment of behaviors such as rolling the eyes, avoiding eye contact, the limp stance, the young male gait or pimp walk/strut, walking away from a conflict situation, turning ones back in a discussion and the female hand on the hip stance (Johnson 1971).

In comparison with AfricanA-merican English (AAE), AfricanA-merican Vernacular English (AAVE) features are said to have retained their distinctiveness over time due to historic patterns of economic and cultural developments among low income AfricanA-mericans (Abrahams 1970; Baugh 1983; DeFrantz 1979; Johnson 1971; Mitchell-Kernan 1972; Rickford 1977; Smitherman 1977). These linguistic characterizations have been reinforced by lower educational achievement levels, limited assimilation into mainstream American culture and isolated residential patterns. Despite numerous efforts to establish the legitimacy of vernacular AAE, its use is highly stigmatized in mainstream American culture. Using AAVE is perceived as a major deterrent to full participation in societal opportunities and is specifically cited as a cause of educational failure, unemployment and social alienation among AfricanA-merican youth (Hoover et al. 1988; McNair-Knox 1985; Sledd 1969; Smith 1977; Williams 1970).

To complicate the situation further, African-Americans evidence a range of opinions about the vernacular and frequently mirror mainstream rejection of its use (Hoover 1975; Schneider 1971; Taylor 1975; Vacca 1975). Middle class African-Americans are frequently reported to object to its use in schools. Outside of school, a typical objection is the following:

> In the process of young people applying for jobs, employers would ask them a question which would elicit a response, "I bees ready for coming here next week." This . . . insertion of "bees" is rampant and, I think, really throws an employer off in terms of what the young person is talking about. "Now that you're finished with me, I bees going home" . . . If we relegate them only to that narrow, limited, provincial dimension of life and language, we do them a disservice . . . I see that they will not go beyond the borderlines of their immediate neighborhood. We have no right to do that to any child (McCrum and MacNeil 1989).

Another study showed that low income African-American parents' hold negative attitudes toward AAVE in school settings. "Parents . . . do not accept Africanized Black English in writing and reading . . . nor in the school domain" (Hoover 1975). In a third study reported by Taylor (1975), low income American parents expressed more ambivalent attitudes toward the use of AAVE. On one hand, they felt that AAVE is inferior to Standard English and that its usage is inappropriate in school domains and constitutes a serious barrier to successful employment pursuits. On the other hand, however, they felt that AAVE usage is more appropriate in certain situations as well as superior to Standard English in expressing some things.

Given the stigma attached to vernacular AAE by mainstream society and the ambivalence of African-Americans as to how, when and where its use is appropriate, one might be inclined to predict its eventual extinction. But just the opposite may be happening. The community of vernacular AAE speakers is alive and well and appears to be reproducing itself in each successive generation, especially among inner city youth. Recent research by Labov (1987) and others indicates that in inner city areas where low income African-Americans constitute a majority population or are isolated, AAVE features are as prevalent as ever. In fact, the grammatical patterns analyzed in Labov's research have led him to reach the highly controversial conclusion that the variant is increasing in its divergence from mainstream White American vernacular norms (Rickford 1987; Spears 1987; Vaughn-Cooke 1987; Wolfram 1987).

Similarly, the East Palo Alto Neighborhood Studies (EPANS) language data collected from working class, African-American female teenagers show a high degree of vernacular usage similar to that reported in previous studies of AAVE. More importantly, teen AAVE provides fascinating content related to teen perceptions and commentary on their environment which should be seriously considered in any discussion of parenting strategies involving intergenerational communication.

A Contemporary Look At African-American Teen Language Divergence: What Do They Be Saying?

The EPANS project is a time-depth study of variation in urban vernacular English. From 1986 to 1988 preliminary research was conducted using Labov's (1984) prescribed techniques: face-to-face recordings of speech; construction of a sociolinguistic interview schedule using conversation modules and friendship networks; and use of techniques designed to elicit spontaneous utterances of vernacular usage. To date, the project has been successful in eliciting a rich sample of vernacular data.* Features such as divergent uses of the copula are present in the speech samples of the interviewees, i.e. 0 (zero)-copula (absence of present tense

* The author has served as Research Associate for the project and conducted all of the interviews cited in this paper. The average length of each interview was approximately 120 minutes.

forms of the verb, "to be," as in "You scared," instead of "You are scared"), and invariant be (use of the infinitive form instead of conjugated present tense forms of the verb "to be," as in "I be going"). These are among the more popular variables investigated in previous studies. For example, the following excerpt from an interview with Foxy Boston (FB), a fourteen year old African-American female, evidences a high invariant BE usage pattern.*

> Don't sometime when you wake up, you BE going, um, after you have a dream, you go, "That's serious! Shoot, I know I do, cause I BE waking up and I BE slurping . . . and I BE going "Dang, that's serious! Guess who I had a dream about, y'all!" And I go to school, I'll go, "Gyahh! Y'all guys—"When I get on the school bus—when I get on the city bus in the morning . . . all our friends BE coming' to pick me up . . . we BE all meeting at the bus stop . . . Then they BE saying, "Guess what girl! . . . Something serious happen yesterday," They telling me . . . Guess what! Something serious happen, girl! Guess who I had a dream about! That's serious, man! They BE going, "Who? Who you have a dream for?" And I tell 'em—they go, "That's serious, dang, that's serious" (EPANS 7-1: 686-700).**

As another example, the following excerpts from an interview with Tinky Gates (TG), a fifteen year old African-American female, shows a frequent zero-copula usage pattern:

---

* The name "Foxy Boston," like those used for all EPANS interviewees, is a pseudonym. Transcriptions use a mixture of standard and non-standard spellings to present a more representative picture of pronunciation patterns.

** EPANS interview and transcript reference information: the initial number is the arbitrarily assigned interviewee identification code; the number following the hyphen indicates the arbitrarily assigned interview tape number, and the numbers following the colon provide the beginning and ending tape counter numbers of the exerpt location.

> It's gon' be like this in my house. Like say, for instance, somebody—somebody was to box my kid, right? Okay, talking' 'bout they—they—they (0) gon' put their foot on them and all this, and they (0) talking 'bout they didn't win the fight, and all this, right? . . . And when the first time that he get beat up, I'm gon' send him right back . . . I sho' am. I say—I say, "You want to get beat up? . . . Nah, you ain't got beat up, nah, go right back. I got a—I got a friend, she (0) my—she (0) my buddy—she (0) my buddy, Keisha. Her mama feel like this—ah was cracking' up. She said, "You didn't beat her up? Go back and get her." I be cracking up. I said, "What?! Go back outside an' get her?" You know? And it be like—you know, you'll be—it's like—it's like you (0) scared, but you ain't, you know. You (0) showing the kid you can't be scared all your life. You got to get out there and, you know, tell them you ain't scared of them someday. Cause it's some kids, they (0) just gon' keep picking—picking, pick-pick-pick . . . (EPANS 12-1: 577-600).

In addition to divergent uses of the copula and many other frequently reported vernacular features, language data from these interviews contain information relevant to parent-teen communication issues. Specifically, they provide a wide range of teen opinions and value statements. Topics prompting the most interesting commentary include male-female sexuality and relationships, teen pregnancy and parenting responsibilities, quality of life in Bay Area African-American communities, drug abuse and school campus violence. The following excerpts from conversations with Foxy Boston (FB), Rhoda King (RK, 13 year old female), Tinky Gates (TG), Asha Jones (AJ, 16 year old female) and Lana Smith (LS, 15 year old female) are representative of some of the more value-laden statements.

Male-Female Sexuality

FB: Some little girls is bad at that school . . . — They fast. They be talking 'bout the boys. They be pulling down their panties. The seventh . . . graders, they be — . . . they act childish still. The eighth graders act like they 21. The eighth graders, they act grown. And then they be telling the ones that acts like they kids do, "Y'all–y'all need to grow up." There's this boy that go to my school, he had on . . . a stretch suit and they pulled them down.

RK: The boys do it, too! They'll -they'll wear sweat pants and then they'll have some jeans under it and they'll walk around with half their jeans hanging out — . . . It's just supposed to attract attention. And some people just ignore it though. It's stupid. The boys do it. Cause they're stupid! All of them except for the nerds. The nerds go around talking to the teachers at lunch break (EPANS 7-1: 150-164).

Male-Female Relationships

LS: Out of a hundred—a hundred percent, about 50% of them (men) will and about 50% of them won't come through for you.

TG: Some of 'em [say]—Why don't you come—live with—you know, I go find you a place or, whatever, you know, you can—you know, you won't have to work.

AJ: But I feel if a girl or a woman do that it's not—I wouldn't do that. I mean, if a man said, um, I don' care if he a millionaire, it all runs out in due time. I mean, you have to work for yourself. You have to have something for yourself . . . (EPANS 12-1: 320-330).

Teen Pregnancy and Parenting Responsibilities

TG: My kids? My generation? They gonna be jus' like m—nah—they'll be different—I'll make my mama gray with my kids. I swear . . . I think I make my—I think my kids would worry my mama too much. You know what, I'm not gon' rely on my mama to babysit my kids. Them my kids. She ain' got no—She ain't had nothing to do with that. Them my kids. No, but no, no, it's sometime that you [will think] . . . "Well mom, you know, can I bring the kids over? You might wanna see 'em." Okay—I see some girls'll say . . . they rely on they mama. Well your mama . . . ain't had the baby. What you want her to do? You know, I got a buddy, . . . and she got a baby, right?

She don't even see him . . . . It's like—It's hers, but it's like—she rely on her mama do everything for the kid more than she do, and I be like—ooh, them your kids. Why you ain't takin' care of 'em, you know? Well, so, she wanna lay up and have the baby, then, then she should be laying up having the consequences (EPANS 12-1: 285-300).

AJ: A boy down here'll say in a minute, "Tha' ain' my baby!"

TG: That ain't my baby! Did I—look, did I see her—Nah, baby, I ain't even seen you before. Where that baby? Yeah, I don't even know you, honey. Uh, when did you get that? Nah child, I cain't even see you, you know—

LS: "You must have seen somebody that look like me—"

TG: They'll say, "Did you ha' my baby?" And they be like—gahh, this man done said this, and I know they feel so funny.

LS: They feel hurt (EPANS 12-1: 336-340).

Quality of Life

(If you are going to convince a stranger to visit East Palo Alto, what would you tell him?)

RK: Nothin'. It's no good.

FB: If they do come, I'd tell 'em it's boring, cause it is. It's nothin to do—

RK: Unless they want to come up here to buy drugs, then—

Well, it's the truth.

(What about Oakland?)

FB: No. Oakland harder, rougher . . . It's more—It's more fighting, more shooting, more drugs and all that there. It's rough in Oakland. When I go down there to spend the night with my auntie and them?—We be, um—I be over my cousins and them and—it be rough there . . . especially in the east part . . . they be shooting . . . They be having the little kids selling drugs and stuff (EPANS 7-1: 70-80).

Drugs and Drug Usage

AJ: I mean, the high is like that (finger snap)!

TG: Yeah! An' they making . . . you look dumb, an' they running scot-free with your money and you sitting there high off of something you ain' even know—an' here this man is running scot-free with your twenty fi—nah baby, uh, uh, nah, I work too hard for that twenty fi' dollars. You better get away from me. I be trying to invest mines into clothes, into my room, and things I want to have. Nah . . . (EPANS 12-1: 257-262).

School Campus Violence

FB: Oh, it's alright. Oh, it—they -they better, cause all the bad people gone— . . . to high school. They—they moved . . . No, no, no the bad people didn't go to high school. The bad people—they went back to Oakland. They was bad. They went back to Oakland. They used to live around here . . . when Dolia an' dem came down here—before they came the school was good . . . But then . . . when Dolia and them came, that's when —that's when they started shooting up there, and then—somebody got stabbed and all this stuff . . . (EPANS 7-1: 120-126).

The interviews also provided a healthy dose of exposure to current slang terminology and meanings. Slang expressions recorded during conversations reflect disturbing perspectives among teens that are indicative of a general failure orientation, negative interpersonal relationships, and acceptance of violence and destructive events in the environment. Selected themes, terms and meanings are as follows:

Theme	**Expression**	**Meaning**
Death	get ghost	leave
Phoniness	clownin'	embarrass
	mask	phony behavior
Sexuality	thick	a nice body
	tenda	attractive person
	the lick	very good, great
	workin' it	sexual play,
Illness	you be illin'	you're sick, you
Violence	kickin' it	relaxing
	bust a move	dance very well or approach a person for romantic interest
	scrappin'	excessive eating
	take a lot out of you	beat someone up
	gangbanging	gang fighting
	shot down	rejected in love
	tear it off	stop being phony
Antisocial role modeling	rogue	friend, buddy
Destitution	to the curb	low, deteriorated, condition of existence

Still another characteristic of EPANS data is the consistent pattern of vernacular usage that took place throughout the entire interview period. The fact that there was no switching to standard speech patterns by the interviewees above, as well as by other teenagers interviewed in the study, confirms the success of interview techniques. No switching also suggests either an exclusive dependence on or a high level of comfort with the vernacular as a medium of communication. In fact, there appears to be both comfort and a hint of willfulness in the teenagers' choice of speech patterns—willfulness reflecting a strong view of language use as an expression of cultural identity. As expressed by Tinky:

> Then it's these . . . Black girls just—act like white girls. I say, "If you want to be white, go change your—color" (EPANS 12-1: 238-240).
>
> (If somebody called you on the phone could you tell from their voice if they were Black or White?) Yeah. (How could you tell?) The way they talk. (Okay, how would you know that it was a White person?) The White person'll talk more proper . . . (Okay, now here's a question. Do you think that Blacks who hang out a lot with Whites start to sound White?) Yeah. They start to getting like oreo cookies, too. (What about—White people who hang out with Blacks?) They be getting on my nerves. They get to being' Black. (You think everybody needs to speak standard English?) No. (Why not?) Why? Because they need to relate with their own heritage (EPANS 13-1: 902-920).

The previous descriptions of EPANS language data offer provocative insights into teen language use behavior and opinions which may prove useful to assessing the scope of intergenerational communication problems in African-American families. The use of Labovian language elicitation techniques, which focused more on content than form and were designed to encourage freedom of expression, proved to be successful in getting the teens to open up and speak their minds without inhibition. Parents may use these techniques as a way to more effectively tap into the vernacular. They may be able to discover what is really happening in the social and emotional world of their teens and bolster their efforts to develop into healthy and productive adults.

Strategies for Bridging the Intergenerational Communications Gap: You Would Want to Stop Checkin' Them and Take Heed to What They Be Saying.

For parents who are concerned about establishing better communication with teens, the importance of treating vernacular African-American English as a resource is crucial for historical, cultural and pragmatic reasons. Historically, linguistic research has validated its legitimacy as a medium of communication which has adequately served the needs of a wide-ranging community of speakers for hundreds of years. Moreover, the prevalence of vernacular features in EPANS teen language data suggests that African-American Vernacular English (AAVE) has continued to develop in spite of perceived improvements in educational and employment opportunities. The transmission of AAVE language characteristics is still occurring across successive generations of African-Americans.

The cultural rationale for treating AAVE is that its use among teens appears to function as an important symbol of peer group solidarity and as a demonstration of pride in one's African heritage. Data from EPANS indicate that AAVE users are making conscious efforts to preserve the cultural salience of the Africanity of African-American language. The cultural chauvinism reflected in Tinky's opinions about speaking standard English and people who attempt to emulate a culture other than their own may explain why the use of the vernacular is so tenaciously exhibited by African-American youth. If so, it may well be an attitude passed on through the legacy of the sixties when African-Americans vociferously proclaimed the right to cultural expression of all aspects of their African heritage. One writer described this cultural chauvinism as follows:

> . . . From . . . a linguistic perspective, even though African-Americans . . . share three fourths of their lexicon, i.e. vocabulary, with Euro-Americans, the African-American's language is not genetically the same as the Euro-American's English . . . [It is different] pre-

> cisely to the extent to which an African-American has been beat, kicked, raped, robbed, used, abused, and made a fool . . . and [lives] in social isolation from the dominant culture . . . (Smith 1977,66-7).

The practical rationale for the appropriate treatment of the vernacular is multifaceted. First, AAVE is clearly the popular mode of expression among African-American teens. It is used in spite of socially prescribed norms and values which disapprove of its use or relegate its function to informal or low prestige situations. Although AAVE operates in conflict with language-based interactions involving the larger society, its existence must be acknowledged and treated with respect. Far too often attempts to ignore or stifle AAVE only serve to undermine the most sincere efforts of parents and teachers to communicate with African-American teens.

Secondly, teen vernacular language may have to be viewed as a reliable means of gaining feedback on the effectiveness of parenting and communication efforts. EPANS language data suggest that vernacular expression conveys more of teenagers' personal concerns, value formation, and responses to peer culture. In order to access this information, parents have to listen and attempt to understand the messages conveyed by informal and uninhibited teen expression. This can be a challenging task because it will require new attitudes and reactions to a highly stigmatized way of talking. However, it can also be an exciting task because of the creativity and freedom of expression afforded to AAVE speakers. If parents can learn to focus more on content than form, they will discover and obtain concrete information that can be used to evaluate the success of their efforts to transmit culturally appropriate values, establish behavioral standards, illicit information about physical and emotional problems, and facilitate the development of a positive self-concept.

Finally, the need to tap into teen language is essential given all the negative influences on teens in low income African-American communities. Also tapping into teen talk is essential because of the complexity of personal development needed by teens to become culturally sensitive and productive members of an ever-changing and increasingly sophisticated technological society. As stressed by Taylor (1987):

> We are at a point in the history of this nation, where because of various technological changes we're able to have all sorts of messages presented to us—many of which are dangerous messages. Through music video, for example—lets just take one message—it is now possible for all sorts of messages about drugs, about families, about promiscuity, etc. to be promoted to us in our living rooms "live and in living color" and in better acoustics than . . . on the real stage. These messages are bombarding the minds of our young people. We need to make certain, . . . in the information age, that we know how to process information—to know what . . . values and ideas and which perceptions are being projected to us . . .

In sum, parenting strategies for bridging the intergenerational communication gap should emphasize attending to messages revealed in teen opinions, values statements and slang terminology as a way of becoming more in tune with the personal issues confronting them on a daily basis. Recommended strategies should include ways to elicit uninhibited teen expression. This can be done by working to obtain the interest and involvement of teens in conversation, and by focusing more on content than on grammar. But most important is that the listener must be neutral and not react against the form of language expressed.

The wealth of insights to be gained from listening to and attempting to understand teen language may prove to be invaluable to the parenting process. Vernacular language expression is a window to underlying messages about teen peer identity issues, behavior norms, and reactions to environmental conditions. Efforts to tap into this expression may create a more positive and non-threatening context for intergenerational communications. Also these efforts may provide an opportunity for parents to demonstrate respect for the integrity of African-American's unique language. Positive interaction between adult listeners and teens may serve to reduce teen resistance to broadening their language usage and may foster more positive attitudes toward the acquisition of situationally appropriate Mainstream-American English competencies.

References

Abrahams, R. D. 1970. "The Advantages of Black English," *Florida FL Reporter.* 8(1,2),27-30,51.

Adams, L. and C. Strouse. 1960. "Kids" in M. Stewart *Bye Bye Birdie* (Musical Score). New York: Strada Music.

Bailey, B. L. 1970. "Some Arguments Against the Use of Dialect Readers in the Teaching of Initial Reading." *Florida FL Reporter.* Spring/Fall 8(1,2),8,46.

Baratz, J. C. 1969. "Language and Cognitive Assessment of Negro Children: Assumptions and Research Needs," *Florida FL Reporter.* Fall 7(2),11-14.

Baratz, J. C. 1973. "The Relationship of Black English to Reading" in J. Laffey and R. Shuy (eds.) *Language Differences: Do They Interfere?* Newark, Delaware: International Reading Association.

Baugh, J. 1983. *Black Street Speech: Its History, Structure, and Survival.* Austin: University of Texas Press.

Burling, R. 1973. *English in Black and White.* New York: Rinehart and Winston.

Cullinan, B. (ed.) 1974. *Black Dialects and Reading.* Urbana, Illinois: ERIC Clearinghouse on Reading and Communication Skills, National Council of Teachers of English.

Dalby, D. 1972. *Rappin' and Stylin' Out: Communications in Urban Black America.* Urbana: University of Illinois Press.

DeFrantz, A. P. 1979. "A Critique of the Literature on Ebonics." *Journal of Black Studies.* June 9(4),383-396.

De Stefano, J.S. 1972. "Social Variation in Language: Implications for Teaching Reading to Black Ghetto Children," in J.A. Figurel (ed.) *Better Reading in Urban Schools.* Newark, Delaware: International reading Association.

DiGiulio, R. C. 1973. "Measuring Teacher Attitude Toward Black English: A Pilot Project." *Florida FL Reporter.* Spring/Fall 11(1,2),25-26,49.

Dillard, J. L. 1972. *Black English: Its History and Usage in the United States*. New York: Random House.
East Palo Alto Neighborhood Study (EPANS). 1986-7. Interview Transcripts. Stanford University.
Fasold, R. and W. Wolfram. 1970. "Some Linguistic Features of Negro Dialect," in R. Fasold and R. W. Shuy (eds.) *Teaching Standard English in the Inner City.* Washington, D.C.: Center for Applied Linguistics.
Harber, J. R. and J. N. Beatty. 1978. *Reading and the Black English-Speaking Child: An Annotated Bibliography.* Newark, Delaware: International Reading Association (ED 149313).
Hoover, M. R. 1975. *Appropriate Use of Black English by Black Children as Rated by Black Parents*. Unpublished doctoral dissertation, Stanford University.
Hoover, M. R. et al. 1988. *Tests of Black Language for Teachers of Bidialectal Students.* Berkeley: University of Berkeley Press.
Jeff, D.J.J. and F. Prince. 1988. "Parents Just Don't Understand." Zomba Productions Ltd. New York.
Johnson, K. R. 1971. "Teachers' Attitude Toward the Nonstandard Negro Dialect—Let's Change It." *Elementary English.* 48(2), 176-184.
Kochman, T. 1972. (ed.) *Rappin' and Stylin' Out: Communication in Urban Black America.* Urbana: University of Illinois Press.
Labov. W. et al. 1968. "A Study of the Non-Standard English of Negro and Puerto Rican Speakers in New York City." *Cooperative Research Report* 3288. 2 Volumes. Philadelphia: U.S. Regional Survey.
Labov, W. 1969. The Logic of Non-standard English. *Florida FL Reporter*. Spring/Summer, 7(1), 60-74.
Labov, W. 1972. *Language in the Inner City: Studies in the Black English Vernacular.* Philadelphia: Univ. of Pennsylvania Press.
Labov, W. 1974. "Some Sources of Reading Problems for Negro Speakers of Nonstandard English" in R. B. Ruddell et al. (eds.) *Resources in Reading—Language Instruction.* Englewood Cliffs: Prentice Hall.
Labov, W. 1984. "Field Methods of the Project on Linguistic Change and Variation" in J. Baugh and J. Sherzer (eds.) *Language in Use.* Englewood Cliffs: Prentice-Hall.
Labov, W. 1987. "Are Black and White Vernaculars Diverging?" *American Speech.* 62(1),5-12.
Laffey, J. and R. Shuy. 1973. (eds.) *Language Differences: Do They Interfere?* Newark, Delaware: International Reading Association.

Lourie, M. A. 1978. "Black English Vernacular: A Comparative Description" in M. A. Lourie and N. Conklin (eds.) *A Plural Nation.* Rowley, Mass.: Newbury House Publishers.

McCrum, R. and R. MacNeil. 1989. "The Story of English: Black on White." A British Broadcasting Service Television Co-production with WNET. New York.

McNair-Knox, F. 1985. *The Effects of Foreign Language Instruction on the Reading Ability of African-American Children.* Unpublished doctoral dissertation, Stanford University.

Mitchell-Kernan, C. 1972. "On the Status of Black English for Native Speakers: An Assessment of Attitudes and Values" in C. Cazden, V. John and D. Hymes (eds.) *Functions of Language in the Classroom.* New York: Teacher's College Press.

National Urban League. 1987. *The State of Black America.* New York: National Urban League.

Nichols, P. C. 1981. "Creoles of the USA," in C. A. Ferguson and S. Heath (eds.) *Language in the USA*. Cambridge: Cambridge University Press.

Politzer, R. and D. Bartley. 1969a. "Standard English and Nonstandard Dialects: Phonology and Morphology" (Research and Development Memorandum No. 46) Stanford: Stanford Center for Research and Development in Teaching, School of Education, Stanford University.

Politzer, R. and D. Bartley. 1969b. "Standard English and Nonstandard Dialects: Elements of Syntax" (Research and Development memorandum No. 54) Stanford: Stanford center for Research and Development in Teaching, School of Education, Stanford University.

Politzer, R. 1973. "Problems in Applying Foreign Language Teaching Methods to the Teaching of Standard English as a Second Dialect" in J. DeStefano (ed.) *Language, Society and Culture.* Worthington, Ohio: Charles A. Jones Publishing Company.

Rhodes, O. 1970. "Some Implications for Teaching Reading to Speakers of Black Dialect." *Viewpoints*. 46(3), 117-147.

Rickford, J. R. 1977. "The Question of Prior Creolization in Black English" in A. Valdman (ed.) *Pidgin and Creole Linguistics*. Bloomington: Indiana University Press.

Rickford, J. R. 1985. "Ethnicity As a Sociolinguistic Boundary." *American Speech*. 60(2),90-125.

Rickford, J. R. 1986. "East Palo Alto Neighborhood Study." Project Proposal for the Stanford University Urban Studies Fellowship Program. Stanford University.

Rickford, J. R. 1987. "Are Black and White Vernaculars Diverging?" Papers from the NWAVE XIV Panel Discussion: VII. American Speech. Spring 62(1), 55-62.

Schneider, M. 1971. "Use Dialect Readers? The Middle Class Black Establishment Will Damn You If You Do. The Black Child Will Damned You if You Don't." *Florida FL Reporter.* Spring/Fall 9(1,2),45-46,56.

Shuy, R. W. 1971. "Social Dialects: Teaching Vs. Learning." *Florida FL Reporter.* Spring/Fall 9(1), 28-33,55.

Simons, H. D. 1976. "Black Dialect, Reading Interference and Classroom Interaction." Paper Presented: Conference on Theory and Practice of Beginning Reading Instruction, University of Pittsburgh, Learning Research and Development Center (ED 155648).

Sledd, J. 1969. "Bi-dialectalism: The Linguistics of White Supremacy." *English Journal.* December 58(9), 1307-1315, 1329.

Smith, E. A. 1974. *The Evolu tion and Continuing Presence of the African Oral Tradition in Black America.* Unpublished Ph.D. dissertation, University of California at Irvine.

Smith, E. A. 1977. "A Case for Bilingual and Bicultural Education for United States Slave Descendants of American Origin." Paper No. 39. Seminar Paper Series. Department of Linguistics, California State University Fullerton.

Smitherman, G. 1977. *Talkin' and Testifyin': The Language of Black America.* Boston: Houghton Mifflin.

Spears, A. K. 1987. "Are Black and White Vernaculars Diverging?" *American Speech.* 62(1), 48-55.

Stewart, W. 1970. "Foreign Language Teaching Methods in Quasi-Foreign Situations" in R. Fasold and R. Shuy (eds.) *Teaching Standard English in the Inner City.* Washington, D.C.: Center for Applied Linguistcis.

Taylor, O. 1969. "An Introduction to the Historical Development of Black English: Some Implications for American Education." Paper given at the Institute on the Speech and Language of the Rural and Urban Poor, Ohio University.

Taylor, O. 1975. "Black Language and What to do about it: Some Black Community Perspectives" in R. Williams (ed.) *Ebonics: The True Language of Black Folks.* St. Louis, Missouri: Institute of Black Studies.

Taylor, O. 1987. "Black Economic Empowerment." Speech presented at the Black Liberation Month Symposium. Stanford University.

Tolliver-Weddington, G. 1979. "Introduction." *Journal of Black Studies.* June 9(4), 364-366.

Turner, L. 1949. *Africanisms in the Gullah Dialect.* Chicago: University of Chicago Press.

Vacca, J. 1975. "Bidialectalism—Choose your Side!" *The Reading Teacher.* April 28(7): 643-646.

Vaughn-Cooke, F. B. 1987. "Are Black and White Vernaculars Diverging?" *American Speech.* 62(1), 12-32.

Weltz, S. 1974. "Reading and Black English" in A. Beery, et al. (eds.) *Elementary Reading Instruction: Selected Materials.* Boston: Allyn and Bacon.

Whatley, E. 1981. "Language Among Black Americans" in C. Ferguson and S. Heath (eds.) *Language in the USA.* Cambridge: Cambridge University Press.

Williams, F. 1970. *Language and Poverty.* Chicago: Markham.

Williams, R. L. 1975. *Ebonics: The True Language of Black Folks.* St. Louis: Institute of Black Studies.

Wofford, J. 1979. "Ebonics: A Legitimate System of Oral Communication." *Journal of Black Studies.* June 9(4), 367-382.

Wolfram, W. 1970. "Sociolinguistic Alternatives in Teaching Reading to Nonstandard Speakers." *Florida FL Reporter.* 62(1,2), 16-23.

Chapter 13

When Education Succeeds: The Cost of Success

Tee Sweet*

I HAVE LIVED AND WORKED in San Jose, California, for thirty-one years. This city has evolved from a small town with an agricultural economy and some light manufacturing to the premier center of high technology in the country. While other American cities struggled with decline of their industrial base, San Jose has grown and prospered. Progress and prosperity has brought with them a number of surprises. Twenty-five years ago when I became active with the San Jose chapter of the National Association for the Advancement of Colored People (N.A.A.C.P.), Blacks lived in approximately four square blocks off of the downtown business district. It was a community. Most people had migrated from the South for job opportunities, worked in what little industry there was in San Jose and eventually came to own their homes. The major issues were discrimination in jobs and segregated housing. If you were Black and wanted to live in San Jose, you had to live in the Black community very much like in the South or any place else in the U.S. I spent most of my time as President of the N.A.A.C.P. struggling against these two barriers. When I compare our circumstances in jobs and housing then and now, Blacks in San Jose were very successful. Blacks now live and work all over the valley, but there is an irony in this. I will briefly address this unanticipated outcome of our success in this paper.

* Written with the assistance of Benjamin Bowser.

First of all, I am writing from experience. What I have observed cannot be found in the statistics about the changing economy and population of San Jose. Furthermore, there are very few in this city who have spent as many hours as I have talking and meeting with Black people over the years, hearing their concerns, sharing their trials and enjoying their victories. We all assumed that once we overcame the barriers of discrimination in jobs and housing, we would then see greater personal freedom, prosperity and more opportunities for our children. What we did not anticipate was that once we reached the "promised land" most of our young people would not be able to take advantage of it. Our young people are now going to integrated schools and, even in the poorest sections of San Jose, are living in integrated neighborhoods. But now they do not have the motivation, discipline and academic backgrounds to enjoy the new high-tech jobs and new housing opening all around them. This is a national tragedy. What is not as apparent is the price those few who are successful have had to pay in self-respect, and historical and social identity with their people.

The Setting and Its Significance

If the U.S. ever does develop a true post-industrial economy, San Jose, California, will be the model. It is the objective of virtually every city and suburb in the nation to develop clean, high-paying, high-tech industries. Those which are now experiencing rejuvenated economies and renewed community development have new modern industries. In this sense, San Jose as a local economy, cultural center and city presently represents what many other cities and suburban communities would like to be in coming years. San Jose is the future for which the nation is striving. Therefore, if you want to know what place Blacks will undoubtedly have in the nation's high-tech future, you should look at Blacks currently in San Jose. While the city has grown rapidly over the past twenty years, it is still not so large that you cannot meet and deal with Blacks in all sectors of the city.

First of all, there is no longer a central Black community. There are many little pockets of Blacks living throughout the city and its suburbs. San Jose and its surrounding suburbs are some of the most integrated metropolitan areas in the U.S. Where you live in San Jose has more to do with social class and income than with race, though there is still some discrimination—primarily in lower-income rental units. Second, there is no large working-class Black community as you find in other large metropolitan areas. The manufacturing jobs that attracted Black people years ago no longer exist. Many of these earlier workers have now retired or have moved away. Blacks in San Jose who do not have education and skills are struggling to survive in a declining job market while the city grows around them. As a consequence, the increasing price of housing alone is making it more and more difficult for a working-class family to live in the area, the Santa Clara valley.

The new Black migrants to the area come from all over the nation and most work in administrative, research and technological roles within high-tech corporations. They are middle class. They are highly skilled. They live where they can afford. And they represent the success stories in many eastern and southern Black families. Over the years I have met many of these new migrants to the Valley. The older professionals come with families and roots in a Black community—somewhere. They join one of several Black churches, are members of the N.A.A.C.P. and the newly formed Urban League, and live and struggle like the Black middle class everywhere else.

But in recent years there is a new group of Black migrants to the Valley. They are single, young, male and culturally unique. They are recent college graduates. Many have professional degrees and could easily be the older children of our established Black professionals in San Jose, though they are not, as I will discuss later. They are in research, engineering and related highly skilled roles. There were only a few of these young people working in the Valley a decade ago. But as the years pass, their numbers increase. Their growing presence stands in sharp contrast to both older, married migrants to the Valley and the national crisis of Black males. Over the years I have talked with many of them and become a mother-figure to some. While my impressions are based on several years of conversations, I shaped my observations for this paper from conversations and interviews with seventeen of these young Black men who are between 25 and 30 years old. I make no claim that my observations are scientifically representative. My comments are impressionistic but fair and will not be found in scholarly literature. What I learned from them is the price they have paid as Blacks and males to be successful. What I have to report is tragic.

Single, Black, Male and Successful

You cannot make quick assumptions about these young men. They make it very clear that being "Black," however you wish to define it, is optional and of little consequence to them. Their skin color is incidental. Their identity is based on their jobs, life-styles and their very conscious sense of economic worth. They are intent on enjoying everything they think White men enjoy, without concern for heritage or race. Most are newcomers to California. Very few of their parents are or were professionals and a surprising number are from small southern towns. They are wary of and reject Black people, but, surprisingly, not one another. They share their sense of a nonracial identity with one another and have a common social network apart from other Blacks. This includes separation from their same age and social class peers who identify with Black people and the Black heritage.

They neither feel obligated to express an interest in civic or community projects nor to take leadership roles. They feel that civil rights organizations such as the N.A.A.C.P. and the Urban League have served their purpose and are joined by those looking for a handout. It does not matter to what political party one belongs because the end result for them, personally, is how much money one can get. Furthermore, they feel that they are replacing the old "black way" of thinking which developed in the 1950s and 1960s and which emphasizes civil rights, traditional religion and ideas about being "Black and Proud." A number are "born again Christians" but at the same time point out that women, money, fun and self are more important to them than civil rights and the old ways. They see no contradiction in their profession of faith and their values.

They are very choosey and critical in their relationships with female friends and wives. It is my observation that they are not more attractive than other Black men in their age group. They are neither athletic nor light-skinned, nor could they pass as Black GQ (*Genthemen's Quarterly*) models. Yet their women are white, or nearly so. And if you ask them why they prefer white women, they respond that their preference has nothing to do with race. They are attracted to women with similar career and recreational interests and these women happen to be White or very light-skinned Blacks.

What I did not know until recently is that, despite their rejection of race and heritage, many of these men know one another. Their relations are out of choice through their work, professional groups and church memberships. I have gotten to know many of them because they refer one another to me as someone in the community to whom they can talk. I suspect that they want to talk with an older community leader who will not reject them because they are not completely comfortable with their break from the "old ways." While they have no definite organization, they do have a sense of themselves as a group. Furthermore, I was surprised to find out that they even have mentors or peer role models from whom they informally seek advice over the telephone or at lunch.

Their high degree of self-importance is based on their college and graduate school degrees. There is nothing about their family or community backgrounds that they feel would distinguish them. What they want more than anything is recognition in their professions. Many are engineers, computer scientists, bankers, lawyers and accountants. I have been invited to some of their get-togethers and have listened very carefully to the conversations. They talk about their college years . . . the fun times.

The few who are married have spouses with college degrees and high-paying jobs as well. These men make it very clear that they would not have it any other way. Having the additional money means even more leisure and more comfort.

Most are separated by distance and by choice from their parents and extended families. And despite having the money, they seldom visit them. When asked about their families, they will tell you that they have a need for privacy and must be financially responsible for only themselves. The distance also makes it difficult for family members to ask them for money. Most of these men live in Sunnyvale and Santa Clara, two suburbs of San Jose, preferring not to live around other Blacks.

Case Descriptions

In the following section I will describe two of these young men. They are composites of the seventeen of whom I have gotten to know and have the fictitious names of "Keith" and "Clifford." They reflect the concerns, values and aspirations of all these young men.

Keith

Keith left Boston when he was seven years old and returned to the South. He was reared by his grandparents, to whom a college education meant very little. They worked very hard to support their children and to raise four grandchildren as well. They wanted Keith to finish high school, find a job and support himself, plus his younger brothers and sisters. What made a difference for Keith was the insistence of a White, female guidance counselor that he go to college. His grandmother gave in and allowed him to attend a southern university.

Keith was the first in his family to attend college and to graduate. He was very pleased to be introduced by his family as a college student and was held in high esteem by relatives and friends. During his vacations from school the girls flocked to him. After college and some graduate work, he was recruited for a job in the Santa Clara valley. He has worked on the same job for six years and is beholden to his boss and company for the advantages he receives—good pay and prestige.

Keith neither misses the girls who once flocked to him nor does he miss his family. After several months on the job, he met a young White woman who works close to him. She is a bookkeeper, was previously married and has a young daughter. They became friends and often met for lunch. It turns out that this was Keith's first serious relationship. Sometimes she packed lunch for the two of them—watercress sandwiches, fresh fruit and a thermos of white wine. If the weather permitted, they ate lunch in the park.

They are now married. She is a friendly woman, takes a tan well and has smooth skin and long hair. She often praises him and helps him with his various job projects after work. She "believes in him" and tells him about better jobs that he might pursue. Going out on the town is always fun. She seldom complains about spending too much money. There are Black women who do the same things and have the same qualities, but to Keith the fact that his wife is White makes a difference.

Keith feels that his wife has grace and very good social skills. She enhances his prestige with his friends. In contrast, Keith believes that Black women tend to be parochial, to seek friends only among relatives and others like them and are adversarial. He gladly discarded his identity with Black women and his family.

While Keith holds that race is no longer important, he sees the inherent conflict in competition with white men. He is very much aware of the need to close the gap between the races and, in particular, between himself and them. He does this by dressing stylishly and expensively, turning in a high work performance, driving a new car, being punctual and through having a White wife. These serve as ways not only to identity with Whites, but also to demonstrate to Whites that he has mastered the larger culture as well or better than they.

Clifford

Clifford is older than most of these young men; he is thirty years old. But they look up to him. He grew up in a family of five in Los Angeles. He was his mother's favorite and she spoiled him with additional freedom to play and watch television after his homework. She worked as a dental assistant and secretary, and also part-time in a department store for the family needs during Christmas. Clifford's father was a policeman who ran the house and was a strict disciplinarian. He neither played with the children nor took them to the movies, picnics or school functions. While Clifford was favored, his home life was not particularly happy.

In retrospect, Clifford points out that his mother did not teach him about fine foods and his family had no sense of the wonderful recreational activities available to them. Furthermore, the Black women who have been in his life remind him of his mother and the limitations of his family. They had little knowledge of the important issues of the day, had very limited lives and wanted it that way. They were uncomfortable in fine places and were very hard to please. Unlike many of his younger contemporaries, Clifford has changed jobs twice in the last six years. In the first, he was passed over for promotion and in the second, he was insubordinate. He blames himself for both of these since he was really angry with his girl friend and took it out on his boss.

Reflecting back to his days in school, he recalled his first Black teacher. She was his eleventh grade U.S. History teacher. He vividly remembers when she got to the sections on the Civil War and U.S. Constitution. He felt that she spent too much time on the issue of slavery which made him very uncomfortable. When she talked about slavery, all the White students in class looked at him. She seemed to be a harder grader and would call his mother for too many little things. She was also strict and called on him all of the time to answer questions. If he could not answer them correctly, he had to stay after school. This was embarrassing and humiliating. On the other hand, he recalls with pride his white college sociology professor. He credits her for introducing him to the arts and to the theater. She was the first person who spent time with him after class talking about things other than classwork.

Clifford spends most of his leisure time in social and recreational activities. He goes out regularly to meet friends at clubs or at their condos for food, drink and sometimes drugs. A major pastime is watching the latest videos. There are strict unwritten rules on the kind of women who are invited to their get-togethers. They are invariably light or white, have long hair, are college graduates and have high-paying jobs. These women must also show independence, self-sufficiency and dress well at all times. To Clifford and his friends Black women are simply out. They are too uptight, no fun, very demanding and very hard to please. Furthermore, they are dull at parties and have nothing to talk about.

While there is nothing like a good party, church is also important in Clifford's life. He seldom misses service. He prides himself on being "born again" and sees no conflict between church and his views on race, family and having fun. But there is an added incentive. Church also serves as a place to meet beautiful (light-skinned Black) women. He attends the Black church with the highest-income parishioners. Here, he feels that the members are established and wealthier than those at the traditional churches—even the building is modern and shows wealth. He is quite pleased that when he walks into church, heads turn with respect and deference.

Reflections

You might want to dismiss these men as immature, confused, isolated cases or simply as examples of what happens to Black men in the West. Nothing could be further from the truth. They are all over and they are often our most successful males in terms of education, professional attainment and economic mobility. While the circumstances of most Black men are indeed tragic, the numbers of these "successful" men will continue to increase slowly. If we are successful in getting more of our young men through college and into professions, Keith and Clifford may seem not to be so extraordinary at all. What is apparent here is not what these young men say and think. It is the psychological and cultural price that they paid to be successful. Through their education and socialization on the job, they have gotten a not so subtle message that being Black is a liability and identifying with Black people will automatically disqualify them from upward mobility in the company. But ironically, it is all right for them to associate with other corporate Blacks like themselves.

So after a generation of struggle in San Jose and the Valley, we have desegregated the workplace and housing. Now most of our young men and women cannot qualify for open opportunities in new jobs and housing. And for those who do qualify, many feel that they have to abandon their identity and association with Black people and their families. This process does not begin when they reach California. It begins in high school, if not earlier. Most of the explanations the men in this essay give for their values, preference for White women and dismissal of Blacks are developed because of what they feel they have to do for acceptance in the White world. The function of these excuses is to help them ignore the real interpersonal racial struggles they experienced in school and continue to experience daily on the job. The race struggle for them and, increasingly, for all of us in the evolving hightech world no longer has clearly visible targets. It is now an underground struggle and psychological war with few rules and guidelines. But the damage that this new kind of struggle creates is as bad as, if not worse than, the old system of open discrimination and segregation. And the casualties are apparent and very much with us.

If we are effectively to address this new new situation of overt rather than covert hostility and its intraracial impact on many of our successful young men, we must first recognize that the situation exists. Most young Black people have not abandoned their race as these young men have and we all live under the same pressures. But their experiences and the way in which they have addressed the pressures of race highlight the stress that all Blacks are under and the cost of disorganization. We must struggle as a group to improve our political and economic status so that we will be respected as a people—not simply as individuals. Numbers and economic power (not simply income) speak loudly and empower change in the way we are perceived. I believe that Blacks as a group must take that action so that young men like these and those who will follow them will see themselves, their parents and community, and not their colleges or employers, as their primary identity.

American society gives negative images of Blacks, especially of Black men. Our youth suffer from a lack of positive images stemming from some of the following:

1. teachers teaching ideas in conflict with Black heritage
2. teachers, White and Black, who have no knowledge of the positive contributions of Blacks to society in the past or present
3. television which demeans and trivializes Black people
4. economically struggling single parent households headed by a parent who knows only failure
5. churches dominated by women and pastors who are out of touch and unwilling to address the issues of the day
6. law enforcement which sees all Blacks as criminals
7. Black organizations which neither have the structure nor the leadership to address covert racism

Too many of our Black youth try to escape into the White world because they feel that we have not accomplished anything worthwhile. They also feel that we cannot help them achieve what they want out of life. We should demand that educators give the same respect and regard to our children that they give to their own. Not only should all children be taught European history but they need to know the histories of Third World peoples and Afro-Americans as well. They should be taught in a positive way so that Black youth will feel comfortable and will be able to build their self-worth.

We need to develop methods to improve the child rearing of single and working mothers. They need to have a positive attitude toward parenthood if they are to rear their own children successfully. Virtually all of the young men on whom I based this essay came to feel at an early age that they had to abandon their racial identities in order to succeed. What they all had in common were family lives where there was a poverty greater than financial poverty. There was poverty of spirit from their parents' day-to-day intellectual, psychological and spiritual emptiness due to their struggle against deprivation and racism. In this sense, parents need to have a sense of humor and be willing and able to communicate with their children about their struggles, failures and successes. Parents should know that it is not enough to simply work and make a living to rear their children successfully.

We need to set up a system of networking, bringing together Blacks that have reached a level of success to serve as role models for others. This group could be organized through a center for speakers, workshops, fun events, etc. Attention should be given to the history of the civil rights movement so that Black children and parents alike can see that progress is made only by people working and making sacrifices for a better future. Finally, all of our communities need to develop a method of reporting worthwhile news that focuses on our worth, successes, wants and needs.

Chapter 14

Black Male Adolescent Development Deviating from the Past: Challenges for the Future

Ronald J. Hudson

THIS PAPER IS AN EFFORT TO EXPLORE the impact of contemporary society on the development of Black male adolescents' identity. These influences include peers, family economic resources and the impact of living in integrated communities. I developed this paper from twenty years of experience as a student, counselor and instructor in predominately white institutions. Over this time I have witnessed a crucial change. Black students have gone from having strong identification with Black communities and culture to a decreasing interest in Black people, their communities and their concerns. The current generation has more historical knowledge and political sophistication regarding Blacks in America. They lack awareness of the significance of developing a strong sense of Blackness while meeting the challenge of upward mobility.

Let me preface my remarks with a definition of the specific population that I am referring to. My work in higher education has taught me that there are in fact two Black populations of male adolescents struggling with identity development—those that have not had access to the avenues of selective education and those that have had such opportunities.

I wish to focus on the latter, the population of upwardly mobile young, Black males. These are our young people who are gaining access to the mainstream and who are held up as educational role models. But many within this group have also posed such questions as "How do I relate (to Black people)?", "How do I talk Black?", "Should I put Black activities on my resumes or mention them in interviews?" These questions vary, but the issue is the same. How does one identify himself ethnically? For longtime observers, the question is, what are the basis and origins of the anxiety associated with identifying as a Black person among upwardly mobile Black youth? I should also note that my focus is on those within this group who have not experienced the "traditional" Black acculturation within their families or communities. They are not studied in contemporary social science literature, but in fact represent an ever-growing proportion of upwardly mobile Black males.

My interest in this subject was also a result of hearing the term "miscellaneous Blacks" (introduced to me by my students), meaning Blacks who do not possess the requisite skills or values to function comfortably or effectively in the broader Black community.

Psychosocial Development

Erickson characterized the period of puberty and adolescence as a psychosocial crisis stage. One's developing identity conflicts with new role expectations and there is reintegration of the past with present and future goals (Erickson 1963). This characterization of adolescent development is then extended with the models advanced by Cross (1980) and Thomas (1971). They address the question: How does one develop a strong Black identity within the cultural dimensions that defined "blackness" in the past with limited opportunities and future goals that do not encourage (and in fact may discourage) that identity?

I have often heard colleagues say that Black students are as culturally diverse as students from other ethnic groups. This assumption by counselors and administrators has resulted in numerous programming errors and in misreading the force behind student-initiated political movements. The most disturbing result is the failure to recognize and respond to the fact that the young men behind these movements are in a continuing struggle to affirm their identity, even when their past experiences have not provided for a solid identification with Black culture.

These young men are products of circumstances. Much of the past literature characterized these Blacks as seeking approval from Whites and as receiving gratification from self-rejection and from rejecting group goals and activities (Thomas 1971). In fact, the process of assimilation that many young and upwardly mobile Black males are undergoing is circumstantial, situational and the result of recent social change. The following analysis will serve to explain, in part, how circumstances and situations impact on adolescent self-concept:

> For the adolescent his or her entire system of self-appraisal is in flux and is more susceptible to changes in the environment, especially political, social, and cultural changes. In the struggle for independence, the adolescent will attempt to evaluate and even to incorporate some of the changing values he or she is encountering. Consequently, the socialization process of the adolescent is crucial in understanding his/her self-concept process (Powell 1985).

Historical research has been cited by Benson that further supports my observations about select groups of Black male adolescents:

> A substantial body of research on race awareness among young Black children in the United States has demonstrated that children as young as two and three years old have absorbed the idea of ethnic variation and are capable of identifying and labeling themselves, and others in ethnic terms. From this age onwards, such children show an increasing sense of the social implications of ethnic variation and begin to produce, the racial attitudes of their society. One of the most striking aspects of Black children's behavior

> in these research projects is what may be inferred as their highly ambivalent feelings with respect to their own ethnic identity. A significant proportion refuse to identify themselves as Black and evidence hostility towards their own ethnic identity (Benson 1981).

I do not agree with many of the conclusions in the literature cited by Benson. Much of this research conducted prior to the era of the civil rights movement was based on the premise that maintaining a Black identity was negative. It was believed by many that ethnic ambiguity may have worked in an individual's favor in his quest to realize the American dream of upward mobility during the 1950s and 1960s.

In contrast, from the late 1960s to the late 1970s there was little tolerance in the Black community for racial ambiguity; this was especially true on college campuses. During this decade, Black pride was expressed by even those students that had limited ties to the Black community, those who my contemporary Black students refer to as "miscellaneous Blacks."

Black Culture and Mobility

Today the concern is not so much the peer pressure to act and look "Black," as it is the personal pressure to feel an affinity and connectedness with the Black community given what is a real or perceived absence of experience. The costs, real or perceived, are also powerful influences on identity development. Kananur Chandra conducted research on Black student concerns in Black colleges and noted:

> The aspirations of the students revolve around a decent standard of living, employment, owning a house, self-development and modern conveniences (Chandra 1976).

The aspirations mentioned above do not differ from those held by Black adolescents and their parents in recent history. But does the development of a strong Black identity serve to compromise the opportunity to achieve material and professional gains? It is my belief that upwardly mobile Black males are experiencing identity conflicts based on past group experiences and future goals. Both past experiences and future goals may not be accurately or realistically understood. It is one's family and primary socializers who pass on accurate or inaccurate, realistic or unrealistic knowledge and expectations. The decline of the civil rights movement has brought further ethnic ambiguity since it played such an important role in Black identity development in the late 1960s. The importance of parents (or primary socializers) and civil rights activism to Black male cultural identity development cuts across all social classes.

Despite what some cloistered analysts say, it is most Black people's experience that racism is still a basis for social stratification and opportunity in the U.S. Individual needs and social identity cannot be effectively addressed without recognizing race.

Meyers and King makes the following recommendation in their article on mental health issues and the Black child. The research agenda proposed must be taken seriously if we are to in fact develop a basis for understanding the process of identity development in contemporary youth.

> New research efforts need to be mounted that are founded on the assumption that the black child is an entity independent of the white child, and not an entity to be known mainly by comparison. Questions about the basic nature of the black child—[what are] his/her coping styles, pressures and demands actually faced, pattern of life span development [and] crises and conflicts that interact to predict successful mastery over the vicissitudes of life—should be central to this research effort.
>
> Similarly, research is needed that concretely specifies the critical variables that define social class for blacks. These variables should be identified not as generalized criteria for all groups, but as specifically significant and meaningful to blacks (Meyers and King 1983).

Research by Dawkins (1981) suggest that social background variables have a stronger influence on occupational aspirations for Black males than any other factor. Dawkins further notes that educational factors were important in predicting educational aspirations, but not necessarily educational outcomes. By focusing on the educational and occupational aspirations of Black males, social class may be a significant factor in influencing occupational outcomes (distinct from aspirations). This raises questions about the influence of social class on self-esteem and how one identifies himself in the present and future context. I raise this point because I feel that high aspirations may be related not only to social class, but also to reinforcement from family members, educational institutions and social contacts (peer associations). What is crucial here is that Black cultural identity may be only optional. For many, having a Black identity may actually be counterproductive if one's goals in the mainstream require assimilating conflicting white values, beliefs and attitudes.

The idea that having a Black identity is detrimental to upward mobility is very evident among Black males who expressed concerns over mentioning their involvement in activities in the Black student community when applying for employment. This is a major debate among students with strong feelings on both sides of the issue: Should I or should I not appear Black in more of a sense than my skin color would define? The influence of past experience should not be ignored in the assessment of how an individual comes to actualize his identity, and how his Black identity will be internalized as a source of power and influence in advancing the causes that serve individual and community needs. The following quote highlights the student debate over Black identity and mobility.

> The Committed Achievers, but not the Activists, stood out for having had contact with more faculty outside the classroom, turning to faculty specifically for help in planning their future careers, finding these faculty contacts more helpful, belonging to more campus groups, holding more leadership positions on

> the campus, having had more experience in campus governance committees and groups concerned with educational policies, and having taken advantage of more campus events with a distinctively Black political perspective. Activism alone did not promote the integration of collective and individual achievement. Activism in a particular context did (Gurin and Epps 1975).

The perception is that the achievers (serious students) see cultivating a Black identity as optional and even detrimental, while the activists see themselves as the "real Blacks." In my experience this is a false distinction. Activists can and often are also achievers and achievers can also be activists. Individuals committed to activism are developing the strength and the tools to excel in higher education and life. Academic achievement is rarely compromised in the student leaders that I have worked with over the years. My main concern has been "overcommitment" which may result in burnout and frustration subsequently impacting academic performance.

The Black Experience and how it is perceived is significantly influenced by living in integrated communities. As some Blacks achieve middle class status, many leave their home community for jobs and education and end up living in some distant white suburb. This means a change in the racial makeup of the community and the schools. The children of these upwardly mobile parents now find themselves in the minority rather than the majority. This change means that these adolescents will see themselves reflected less in the school curriculum and in the social interest of their peers. This was described to me by one young man as the "biggest emotional downer I went through in life." He felt an immediate feeling of powerlessness. He went on to say that, although people around him were not hostile, he did have to function in a setting that was White and "do the White thing or nothing at all."

The impact of living in a White community is a concern for me regarding my own children. I put a great deal of effort into developing their Black library, taking them to major Black events and participating as actively as possible in their academic activities. I also take particular care to ensure that their interest in positive Black role models and historical figures is legitimized in school. Also a trip "home" (inner-city Los Angeles) does not hurt—I need that much worse than they do.

There is another smaller group of upwardly mobile young Blacks whose parents live in the ghetto, but have received their secondary education in schools located away from their home community. These schools may be public, private and, in some cases, exclusive preparatory schools. This group also has serious questions regarding the impact of the school versus the impact of the home and ghetto community. In contrast, students who live and have been educated in Black communities do not generally separate themselves from their culture and social identity. This was made clear to me by many of these students passing through my Afro-American Psychology courses over the years that they are in the class to get an academic perspective on Black life. They have the "identity thing" together and have no questions about who they are.

The impact of a Black cultural environment could well explain the process of identity that many of the students I speak about may have experienced. Jackson et al. wrote:

> Self-worth and self-conceptions are formed under the auspices of the family/primary group. In the homogeneous racial environment there are fewer occasions than in the heterogeneous environment for negative messages regarding group membership to directly impinge on personal identity development. Thus, the homogeneous environment can help to foster a high degree of individual compartmentalization. Once the development of self is established, integrating conceptions of one's relationship to the group and understanding the group's status in society can be achieved through exposure to images such as art, stories, history, and culture.

They further expand on the role of the family:

> The family's filtering of input from the large society is reduced as a broader range of experiences is encountered. As the minority individual gains more intergroup experience, however, the family has an increasing role in interpreting these experiences. This particular role is critical for maintaining the integrity of the already developed early personal identity as well as the developing conceptions of group identity (Jackson et al. 1981).

Based on earlier research, the role of the family is most crucial in identity development, particularly for Black males, because of the impact of social forces on decision-making and aspirations.

The challenge of identity development for biracial adolescents is of even greater concern. The number of biracial adolescents that I have come into contact with has increased over the years, although I have witnessed a decrease in their problems of identifying with the Black student community. I attribute my observation to the flexibility of racial identification within Black communities. It is personal adjustment rather than group identity issues which remain foremost for this growing population. Gibbs (1987) notes in her conclusions: "As these biracial children increase in the population, many will manage to achieve truly integrated identities; chronic identity conflicts, however, will continue to plague many. This latter group will pose a growing challenge to mental health practitioners in the twenty-first century."

White (1984) characterizes the period of adolescence as one of "choices and balance." Choices will become more difficult in the future if in fact a solid sense of belonging in American society is not realized. A fifteen-year-old today may not have the experience of standing on his front porch during the evening and watching his city ablaze due to racial conflict. Nor will he witness the violence and the murders of Blacks and others who carried on the struggle for racial equality and ask as I did, "What does this mean for me?" Racism is very much alive and possibly more covert and confusing for these young men. They too will demand a part in the American dream as a result of their educations.

Parents, educators, community and mental health professionals must take a proactive role in preparing Black male youth with the requisite skills necessary to survive and contribute to Black society. The requisite skills that have served to bring Black Americans through centuries of racial oppression include authenticity in experience, resilience, interrelatedness and kinship. These skills, which are only a few of those mentioned by White (1984), are the very qualities that are threatened when identity development in young Black males is lacking due to a loss of family and community-based historical influences.

The potential for the emergence of two Black communities based on those who do have and do not have a racial identity is a reality. The task for parents, educators and mental health professionals is to work to prevent this ideological chasm. Black men of the future with the most political, social and economic influence may be those that are the least committed and most lacking in the intellectual and ideological faculties necessary for moving the Black community into the twenty-first century.

References

Benson, S. 1981. *Ambiguous Ethnicity.* New York: Cambridge University Press.

Chandra, K. V. 1976. *Black Student Concerns in a Black College.* San Francisco: R. and E. Research Associates.

Cross, W. E. 1980. "Models of Psychological Nigrescence: A Literature Review," In R. Jones (ed.) *Black Psychology.* New York: Harper & Row Publishers.

Dawkins, M. P. 1981. "Mobility Aspirations of Black Adolescents: A comparison of Males and Females." *Adolescence.* 16,63.

Erikson, E. H. 1963. *Childhood and Society.* New York: W.W. Norton.

Gibbs, J. T. 1987. "Identity Marginality Issues in the Treatment of Biracial Adolescents." *American Journal of Orthopsychiatry.* 57,2.

Gurin, P. and E. G. Epps. 1975. *Black Consciousness, Identity, and Achievement.* New York: Wiley.

Jackson, James S. et al. 1981. "Group Identity Development Within Black Families," in Harriett P. McAdoo (ed.) *Black Families*. Beverly Hills: Sage Publications.

Meyers, H. F. and L. King. 1983. "Mental Health Issues in the Development of the Black American Child," in Gloria J. Powell (ed.) *Psychosocial Development in Minority Group Children*. New York: Brunner/Mazil, Inc.

Powell, G. J. 1985. "Self Concepts among Afro-American students in Racially Isolated Minority Schools: Some Regional Differences." *Journal of the American Academy of Child Psychiatry*. 24:2, 142149.

Thomas, C. 1971. Boys No More. Beverly Hills: Glencoe Press.

White, J. 1984. *The Psychology of Blacks*. Englewood Cliffs, NJ: Prentice Hall.

Chapter 15

Hurling Oppression: Overcoming Anomie and Self Hatred

James Moss

Power

The presently perceived expendability of Black males is a consequence of the white exercise of power. *Power* is the monopoly over options available to one group at the expense of one or more vulnerable groups. White males exercise controlling vetoes over the aspirations and choices of Black males in almost all competitive arenas of American life. Abundant evidence exists to deny any genetic factors to explain this phenomenon. Rather, a combination of historical and geopolitical forces serve to account for the depowering process that has occurred.

Depowerment is the employment of strategies directed at minimizing the options, choices and opportunities by the powerful over their less powerful competitors. In other words, whole groups of people do not depower themselves. They are victimized by those whose interests and resources assure their domination over those less favored. The objective of depowerment is to render powerless those seen as threatening to the maintenance of the status quo. *Powerlessness* is the functional absence of options in the struggle to attain parity with those in power. Innovative strategies, designed to redress the imbalance of power between the powerful and the powerless, lies at the core of the *empowerment* process—gaining control over one's own identity and well-being.

Where powerlessness becomes the usual rather than the unusual feature of human existence and efforts toward empowerment are consistently frustrated, a state of anomie will develop. This is true for individuals and groups historically and in the present. The struggle for power and against anomie is especially true for Black men and explains a good deal of Black male behavior.

Anomie

What most observers of Black behavior do not realize and take into account is that Black people are fully assimilated into American culture and have been for generations. Conditional assimilation has occurred even though Blacks have not been allowed to fully participate in American life. Blacks are striving to achieve the same cultural and personal goals as White Americans. With successful striving comes a sense of balance between cultural goals and individual or group satisfaction. Where cultural goals are frustrated, a state of anomie develops (Merton 1949). In the struggle against anomie and to attain power, Blacks have employed a variety of defensive mechanisms in order to physically and emotionally survive. The following are some of strategies the powerless employ in confronting power structures that appear to be unyielding.

Conformity

Oppressed minorities may sacrifice their cultural identities for the sake of blending in with the majority. In some cases, the oppressed so fully identify psychologically and behaviorally with their oppressors that little, if any, of their original group identity remains (Birmingham 1977; Frazier 1962; Johnson 1927). The powerless who "overconform" reject the notion of opposing either the means used by those in power to achieve their goals or the ends which the powerful have legitimized for the whole society (Bettleheim 1958). Examples are slaves who sided with their masters against other slaves and, more recently, Black neoconservatives who identify with the powerful even when those in power are clearly against Black people's interests.

Innovation

By relying on the strategy of "innovation" in order to empower themselves, the oppressed minority members retain their loyalty to the system, but oppose the second-class status assigned to them. Blacks have sought to overcome the stigma of second-class status by making recourse to ever-changing strategies in the hope that with each effort some new gains will be registered for the group. The gradual improvement in race relations for Blacks in the U.S., has resulted from both legal and extralegal struggles to ease the extent of their oppression in the U.S.

Ritualism

Where the power of oppression far outstrips the resources of the powerless, the latter may view resigning themselves to their fate as the better part of valor. Conscious of the privileges and rewards that go to those in power, the oppressed are convinced of the seeming impossibility of their ever achieving such status for themselves. The "learned helplessness" of the majority of Black American males, the political subjugation of Blacks in South Africa, and the caste discrimination of the Ainus in Japan are recent illustrations of the strategy of "ritualism" or resignation. This strategy serves as an escape from confronting the reality of limited options to effective societal change (Whitaker 1973; Moss 1986).

Retreatism

Retreatism is when the oppressed reject both the culturally approved goals and the legitimate means for achieving those goals. Individuals and groups who have experienced sustained periods of alienation within their society have chosen to or been required to be "in the society but not of it." The homeless, underclass Blacks and teenage Black youth are all populations in the U.S. whose existence on the periphery of the society appears as the only option open to them (Glasgow 1980; Moss 1982).

Separation

One reaction to powerlessness and anomie is to physically remove themselves from the environment of their oppression. No longer willing to subscribe to either the prevailing values of their society or their second-class status, they have elected to seek a social order more consonant with their beliefs and commitments. During slavery and since, some notable Blacks have sought to separate themselves both physically and psychologically from White society within and outside of the U.S.

Rebellion

If all else fails and there is no relief, even for a moment, from frustration and powerlessness, the powerless rebel. Black urban riots against ghetto conditions were classic examples of unorganized rebellions. Slave insurrections were cases of organized rebellion. And under both slavery and second-class citizenship there are countless cases of individual rebellions. The disproportionate number of Black men in prison is a measure of individual rebellion against the social order.

Theory and Process

When we consider the dimensions of power along with the various strategies Blacks have used for empowerment, we can see the African diasporic dilemma. There is a close relation between social structure organized to exclude Blacks from power, the resulting social psychology of oppression (powerlessness) which leads to anomie and Black strategies for survival and empowerment. The following is a model:

Social→ Structure	**Depowerment→**	Powerlesness→	Survival/ Empowerment
Slavery	White Violence	Anomie	Conformity
			Innovation
Jim Crow			Ritualism
Segregation	Racism		Retreatism
Dual Labor			Separation
			Rebellion

All of the social structures that Blacks have lived under in the New World have had as their goal either the exploitation of Blacks or their exclusion. This goal has been achieved through violence or a generalized belief in Black inferiority and subordination (racism). The consequences for Blacks have been powerlessness to achieve, frustration at every turn, and both group and personal alienation from meaningful participation in general society. Anomie in turn has energized the will toward empowerment which has been acted out in the six major strategies. The value of this model is that it keeps all of the components of Black subordination in view. We see history and social structure, social conditions and then strategies of accommodation and empowerment.

One of the main problems that oppressed people experience is conflict within the group. We have had no clear way to understand these conflicts in the context of either oppressive conditions or social structure. The above model provides that. Conflict among Blacks occurs largely around the selection and advocacy of appropriate empowerment strategies. Variations in the conditions of powerlessness due to differences in social structure or differences in the position Blacks have in society lead to different views of what are appropriate strategies of empowerment. Afro-American history is full of conflict between advocates of different group strategies. Also each major historic period in Colonial African, Afro-American, Afro-Caribbean and Afro-Brazilian history could be analyzed with this model. We could better understand variations in the behaviors of Black peoples in contemporary African and Afro-diaspora as well.

Historic Cases

The process by which western European social structures have depowered Blacks that in turn have led to anomie and efforts of empowerment and survival are apparent in history. The precolonial and preslave histories are so very important because they are the primary evidence that Black people are not culturally or inherently disposed to self-hatred and disorganization. Before slavery Africans lived in highly-developed social systems that had clearly defined and often complementary roles for men, women and children. Matrilineal descent gave a special status to women. It was noted that African queens have often ruled African tribes and among some African groups, women were active participants in discussions of public issues (Du Bois 1939). This was centuries before European women were given similar regard.

African families often combined with other African families to form political states, and when political rivalries threatened the unity of the state, larger villages and tribes were brought together in empires such as Mali and Songhay. A division of power between near and remote geographical regions served to effectively defuse efforts on the part of any single political entity to seek domination over another (Franklin 1956). Power was omnipresent in the traditional African community. Although it permeated every aspect of African life, power was diffused within the family and throughout the village and state. Ultimate power was external to the community and rested in the hands of the gods, spirits and departed ancestors. In this context, the person was important, but his significance was not allowed to overshadow or diminish the importance of the larger community. Again this sophisticated form of social organization and manner of controlling conflict centuries ago has still not been achieved by contemporary Western nations. Nor did African families and state management show evidence of inferior social organization, backwardness or self-hatred.

Slavery

Slavery introduced depowerment and anomie to Africans. All of the strategies Blacks have used to gain empowerment were developed then. The enslavement of Africans was a total institution and a four hundred year old laboratory of dehumanization and debasement. Those who survived did so because of their ability to creatively and conditionally struggle for empowerment. The belief that Africans only conformed to slavery is the result of merely looking at the surface. When slavery in the U.S., the Caribbean and Brazil are examined, any loopholes in the rules were exploited (innovation). Dance, song and religion took on multiple meanings (ritualism). In the *American Slave Narratives* former slaves spoke of times when they had to simply take the abuse and hope and wait for another opportunity to seek empowerment (retreatism).

Slaves ran away, escaping slavery completely (separation). Then there were insurrections—attempts to destroy the slave system. Strategies of empowerment were combined. The formation of the Seminole nation in present-day Florida was a case of separation and rebellion. Former slaves and Indians fought a guerrilla war with slavers. In Brazil the "Republic of Palmares" was formed by runaway slaves and lasted for sixty years. And then there was the successful Haitian rebellion in the Caribbean. Slavery and the years of racism after slavery have taken their toll on all Blacks. Each sex was singled out for particular treatment. While both sexes were exploited for their labor and sexuality, men were and still are a particular threat. In patriarchical societies such as Great Britian, Spain and Portugal it is the role of males to seek power and control. Slave leaders and later, Black community leaders have been men. The leaders of the rebellions and insurrections have been men. Black men are to this day viewed as more serious potential competitors with dominant white men. Putting particular emphasis on depowering Black men has been crucial to controlling Black people.

It is significant that racism is a relatively recent development which came out of late eighteenth century defenses of slavery against abolitionists, former slaves and others (Cox 1976). Racism is "a universal, behavioral system, whose generating force is power, and whose manifest objectives are the cultural, social stigmatizing and stereotyping of a whole people" (Moss 1986). Racism's significance is that it was not simply a justification of slavery, it was justification and a blueprint for the continued depowerment of Blacks and unfair and disproportionate empowerment of Whites, regardless of the social system. Racism is purposive, goal-orientated and contributive to the maintenance of the existing unjust social system. Walter Lippman once warned against "believing and then seeing," but for racism, this caution becomes a caveat. By their color, Blacks are seen as inferior in all important respects in relation to Whites.

Jim Crow

After slavery was abolished in 1883 in the Caribbean, in 1865 in the U.S., and in 1888 in Brazil, racism was incorporated in both the legal and extralegal mores throughout the entire fabric of American societies. Since 1865 racism has been both the justification and behavioral blueprint for continued subjugation of Blacks—depowerment. Plantation slavery has been replaced with an industrial wage economy and the industrial wage economy may be transforming into a post-industrial economy. But whatever the economy, the effects of racism have been consistent—continued depowerment and anomie for Blacks. Racism is in fact an ideological and behavioral more for continued psychological and physical violence of the older slave system against Blacks over one hundred years later. John Hope Franklin wrote:

> Beginning in 1870, Southerners enacted laws against intermarriage of the races in every state. Five years later, Tennessee adopted the first 'Jim Crow' law and the rest of the South rapidly fell in line. Negroes and Whites were separated in the trains, in depots and wharves. Toward the end of the century, the Negro was banned from White hotels, barber shops, restaurants and theaters . . . By 1885 most Southern states had laws requiring separate schools . . . and in 1896 the Supreme Court upheld segregation in its "separate but equal" doctrine set forth in Plessy vs. Ferguson (Franklin 1956).

Segregation was not simply an insult. It was a form of institutionalized violence. It was a daily reminder that you were considered inferior. And as in slavery, if you openly resisted you would be dealt with violently. The 214 lynchings at the turn of the century were a form of violent depowerment of not simply the victims. They were reminders to all other Blacks of what could happen to them if they "stepped out of place." Between 1882 and 1937 there were 5,112 lynchings; more than two-thirds were of Black men—reminders. In addition, these lynchings were superseded by what Oliver Cox described as "white punitive riots." Throughout this period White mobs massively attacked whole Black communities to intimidate, to depower, to roll back any gains and to keep them in their "inferior" place.

The Civil Rights Movement

Since slavery Blacks have sought empowerment in whatever way they could. The nonviolent civil rights movement of the 1960s was an innovative response. Prior to television and its ability to show events in one place all over the world, Dr. Martin Luther King Jr.'s nonviolent tactics would have been suicidal—invitations to more punitive white rioting and lynchings. But exposure of such obvious injustices led to change and toward empowering Blacks in the South. But what was not changed was the basic racism among

Whites which made slavery and Jim Crow possible and manifest in the first place.

> Why do white people seem to find it difficult to understand that the Negro is sick and tired of having reluctantly parceled out to him those rights and privileges which all others receive upon birth or entry into America? I never cease to wonder at the amazing presumption of much of white society, assuming that they have the right to bargain with the Negro for his freedom. This continued arrogant ladling out of pieces of the rights of citizenship has begun to generate a fury in the Negro. What the Negro wants—and will not stop until he gets—is absolute and unqualified freedom and equality, here in this land of his birth, and not in Africa or in some other imaginary state (King 1968,36).

Blacks have never had a complete consensus on what is the most appropriate response to White depowerment and their condition of powerlessness and anomie. During slavery Blacks who believed conformity, ritual or retreat were the only possible reactions to their condition were threatened by those who plotted separation and rebellion. The famous W.E.B. Du Bois and Booker T. Washington debate at the turn of the century was over the merits of innovation and rebellion versus conformity and retreatism as the proper response to Jim Crow. There were conflicts within the civil rights movement initially between Martin Luther King, Jr. (innovation-rebellion) and Roy Wilkins (conformity), and then between King, Wilkins, Whitney Young and the Black Power advocates such as Stokely Carmichael (separation-rebellion).

The Present

The innovative strategy of nonviolence for empowerment was able to gain concessions in public accommodations and voting rights in the South. It was not very effective for addressing the economic racism and segregation of the North. Despite greater personal freedoms, the intensity of depowerment and anomie were very apparent in the ghetto riots (rebellions) of the 1960s. Alienation and powerlessness were also apparent in the rise of the Black Muslims (separatism), Black Liberation, urban-based Black Power, Black cultural nationalism, Black students unions, Black studies, and Black Panthers movements. All of these movements had elements of ritualism, retreatism, separatism and rebellion within them. The demise of these movements does not mean that racism is no longer the operative blue-print for Black depowerment. The demise of these movements means that Blacks now face anomie, alienation and the violence of racism as individuals and without a group framework for understanding their plight and for resistance.

The individualization of Black oppression is very apparent, especially in the lives of Black men. The evidence includes the high incidence of drug abuse, crime, Black-on-Black murder, imprisonment, suicide and mental illness. The breakdown of Black families and communities must also be included. These events are inconsistent with the empowerment strategies of conformity, innovation, separatism and rebellion. To kill Blacks is also inconsistent with retreatism and ritualism. What we now have in Black American life is disorganization and disarray around group responses to racism. As a consequence, the experiences of depowerment, powerlessness, alienation and anomie have fallen to the individual level to understand, interpret and resist. It is a wonder that Black self-destruction is not greater and more rapid. As a psychoanalyst, I bear witness to the imposed psychic violence and resulting destruction Black men are now struggling with.

Psychic Violence

Black women and Black men, especially, are under attack as individuals and members of the race—even when identification with the latter is rejected. The psychological attacks come as innuendos, implied meanings, being treated impersonally, and being looked over and through as if you were invisible. It is being insulted and not knowing whether it is because of you personally or because you are Black. It is to be always suspect, never good enough and the odd man out. It is to be stereotyped and politely reminded "who you are." And if you protest, it is to be told that you are too sensitive or that everyone (Whites) is treated like this as well. Dr. Alvin Poussaint described a personal experience that is an example of what Black men regularly experience in some small measure.

> Once last year as I was leaving my office in Jackson, Mississippi, with my Negro secretary, a white policeman yelled, "Hey boy come here!" Somewhat bothered, I retorted: "I'm no boy." He then rushed at me, inflamed, and stood towering over me, snorting, "What d'ja say, boy?" Quickly, he frisked me and demanded "What's your name boy?" Frightened, I replied, "Dr. Poussaint; I'm a physician." He angrily chuckled and hissed, "What's your first name, boy?" When I hesitated, he assumed a threatening stance and clenched his fists. As my heart palpitated, I muttered in profound humiliation, "Alvin." He continued his psychological brutality, bellowing, "Alvin, the next time I call you, you come right away, you hear?" I hesitated. "You hear me, boy?" My voice trembling with helplessness, but following my instincts of preservation, I murmured, "Yes, sir."
>
> Now fully satisfied that I had performed and acquiesced to my "boy status", he dismissed me with, "Now boy, go on and get out of here, or next time we'll take you for a little ride down to the station house!" No amount of self-love could have salvaged my pride or preserved my integrity. In fact, the slightest show of self-respect or resistance might have cost me my life. For the moment my manhood had been ripped from me.

Dr. Poussaint went on to explain that this event took

place in front of a Black woman, in public view for everyone to see.

And regardless of his status, he was reminded that no Black man was as good as any White man. He was helpless and powerless to do anything but conform and internalize his rage and hatred. This same incident is played out every day. But the policeman is now a bank, an employer, the unemployment office, the welfare agency, White coworkers, the corporate culture, the crack cocaine distributors, the union and even the White bum on the street. Whole Black communities are held hostage to impersonal and powerful White institutions—banks, real estate speculators, organized crime and the stigma of being regarded as "inferior."

Even the Black middle class members who have "escaped" the ghetto are held up as examples of America's fairness to those who work hard. The Black middle class male and his family may be victims of "false class-consciousness"—perceiving themselves to belong to a class that cannot be supported or sustained in the market place. The vulnerability, frustration and disillusionment of the Black middle-class may be closer to that of their less fortunate brothers than they may be willing to recognize or acknowledge.

The unwillingness of some young Blacks to experience common cause with their less affluent peers was noted by the author recently in talking with a group of Black students at a college that draws its population mostly from the middle class. These young Blacks are losing sight of the conditions of the oppressed majority and find little about them with which to identify—not even their color. In my practice as a psychoanalyst, I am seeing more and more of these young Black men in their thirties and forties coming into treatment to deal with issues around their racial identity, anger, isolation and anomie. The fragility of the middle-class Black male's identity is seen in the following comment by one of them: "As a Black, you can have a house in Sag Harbor, you can have an IRA, you can have all the material things, but you still can't walk through Howard Beach" (New York Times 1987,28).

The meaning here is not simply that this young man cannot walk through Howard Beach. It is never knowing, regardless of where you are, when and if you will be insulted, humiliated, dehumanized. It is to have destroyed in some unanticipated way what little security and progress you have made.

Conclusion

This country was created out of the confrontation of the common man with the arbitrary power of the Crown of England and subsequently inspired by the democratic outcome of the French Revolution. It is striking to find such a process of liberation so anathema and repulsive when advocated by others. Throughout the history of the Black man in this country, laissez-faire capitalism and its subordination of all human needs to the requirement for maximizing profits dooms the Black man to the visible, permanent status of the excluded. By all reckoning, his is the longest, most enduring population confined to the "surplus labor reserve" and to experience anomie.

To be excluded is to be denied worth and value by those holding the power to allocate resources. It can hardly be expected that those rejected and excluded by the arbitrary dictates of the operation of the economic market can through their own efforts force their way into a system closed to them. A caveat of power is that it rarely voluntarily abrogates itself to others. For the Black man the American social system remains closed. A token few are permitted "in" to justify the appearance that the structure is open and egalitarian. But the maintenance of the status quo with white supremacy remains the order of the day (Moss 1960). And that means most Blacks will be not only relegated to the ghetto, but will be left to continue experiencing intense alienation, anomie and self-hatred.

Separate areas or ghettos fit amazingly well into what Marx referred to as the "surplus labor reserve." The fact that the plantation colonial society and now Black ghettos serve the purpose of capitalism has not been lost on a number of Black leaders. In this observation, their alienation is apparent as well. W.E.B. Du Bois was for a long time a socialist, and at the time of his death he was a member of the Communist Party. Both A. Philip Randolph and Bayard Rustin had socialist orientations and connections (Johnson 1965). Breitman indicated that after his visit to Mecca, Malcolm X turned toward socialism (1966). And the FBI hounded Martin Luther King, Jr. for allowing a professed socialist and alleged communist to actively work with the Southern Christian Leadership Conference (Garrow 1986). Finally, Paul Robeson, lived for many years in the Soviet Union and received one of its highest awards.

Anomie is also apparent when we consider the numerous Blacks who have sought political and cultural freedom through emigration to Europe and elsewhere. The various colonization efforts of Black Americans to establish separate states and institutions within the U.S. comes out of the same powerlessness. Can Blacks be expected to conform, to innovate, to be ritualistic, to retreat, to separate and to rebel forever? No amount of psychotherapy can help Black men adjust to an inherently inhuman and alienating condition which singles them out for both physical and psychological violence—powerlessness.

If the Black male is an endangered species, most have engaged this status with patience, courage and resiliency. Those of us in the mental health profession know that our patients did not impose their emotional deficits upon themselves. They are the product of the fragility of the individual and cultural constraints that inhibit their ability to "become all that they are capable of becoming." The Black male has historically demonstrated that given the entitlements accorded to all others in society, he is fully capable of contributing to the process of his own self-empowerment. American society must allow him to do just that.

References

Bettleheim, B. 1958. "Individual and Man's Behavior in Extreme Situations" in E.E. Maccoby et al. (eds.) *Readings in Social Psychology.* New York: Holt.

Birmingham, S. 1977. "Strivers Row." *New York Magazine*. May 27. pp. 30-35.

Breitman, C. 1966. *The Last Year of Malcolm X*. New York: Alfred A. Knopf.

Cox, O. 1976. *Race Relations: Elements and Dynamics*. Detroit: Wayne State University.

Du Bois, W.E.B. 1939. *Black Folks: Then and Now*. New York: Holt.

Franklin, J.H. 1956. *From Slavery to Freedom*. New York: Alfred A. Knopf.

Frazier, E.F. 1962. *The Black Bourgeoisie*. New York: Collier.

Garrow, D.J. 1986. *Bearing The Cross*. New York: Morrow.

Glasgow, D.G. 1980. *The Black Underclass*. San Francisco: JosseyBass.

Johnson, J.W. 1927. *The Autobiography of an Ex-Colored Man*. Garden City, N.Y.: Garden City Publishing Company.

Johnson, O. 1965. "Marxism and The Negro Freedom Struggle." *Human Relations*. 13:1, 21-39.

King, M.L. 1968. *The Wisdom of Martin Luther King*. New York: Lancer.

Merton, R.K. 1949. *Social Theory and Social Structure*. Glencoe: Free Press.

Moss, J. 1960. "Currents of Change in American Race Relations." *British Journal of Sociology*. 11, 232-234.

Moss, J. 1982. "Unemployment Among Black Youth: A Policy Dilemma." *Social Work*. 27:1, 47-52.

Moss, J. 1986. "Power and Powerlessness: Some Implications for Social Work Practice." Unpublished.

The New York Times. 1987. "New York's Racial Paradox: Amid Progress, Growing Tension." March 29.

Whitaker, B. 1973. *The Fourth World: Victims of Group Oppression*. New York: Schocken.

Chapter 16

The Literary Empowerment of Black Male Youth

Daphne Muse

THERE IS NO GREATER TOOL OF EMPOWERMENT than the constantly nurtured, intellectually expanded, culturally enriched, and spiritually maintained mind. For more than two centuries, Black authors throughout the world have created books as one of the primary sources of that empowerment. Through the adaptation of legends and folktales, the rendering of new experiences, the writing of magnificent biographies, the culling of intricate mysteries, Charlemae Rollins, W.E.B. Du Bois, Countee Cullen, Jessie Fauset, Arna Bontemps, and Shirley Graham DuBois established a precious literary legacy for us. And contemporary authors like Alice Walker, James Baldwin, Eloise Greenfield, Virginia Hamilton, Walter Dean Myers, John Steptoe and Lucille Clifton have continued this often ignored but incredibly endowed legacy.

Until the late sixties, the existence of Black children's literature, though published since the late nineteenth century, remained relatively unknown. And the children's works that major scholars like Du Bois—who along with Jessie Fauset wrote, edited and published *The Brownies Books* (a children's magazine) from 1922-24—remains almost totally obscure. Along with some of the other revolutionary sweeps that began in the late sixties and moved into the early seventies, there was a virtual explosion in children's literature. Though many aspects of that revolution gained high visibility, far too few were directly impacted by the dawning of a literary explosion whose sounds have been muted by television, and gratuitous violence. But this explosion has changed the tone, tenor and character of all children's literature and turned many of the "classics" on their heads.

But those who did feel the effects of these books hail the achievements of these authors and hold dear the impact they have had on their lives. Harrison Simms is the codirector of the Oakland Men's Project, a community-based organization that addresses the issue of male violence in everyday family, school, work and community life. Simms fondly recalls, as a young man, a steady literary diet of Baldwin, Hughes, Lester and Braithwaite. "I had a passion for characters named Jesse B. Simple, Malcolm Little, folklore that spoke of conjure women and spider tales; and poems that promised a vital future.

"While I was growing up in Cincinnati, Langston Hughes was especially a giant for me. He wrote of real people in a real world with feelings that ran from the extraordinary to the most mundane. I have gotten through some of my life's most difficult times because their words resounded in my mind and helped to ground me," notes Simms. So taken was Simms by Baldwin's *The Fire Next Time,* he still readily quotes from the novel. "I remember every passage of that book. And Baldwin's death made me think about reading the novel again."

As the father of a nineteen-year-old and a five-year-old, Simms has very strong feelings about reading to his children. "I think one of the crucial losses Black youth have suffered is not being read to on a regular basis. When that doesn't happen, the door of intellectual inquisitiveness never opens. I want to see those doors opened along with the social and economic doors that are slowly opening up," Simms says pensively.

Scholars, educators, counselors, pediatricians and parents themselves have noted the fact that a real bonding takes place when you read to children. It creates a comforting vehicle for asking questions and it allows children to see how the complex and sometimes mysteriously interesting aspects of life are addressed either metaphorically or realistically.

According to Dr. William Smith, an Oakland-based psychologist, "Reading, especially the reading by a parent to a child is a real interpersonal event. Apart from what is being read, it seems to me that a lot of parents could make reading more exciting and subsequently strengthen the relationship with the child even more." But when asked what he might recommend for Black teenage males, he hesitated and said, "I really don't know what's out there to recommend." Smith notes that books didn't really begin to affect his life until he was in college. "*Native Son* was certainly an important book for me. It helped me put the civil rights movement in perspective."

When asked if he would like to see himself as a child in a book, Smith pauses to think and then snickers. You know, I would want to be included in an upbeat adventure story in which there was a certain kind of order, stability and a family. But there would also be change and a certain amount of danger. Oh, and I would have to wear sunglasses. When I was growing up, my dad wouldn't let me wear sunglasses because he said it was dangerous and the police were always on the lookout for Black boys and men with sunglasses on."

Four year old Elijah Dessisso's literary diet is just as solid and diverse as his nutritional diet. "Sometimes I read by myself to be by myself and with myself and get to know myself," Elijah says with a reassuring smile. His parents began reading to him not long after he was born and at four, he has a very distinct sense of what he likes to read and why. King Shabazz and Toni Polito from Lucille Clifton's *The Boy Who Didn't Believe in Spring* are some of his favorite characters. In the middle of a vacant forgotten lot, King Shabazz discovers spring in the form of a flower bursting through the rubble-cluttered lot. He invites his friend Toni to join him in sharing in the moment of that discovery.

While Elijah diligently reads books that are culturally specific, he diversifies his literary diet with comic books, traditional tales and all kinds of fantasies that children so eagerly attach themselves to. When asked what his favorite books were he said, "The books I like the most make me think about applesauce and transformers." He pointed to his select pile which included a range of traditional and culturally specifically stories. The stack was topped by Virginia Hamilton's collection of folktales *The People Could Fly.* And, his mom confirms that he loves applesauce and transformers more than anything in life.

Malik Wilson is a ten year old living in Ann Arbor, Michigan. He's been involved in his school's battle of the books program and looks forward to reading even more of the big boys' books. This year he has read sixteen short novels and four biographies. "I really like *Charlie and the Chocolate Factory, MC Higgins The Great* and *The Planet of Junior Brown.* I really like novels and biographies and especially like to read books about Native American and Black people. The last Native American book, *The Indian in the Cupboard,* was problematic," he states with a voice of both maturity and authority.

"But I don't just read for school or my parents. I read for pleasure too. If I could write a children's book right now, I'd write a book about a boy in elementary school who is being neglected and nobody likes him or cares about what he thinks about things," remarks Malik insightfully. "The books I've read have taught me so much about the civil rights movement and times that once were."

In recent years, the research clearly points to the critical importance of cultural literacy. Researchers and educators like E.D. Hirsch, Jr., Dr. Wade Nobles and Dr. Joyce King, while underscoring the importance of functional literacy, have produced conclusive evidence that students read more fluently and with greater understanding when they have background knowledge of the past and a sense of the present.

Dr. Nobles, the director of the Institute for the Advanced Study of Black Family Life and Culture, is a strong believer in the affirmation of who we are as a people and has put tremendous time and energy into bringing to young Black people a basic understanding of the cultural and intellectual underpinnings of our peoplehood. Developing historical sketches from research, adult, and young adult fiction, Nobles has conducted workshops focusing on Black male teenagers with the objective of having them look at the lives of well known leaders to point out how they too have had to struggle with many of life's day-to-day issues. Nobles is tremendously effective in demystifying the lives of our leaders and pointing out the potential that exists in the young people he sometimes works with and bases his research on.

Dr. Joyce King, who also serves as a curriculum consultant for the California State Department of Education, is quick to point out that cultural literacy is a critical component of intellectual breadth. Though there are things that are indeed universal, there are also things that are culturally specific.

And, it is those very specifics that are essential for ongoing empowerment of Black people. King has played a key role in the cultural diversification of the curriculum for the state of California. "Our work has created the potential for more input from minority authors into the curriculum offerings." But unlike California, most states still have gaping holes in their curricula when it comes to addressing both the cultural and intellectual diversity of its citizens.

According to booksellers across the nation, major publishers and the Association of Booksellers for Children, since 1968 children's books have become one of the hottest sellers in the industry. But according to award-winning author Eloise Greenfield, Black authors still have to struggle to get their books published. Greenfield, who has a solid, twenty-year record in the field, says, "We know the potential these books have for redirecting our youth. For the most part, these publishers rate a zero on the social consciousness scale."

Though most of her books are written with children between the ages of 5-11 in mind, many of Greenfield's characters are teenagers. There's Reggie in *Honey, I Love* who thinks he's Kareem and not somebody's brother. And there's Larry, Genny's stabilizing and rather wise brother in *Talk About a Family.* He's due to return from the army soon and Genny has pinned her hopes on him to serve as a healer for some real family conflict.

Not only is Greenfield an insightful writer, but she's a excellent chronicler of familial transitions and all of her books realistically deal with the myriad of complexities that exist in all families. She was one of the first children's authors to compassionately and correctly include physically disabled children in her books. Both *Alesia* and *Darlene* have disabled characters as the protagonists. *Alesia* is an especially poignant book for young Black males because it undercuts stereotypes related to disability, social acceptability and sexism.

Though Greenfield writes on universal themes from a culturally specific perspective, she firmly states that "Children's books should also point the way toward progress as humans; progress that frees people from the kinds of restrictions imposed by racism, sexism and classism."

Illustrator Tom Feelings renders some of the most mystically powerful and realistic images of Black people of any contemporary illustrator. His work reflects the pride, intellect, anger and hope that swell within the our youth. His comprehensive illustrations of slavery tell of that "holocaust" in ways as compellingly as W.E.B. DuBois. He is currently at work on a picture book for teenagers. "Along with the slavery book I've been working on for several years now, this book is probably one of the most important I've ever done," states Feelings with the firmness of commitment resounding in his voice. "I see the need to challenge the spirit of young Black people and show them that the cynicism can be redirected and the truth faced without despair."

"I want to see all the feelings housed within the souls of our youth expressed," says Feelings with unwavering conviction. "Whether it's despair, cynicism or rage, whether it's yearnings and longings for compassion, the need for understanding or the joy of accomplishment. Whatever that range of feelings encompasses, I want it to put the readers in touch with all their feelings. I also want to move through the other side to a better sense of self-esteem. The vestiges of slavery are still very much with us and we're talking about people who look at themselves under the heavy weight of that history and continue to see themselves as ugly."

"People constantly urge and encourage me to get my work in the Metropolitan Museum. But believe me, it is more important for me to put my work into the hearts and minds of young Black people, thereby endearing them to themselves, than it is to put it in the Metropolitan Museum. My mom gave me the freedom to use my imagination and I want my work to help them do the same," states Feelings adamantly.

Not only is it important for parents, educators, teachers, pediatricians, counselors and other professionals to become aware of this richly engaging body of literature, but it is just as important for them to read and question it as well. Many of the books written by Virginia Hamilton, Walter Dean Myers, Eloise Greenfield, Alexis Deveaux, Langston Hughes and Sharon Bell-Mathis are splendidly funny, courageously reflective, poignantly tragic and infinitely wise in their characterizations and content.

Reading often erases limitations in life, and what was once a day dream can eventually manifest itself as a reality. Biographies of people like Fannie Lou Hamer, W.E.B. Du Bois, Benjamin Banneker and Katherine Dunham are real proof of that. Everyone should be encouraged to dream their own dreams.

But for many of this nation's sweet-faced, bright-minded boys and emerging young men filled with violence, dreaming their own dreams has yet to dawn upon them because values are being imposed upon them that wreak havoc with the very fiber of their souls. Gangs become their community while torture and murder are the only vehicles they know how to use for expressing their anger, rage and lack of empowerment. For them, touching the larger world, working through the despair and arriving on the other side of hope seems as remote as walking to Mars on a banana leaf crutch.

But there were often times when Malcolm X, Anthony Burns, Nat Turner, Sojouner Truth, Jesse Jackson, and Harriet Tubman and others felt the same way. The fact that all of these people rose up out of the ashes of adversity and marched forth to the tune of hope can serve as active, realistic role models for these tormented and dejected spirits.

Seventeen year old Damari Drumright will never forget the impact *The Autobiography of Malcolm X* had on his life. "I was stunned, inspired, enraged and then somehow spiritually soothed. That book has been one of the most powerful experiences in my life and I can see myself reading it over and over again when the need arises to better understand and deal with so many things I don't understand. If he were still alive, he could bring so much understanding and reassurance to so many people," says Drumright.

Over the past twenty years, *The Autobiography of Malcolm X* seems to be one of the books most widely read by young boys and men in the Black community. From pimps to prisoners and preachers, they all extol and appreciate the virtues and power of this brilliant and compassionate man.

A young man in prison once told me that the fact the autobiography chronicles Malcolm's growth from "his out-of-his-criminal mind into a more loving and embracing mind was what gripped his soul the most. I saw how he did it and it wasn't miracle work. I know it's my own growth and hard work that will get me out and keep me out of prison. And I can't wait to read this book to my thirteen year old son."

"I'm just beginning to really read," says fifteen year old Lamont Curry. "I didn't think I could get excited about reading, but I just finished reading *Catcher in the Rye, Native Son* and *Grapes of Wrath*. I'm just learning about stuff and it's making me think and I'm a little scared by some of it but I'm excited too. My parents leaned on me for a long time too. I just never thought a book could excite me."

Not all the literature is great or even good. And there seems to be a tendency to rewrite the same stories. Children's books and stories about Martin Luther King, Jr. abound. Though Dr. King certainly was eloquent, brilliant and one of the major leaders of the twentieth century, we have yet to write the witty, historically relevant or compassionate stories of the scores of ordinary and unsung heroes and heroines, people who improve the quality of our lives in humanistic, spiritual and material ways.

Virginia Hamilton, Langston Hughes, Eloise Greenfield, W.E.B. Du Bois, Walter Dean Myers and scores of others have established a vital literary legacy for our children; let's celebrate that legacy by passing it on. And let us pass on creative as well as inspiring ways for our young people to become involved with this legacy. In conjunction with prison sentences, sentence our youth to literacy as an incentive for cutting the prison or probation time. Mandate that literacy be a requirement for completing probation.

None of us have led simple, uncomplicated lives, and the more these young men can read about others who have dealt with the racist and other obstructionist obstacles placed on life's path, the more they can begin to have concrete role models that take them from despair to hope.

Sources and References

Scores of biographies written of creative, famous and community-based Black leaders have been written over the past forty years. Many of them focus on famous athletes, entertainers, inventors, scholars and politicians, including Paul Robeson, Jackie Robinson, Rosa Parks, Katherine Dunham, Langston Hughes, Jesse Jackson, Stevie Wonder, Dr. J, Frederick Douglass, George Washington Carver, Fannie Lou Hamer, children involved in the civil rights movement and many others, available in most public libraries.

In those public libraries, at rummage sales and in thrift stores, some of the world's greatest literary treasures can be found. Even some supermarkets are beginning to stock children's books that encompass the Black Experience. And remember, many bookstores have readings and invite the public to meet the authors and illustrators. Check with your local bookstore about such events.

But there is one book that you don't even have to leave home to find: your family photo album. Filled with stories, photographs and precious moments of generations of people, this treasure can often be the jumping-off point for understanding more about your own life through the lives of others with whom you are familially connected. Great pleasure and amazing insights as well as family history can be uncovered by sitting down and discussing the photos in these albums. You can join with your family in writing stories to match the photographs or making up stories about those members of your family about whom you know little or nothing. And keep in mind that every family is culturally, socially and economically diverse. We all have "characters" in our families, some of whom are more colorful than others.

With solid grounding in cultural literacy, children and young adults should be encouraged to move into the larger realm of world literature in order to have an even stronger sense of themselves in juxtaposition with the rest of the world. Though this is a culturally specific bibliography, it should only serve as a reference point for an even broader literary and life-enriching experience.

Books for Teenage Boys to Read to Younger Children

1. *A Guide to Resources for Black Boys*—Daphne Muse, contributor (National Black Child Development Institute, Washington, D.C., 1988). This guide includes a range of titles appropriate for boys and young men between the ages of birth and 18.
2. *Afro-Bets ABC Book*—Cheryl Willis Hudson (New Jersey, 1987). Using both imaginative and culturally intriguing blends, the author has developed a series of books that teach basic skills while conveying historical information and cultural traditions.
3. *Afro-Bets 123 Book*—Cheryl Willis Hudson (Just Us Books, New Jersey, 1987).
4. *Bubbles*—Eliose Greenfield (Drum and Spear Press, Washington, D.C., 1971). This story sensitively portrays the trying and sometimes lonely experience a young boy encounters when he wants to share the fact that he has learned how to read.
5. *Daddy is a Monster . . . Sometimes*—John Steptoe (Lippincott, New York, 1980). These spirited reminiscences of two children take a real look at anger and how it brings out the monster in their daddy.
6. *Everett Anderson's Goodbye*—Lucille Clifton; illustrated by Ann Grifalconi (Holt, Rinehart and Winston, (New York 1983). This story is about a young boy yearning for his father when he is confronted with the realities of death by moving through the five stages of grief: denial, anger, bargaining, depression and acceptance. He comes to

realize that death cannot stop the love he has for his father.

7. *Folktales of the Yoruba People*—Angela Fantanez de Fleming (Visual Arts Research and Resource Center, 1987). These are longstanding, imaginatively woven tales that speak to the spiritual and intellectual traditions of a proud, West African people.
8. *Justin and the Best Biscuits in the World*—Mildred Pitts; illustrated by Catherine Stock (Lothrop, Lee Shepard, 1986). Ten-year-old Justin believes cleaning up his room and cooking are women's work. He longs for a brother. Justin's beloved grandpa comes to visit and takes Justin home with him. There Justin learns that grandpa knows a thing or two about women's work. He makes the best biscuits in the world and we are anxious to find out if grandpa's biscuits can win at the bake-off contest during the annual rodeo.
9. *My Daddy Don't Go To Work*—Madeena Spray Nolan (Carol Rhoda Books, 1978). The book presents a loving family caught up in a situation that reveals the strength of their relationships. Written with insight and empathy, it is about an urban Black family dealing with the father's unemployment.
10. *The Boy Who Didn't Believe in Spring*—Lucille Clifton (Viking, New York, 1973). King Shabazz and his friend Tony revel in the joy of finding spring in the midst of a cluttered lot in the heart of New York City. A Spanish version of this book is also available.
11. *Who Looks at Me*—June Jordan; illustrated with twenty-seven paintings by artists including Romare Bearden and Andrew Wyeth. (Dial, New York 1969). The eloquence of this poem is reinforced by works of some of the world's greatest artists.

Imaginative and Fun Books for Teenage Boys

1. *And I Must Hurry for the Sea Is Coming In*—George Mendoza (Prentice Hall, 1971). A young Black boy is pictured as the masterful captain of a large, beautiful sailboat. The surprise ending points to the fact that the boy is really sailing a toy boat in a fire hydrant.
2. *Anthony Burns: The Defeat and Triumph of a Fugitive Slave*—Virginia Hamilton (Knopf, 1988). Based on court records, newspaper articles and other primary sources, Hamilton has written a compelling novel about a twenty-year-old man who fled from Virginia to Boston and was captured under the Fugitive Slave Acts. Violent riots shook Boston during the trial and federal troops were called in to guard the streets. The novel portrays Burns as a child on the plantation, as a slave desperate for freedom, as a prisoner struggling to maintain his faith in humanity, and as a short-lived free man.
3. *Breadsticks and Blessing Places*—Candy Dawson Boyd (Macmillan 1985). 12-year-old Antoinette Doublass is having difficult with word problems and worries that she will not pass the entrance tests for MLK Academy, a public prep school, that she yearns to attend. Then she loses one of her best friends. What did it matter to make plans when death could just snatch your life away?
4. *Childtimes*—Eloise Greenfield and Lessie Jones Little; illustrated by Jerry Pinkney (Crowell 1979). This is a three-generation memoir in which mother, daughter and grand daughter tell of their childhoods which they poetically call childtimes.
5. *Fast Sam, Cool Clyde and Stuff*—Walter Dean Myers (Viking, 1975). This story recounts the adolescent years of a Black boy in New York City and his close-knit group of supportive friends. It destroys many stereotypes about young blacks in urban environments.
6. *Great Gittin' Up in the Morning: A Biography of Denmark Vesey*—John Oliver Killens (Doubleday 1972). This is the biography of a free Black man in Charleston, South Carolina, who was destined to lead a major slave rebel-

lion. As it breathes with the passion of Vessey's commitment, the reader also gets a real sense of the intensity of slavery.

7. *Just Us Women*—Jeannette Caines; illustrated by Pat Cummings (Harper and Row, 1982). This is a wonderful story that clearly speaks to the bonding that goes on between women. Aunt Martha and her niece jump up one Saturday morning and hop in the car for a ride to North Carolina. On the way, they explore great roadside places and conversation.
8. *Kaffir Boy: The True Story of a Black Youth's Coming of Age in Apartheid South Africa*—Mark Mathabane (MacMillian, New York 1986). The autobiography of Mark Mathabane graphically portrays his daily struggles to maintain human dignity amid brutal racial hatred. His personal courage is a testimony that what one needs to survive subhuman conditions is an indomitable will not only to survive but to triumph. One also needs an unshakeable belief in one's own worth.
9. *Listen for the Fig Tree*—Sharon Bell Mathis (Viking Press, 1972). A compelling story about a blind teenage girl whose independent spirit enables her to shoulder inordinate responsibilities. The novel gives excellent portrayals of the girl and several men including her father (who is murdered early on in the novel), her "boyfriend," and a gay neighbor who comes to her aid during a rape attempt.
10. *Little Man, Little Man*—James Baldwin and Yoran Cazac (Dial Press, 1975). Authored by one of America's most prolific writers, this is the story of two young boys, W.T. and T.J., coming of age in Harlem. The parallels in this novel are truly similar to the dilemmas and complexities many urban youth face in growing up.
11. *To Be a Slave*—Julius Lester; illustrated by Tom Feelings (Scholastic Books 1986). These first-hand accounts are written from interviews with former slaves.
12. *Walk Together Children: Black American Spirituals,* selected and illustrated by Ashly Bryan (Atheneum, New York 1975). Here are twenty-four spirituals, including "Let Us Break Bread Together on Our Knees" and "Go Tell it on

the Mountain," accompanied by woodcuts.

13. *Yellow Bird and Me*—Joyce Jansen (Clarion Books, 1986). In this sequel to The Gift Giver, Doris is annoyed by Yellow Bird, a boy with dyslexia and his dependence upon her for friendship and reading assistance. As they both cope with Ms. Baker, an insensitive teacher, Doris learns that she may need Yellow Bird, too.

Chapter 17

Encouraging Constructive Parenting Through Humane Portrayals of Black Fathers

(or Rock Steady—

Let's Call this Song Exactly What It Is)

Peter Harris

> Send me some hair of the children's hair in a separate paper with their names on the paper . . . You know how I am about my children. You know I am one man that do love my children . . . —Unidentified enslaved African-American man writing to his wife who'd been sold from him before the Civil War (from Herbert Gutman's *The Black Family in Slavery and Freedom,* 1720-1925)

IN 1971, ARETHA FRANKLIN'S SONG "Rock Steady" was a Top Ten hit. This spring, the Whispers broke-back bad and smokin' with their own song called "Rock Steady." The lyrics are different, yet that term—"Rock Steady"—means the same in both songs, means the same, in fact, whenever any brother or sister sings or says it. "Rock Steady" means to be locked in the groove, on the case, right on and doin' the do like you supposed to do.

I love how these two songs, sixteen years apart, connect generations, rekindle memories of special communion and express a unifying vibe. Black fathers, as the quote opening my remarks illustrates, have a tradition of Rock Steady. The Black father who asked for his children's hair is what I like to call a genetic dancer, a father who combines responsibility with dedication and the imagination to become an artist. Genetic Dancers Rock Steady to music that is silent to the naked ear and invisible to the open eye.

All Black fathers, contrary to stated or unstated public opinion, are Genetic Dancers, either for real or within the realm of potential. I believe all Black males who are educated by serious Black adults of either gender are aware of the sacred mystery of fatherhood. They love their children deeply enough to want to do the right thing by them.

All Black fathers have the artistry within them. They can draw upon it in times of joy and sorrow, triumph and crisis, if they are encouraged to Rock Steady within the tradition of responsible Black male parenting. That artistry is the style, distinction and influence that a serious Black father brings to raising his children. That artistry is everything particular—smells and touch, talk and attitudes—that a father impresses upon his children. Genetic Dancers become art, I believe, when they apply their imagination to parenting in the way Michael Jordan plays basketball or Vincent Harding writes about history.

In other words, Black fathers have the greatest tools with which to shape themselves into heroic figures for their children: they have their minds and they have their culture.

Now, many folks complain that Black fathers dance to some song other than "Rocky Steady," maybe "Papa Was A Rolling Stone." After all, some statistics say that upward to 50% of African-American families have women as their primary guardian of children. Papa must be a rolling stone, the thinking goes, or else why ain't daddy at home?

I'm not one to ignore reality, but I'm also not about letting statistics tell my story. First off, I have been the victim of these numbers. I have heard the comments about my own lack of dedication after I separated from the mother of my children. Those comments came from people who didn't know the circumstances of our separation, nor did they know why children, to whom I was and am deeply devoted, weren't living with me or visiting me. So without knowing the scoop, they told the story—wrongly. For although family composition numbers obviously tell us there are major changes in the Black family, they really only outline the changes. They don't capture the specifics about each of the families represented. Within the aggregate, there are categories—widows, divorcees, teen parents, women whose children's fathers are away in the armed services—that allow us to see more clearly what the general numbers obscure. And certainly those numbers count sisters who wanted the child but not the father, whose religious convictions compelled childbirth instead of abortion, who refused to allow their children to see, visit or live with their fathers.

But suppose we, for a minute, accept that those numbers say that Black fathers are not Rock Steady, have never been Rock Steady and just don't Rock Steady by nature. Let's look right square into the idea, and ask ourselves what our responsibilities would be then. How would we turn what would obviously be lames into Genetic Dancers?

By bad-mouthing them as low-life niggers?
By marrying men from other cultures?
By reducing brothers to sperm banks?
By attacking the social causes—lack of jobs, welfare incentives, prisons, dope?
By disregarding their ideas and opinions about child rearing?

I think a fundamental and challenging first foundation for changing such Black fathers for the better would be to first rekindle their essential humanity. Find the individual men behind those figures and discover their human universe. We must portray them humanely, as full-fledged human beings willing to do right. We must not avoid openly revealing their flaws, their backwardness or the times they stray from the values and standards of our core culture. But we must raise our vision, our expectations, our basic perception of these men.

I'm not saying anything new either. As a people, we've continuously rejected the White supremacist mythology about Africans. And wherever Tarzan and his descendants appear—whether they yell from the pages of publications or silver screens or down South, up South, east or west—we just dog him and dare him to yodel again. And to protect us, our most imaginative men and women reaffirm our right to existence on the planet by telling our tales and stories, distilling our humanity into dialogue and movement so that we can recharge ourselves and pass it on, pass it on . . .

To put it bluntly, I reject the common mythology about me. I suggest that we all accept Black fathers. Period. Not as male mothers. But as men who are basic companions to mothers in the development of our children. This is the standard we are upholding anyway, when we get pissed with those brothers who do not help to raise their children, or refuse to pay equitable child support, or don't take time to be and do with their children, or try to live by the double standards of the Male Get Over.

Our best tradition demands and inspires responsible Black male parenting, and I'm convinced that the so-called average Black father subscribes to this tradition. He should become the building block with which we construct the healthiest changes within Black fathers.

I'm not saying that showing a brother on TV changing diapers is going to—presto!—make a child abuser seek counseling. What I'm saying is that it's time we changed the ground rules, changed the symbols of reality to reflect capability, involvement, and possibilities. Our children are growing day-by-day and we can contribute so much to their mental health by confirming and celebrating the lives of their fathers. Many Black fathers are heroes to their children. We should validate their choices to become fathers. We should listen to their voices.

Black mothers have traditionally been able to draw on this nourishment. Even a sister who is depressed from divorce or lack of work, perhaps, is connected to an umbilical cord of literature, images, history, connected to, maybe, Lorraine's Lena Younger, or Ntozake's self-affirming women. She can—and is definitely being encouraged to—drink of her-story to keep on Rock Steady till times get better or until she joins with others to make times better.

In these times, Black fathers are contributing to the development of their children, but do so without encouragement and celebration. They're shown as Blues Brothers rather than Soul Men. Imitations of who? White fathers? The men who walked across unmarked borders after emancipation to reunify with their children and wives, for example? The men like Abram Scriven, quoted by Gutman from the 1858 note that said, after he was forced from his wife and children by slavery: "If we shall not meet in this world, I hope to meet in heaven—my dear wife for you and my children my pen cannot express the grief I feel to be parted from you all."

Modern Black fathers are rarely compared to the men who sharecropped or ran their own farms. Men who worked night shifts, part-time, or ran their own businesses.

Let's humble ourselves to reject any down-pat definitions of our fathers, accept that they have something to teach us and demand that they share imaginative, constructive, unique, and serious ideas.

If we want genetic dancers—men whose positive self concept is based on being more than just breadwinners—than let us tap into the deep pool of Black men for fresh ideas about Black child and family development. I do not mean looking to them as omnipotent Mistra-Know-It-Alls, to use Stevie's phrase. Nor is this a call for The-Man-From-Do-as-I-Say-Do! It is just promoting these brothers as the first line of expertise about themselves and their own lives. We have not asked Black fathers about fatherhood! *Genetic Dancers* magazine—and all such efforts to communicate with Black fathers—will raise the quality of our problem-solving efforts, set new standards for cooperation between parents and help Black fathers meet the traditionally exacting standards laid down by their ancestors.

Genetic Dancers will continue to explore the artistry within African-American fathers. As the first and only magazine to ever see Black fathers as unique individuals worthy of creative reflection, it must unearth the dedication of these men. But it will also have the courage to face any flaws and backward attitudes some brothers display to the detriment of their children, their mates and themselves.

As publisher and editor, and as a father myself, I pledge first to raise my own children and to contribute to the development of all Black children and young people I know or meet. Secondly, I pledge to anchor *Genetic Dancers* on the best of the tradition of Black fatherhood, stretching without hesitation back to Africa, in much the same way as The Whispers called back to Aretha when they hit the charts with their style of Rock Steady.

I am a Genetic Dancer, Rockin' Steady for my son and two daughters. I urge all of us to "move your hips with the people from side to side" like Aretha said, as we unearth the motherlode of seriousness within our past and mine the fatherlode lying just under the surface of our times. Read the folklore, the poetry and fiction, admire and buy the photos and paintings, listen to the old men, encourage the younger brothers doing their do with their kids on the subways and buses, in the parks and grocery stores, at the marches and rallies. And then "let's call this song exactly what it is. What it is! What it is!"

Chapter 18

Conclusion

Benjamin P. Bowser

THIS COLLECTION OF ESSAYS has looked at young Black men in the social context in which they live. The central theme which unites these essays is that individual and group behaviors cannot be understood or changed without taking into consideration the institutions that shape opportunities and create the social environments in which young people must cope and define their sense of self. Central to the problems of young Black men is their marginality to opportunities and participation in the economy and general society. Young Black men have not simply gone mad nor have they rejected their parents' dreams for a better life. It is no coincidence that in 1989 young Black men are part of the first generation of Afro-Americans who have no clear purpose in life and look forward to no future role, no matter how inferior, in an economy that no longer needs strong backs and manual labor (Anthony Lemelle, Walter Stafford and Robert Staples). Black adolescents are in fact responding to the actual conditions in which they find themselves. They are coping against two external barriers—decreasing opportunities for economic participation in American society and the generalized view that they are outsiders, troublesome, dangerous, and morally and intellectually inferior.

Any class of people with no place in post-industrial America will be ignored and controlled until they destroy themselves or disappear. Drug addiction and trafficking play central roles in controlling and destroying the Black future. As long as the poisons of heroin and crack-cocaine are self-administered, Blacks will continue to be characterized as dangerous, worthless, incapable of self-discipline and devoid of morals. But, more importantly, the function of drug trafficking in Black communities is not only to employ the unemployed, but to prevent the conditions that dispose self-destruction from being seen for what they are and from ultimately being challenged.

Parents and Crises

Today's adolescents in large part mirror their parents. The current generation of Black parents with adolescent children is the most fully urbanized and mainstream-acculturated group of Afro-Americans in this country's history. They are the first generation of Afro-Americans who have broken with folk traditions and the "old school." They are the most urban and the most educated. They were reared like their White peers on a common electronic media and fully expected to achieve the American dream because of the gains of the civil rights movement. And like past generations of Americans they expected that their children would do even better.

What the current generation of Black parents did not anticipate was that their children would face new, more subtle and more effective forms of racism and discrimination along with diminishing opportunities. Nor did they anticipate that their children would have to grow up in communities under siege from drug addicts and traffickers or in suburbs where their racial identity would be synonymous with failure, deprivation and inferiority. They did not anticipate that they would have so little impact upon their children and would have to compete for their children's allegiance with fads, fashions and values set by advertisers and athletes as well as peers who clearly lack direction and adult guidance. The greatest irony is that many of the young people who do achieve the "American Dream" find that a condition for participation in the mainstream is to reject identification with Black people and to have nothing to do with Black communities.

Two central crises are reflected in the problems of educating and parenting Black children in general and males in particular. The first crisis is in expectations of the future. Most Black males do not enter adulthood with life prospects anything near what their parents had initially hoped for. Not all young Black men end up as high school dropouts, as users and sellers of drugs, as murderers and their victims, as unemployed, as irresponsible fathers or in jail. The growing number of troubled Black youth who concern us all are really just the most visible part of a larger group. For every one who ends up as a statistic for what is wrong there are many more who struggle to actualize their potentials but ultimately fail to achieve their dreams. Many talented young Black people graduate from high school and do NOT go on to college, do not have jobs with a future and do not have an apparent purpose in life. The core of this first crisis is that the majority of Black youth who come of age each year are nowhere near the American dream nor are they on track toward achieving it.

The second crisis is, in a way, far more serious than the first. It is a crisis of explanation and action. Gains in civil rights and access to new educational and job opportunities should have made the tasks of Black parents easier than in the past. But just the opposite seems to have happened—parenting is more difficult. Our young people are not succeeding and there is a great deal of confusion as to why not. What makes matters worse is that there is no consensus on either the causes of our youth crisis or the solutions. This crisis of explanation is not due to the uniqueness of the problems or because the solutions have never been formulated. As drug addiction and trafficking have taken our attention away from root causes, a small, new, well-supported group of Black interpreters speak for the wealthy and powerful who know that their interests and decision-making have created the conditions under which Blacks are struggling. The purpose of these new Black spokesmen is to see that attention focuses on anything but continuing racial discrimination, the presumption of black inferiority and general institutional racism. As long as Black people have no consensus on the causes of all of their crises, no strategic action can be taken. Those who feel that their interests are served by continued Black subordination must be taught that implementation of real solutions so that young Black people can fully participate in the economy will mean changes in the nation's priorities and a transformation of how the wealth and resources of this nation are used.

Reasons for Optimism

There is nothing really new about the conditions of young Black men. The same victim blaming, covert discrimination, denial of opportunity and negative public view of Black adolescents assailed prior generations of Black men. The only difference is that now there are far more Black men on the periphery of the economy than in prior generations. The lack of consensus around causes and the resulting lack of leadership around solutions have taken a tremendous toll in broken communities and lost time and lives. Yet the causes of today's conditions are not fundamentally different than in prior decades. In the same way, the solutions are no mystery—jobs from which one can support a family, real opportunity and a general belief on the part of Whites that Black lives have the same intrinsic worth as theirs.

The prospects of positive change, especially around national priorities, may seem for the moment quite dim. But the authors who contributed to this collection of essays are anything but pessimistic. There is an underlying optimism here. They have a spirit which calls for us to seize the times. Black people are starting to organize at the community level and to fight back, as Hardy Frye has pointed out. Those who obscure the real issues either out of conviction or opportunity cannot confuse people at the community level. It is in everyday life that ordinary Black people experience continued racism in the workplace and in their children's lives. They cannot deny what they see. The authors of these essays have a number of points to make and advice to offer for personal and community action. Each essay has its own unique contribution and cannot be adequately summarized. What follows is a selective review of the authors' points and recommendations for action:

Crucial Insights

1. The seemingly bizarre behaviors of young Black men are coping behaviors which have become a subculture of resistance to external stigmatization and forced criminal identities (regardless of whether or not the youth have committed crimes). To be young, male and Black in America's welfare state is to be associated with danger, trouble and criminality. Behind the stigma are young people who are perceptive of how they are regarded and act out in defiance. They also know that they are not valued and are isolated from mainstream opportunities (Lemelle).
2. If you want to know what is going on with Black teens, listen to them talk with each other in their vernacular. You will hear them express their values, concerns, fears and goals. They have a wide range of opinions. Parents and others who listen to them can gain insight on how to approach and relate to these young people (Knox).
3. As long as the only priority of the wealthy and powerful in this country is profits, profits and more profits, more and more Afro-Americans (and other economically marginal people) are going to be forced to the periphery of the mainstream and out of the economy. Eventually enough White Americans are going to realize that this is their future as well. Any real solution to the continued economic disenfranchisement of Americans due to the internationalization of the domestic economy will require major structural change (Stafford and Staples).
4. The initial impetus for change will come from the community level. A general social movement is underway which will produce both ideas and leaders who will address the decline of Black community life. The federal government clearly lacks the political will to address the issues facing Black Americans. The only place where Blacks can initially exercise influence and make demands which have to be responded to is at the local level (Frye). Here the people "will assemble to determine the cause and the remedy" (King and Mitchell).
5. The general social movement now underway will do

what it can at the community level. But what neoconservatives miss is that community self-actualization will not compensate for a deteriorating economic base and real barriers to opportunity. There will have to be a national effort, initiated at the community level, to begin job training, provide adequate housing, school enrichment programs, comprehensive health care and more aggressive action against racial discrimination (Frye).

6. While there are subtle changes in how racial discrimination is acted out, it has not declined or disappeared. Racial discrimination and the presumption of White superiority are still pervasive and are still central to the assault on Blacks' self-esteem. A social structure that covertly excludes a segment of its population sets up a condition where they live a social psychology of oppression. The results are behaviors characterized by conformity, ritualism, innovation (reform), retreatism, separatism and rebellion (Moss).

What Can Be Done?

1. Parenting is much too important to be left to chance or to tradition. Part of the general social movement to reinvigorate Black communities should include parent training and support groups to share insight, strategies and experiences (King and Mitchell).
2. There is a crucial need to bring back the tradition of community parenting where adults take responsibility for children and teens wherever they are and regardless of whether or not they are the natural parents. Parenting is a collective rather than an individual task. Being "the children of everyone" can be an important cofactor in regeneration of the community and in successful parenting (Mitchell).
3. An important early objective of community activism should be the development and implementation of community family agendas where African-American values are passed on to young people. Black adolescence

cannot be left to just happen. Families and community need to plan and guide the adolescent-to-adult process (Goddard).

4. The education of Black adolescents cannot be left up to the "regular" school curriculum. Black adolescents need special attention to offset stigmatization and the general expectation that they should not and will not succeed. This means the development of in-school and community-based enrichment programs. The academic achievements of young Black people must become central to Black community reform and redefinition. If nothing else, a corps of community educational advocates can be formed who will serve as personal advocates for young people whose parents are unwilling or unable to interact with the schools (Bowser and Perkins).
5. It may be impractical for large numbers of Black parents to educate their children at home. But it is not impractical to develop a home study curriculum to supplement and off-set the ways in which the Eurocentric school curriculum and teachers degrade Black self-esteem and ignore the role of African peoples in developing Western civilization and technology (Weusi-Puryear).
6. It is crucial that parents personalize and share their experiences, struggles, successes and failures with their young adults. This sharing need not be always heavy and serious minded. A sense of humor can do wonders to communications. But most of all, effective parenting does not simply happen out of making a successful living and leaving education and the teaching of values up to television, peers and school (Sweet).
7. There will have to be community-level education where local residents are trained to give presentations on a variety of topics and to conduct seminars. Community newsletters need to be published which can give attention to problems and successes, and act as a forum for discussion of local issues. Young people can be congratulated for their successes and extraordinary community contributions can be recognized. The publication of the names and addresses of drug dealers and the auto license numbers of drive-in drug buyers can be an effective way

of isolating destructive elements (Sweet).

8. One of the most effective and overlooked ways to educate and impart values is through reading novels, histories and biographies written by and about Black men and women. Black young people and adults alike need to turn off the television and come to enjoy reading to educate and affirm themselves and their social identities (Muse).
9. Finally, Black and White students need proactive training in cultural sensitivity and must be taught to see beyond stereotypes and myths (Hudson).

The implementation of these points would have a tremendous positive impact on the Black community's effectiveness in coping with continued racial discrimination and economic marginality. At the heart of these recommendations is establishing community control over itself and reaffirming the influence of parents and parent surrogates in the lives of young Black men. The experiences of the past two decades have shown us that even gaining political and economic representation as mayors and members of congress is not sufficient to gain inclusion into the mainstream. As long as Black people are still regarded in the culture as inferior, subordination need not be forced. Blacks impose subordination upon themselves. This leads to a crucial point which Black teens have conveyed to us.

Appropriate Goals

All parents want their sons and daughters to go to school, do well and then be well employed in order to live the good life and to be able to support their families—the American dream. What does this really mean? Most parents are really asking their young people to buy into the mainstream for material comfort. The "dream" is really to be or to remain solidly in the middle class. The parents' presumption is that being in the middle class is certainly a sane life-style, is morally worth pursuing and is economically easier than being in the working or lower class.

While parents are dreaming, their young people are seeing a reality that looks quite different. Middle-class respectability and pursuit of material comfort cannot hide behaviors which have become increasingly associated with what it takes to be really successful. What parents overlook and the young people see is that in the mainstream it is alright and even necessary to be self-centered, to cheat through deception, to lie by impression management and to do whatever needs to be done in order to maintain profits and to stay in power. This is what you have to do to get ahead. The Reagan presidency and the arrogant celebration of materialism over the last decade (during the formation years of today's adolescents) removed any remaining pretense that fairness, honesty and decency were synonymous with material success. There is now very little moral difference between the behaviors of "legitimate" businessmen, government officials and dope dealers. The only real difference is that the businessmen and government officials have power and respectability, while dope dealers have neither. What the respectable and disrespectable have in common is that both are in "business" for money and acclaim and can delude themselves into believing that their behaviors are not exploitive and destructive.

If all the crises that afflict Black America suddenly disappeared tomorrow along with Black self-destructive behavior, we would still be in a great deal of trouble. Day-to-day family life and rearing adolescents would still be very difficult. America even without the racial crisis is a land where the people are exploited by business in the name of profits and where a democratic government does not work for the "little man." Americans with their exaggerated sense of individualism are left to struggle to maintain a faltering standard of living and illusions of forever being able to improve on the "American dream."

It is no exaggeration that the majority of Americans will at some time in their lives experience serious emotional problems and will never see their problems as generated by the culture in which they live. Addiction and codependence are also becoming the norm. One need not be a substance abuser to be an addict. One can be addicted to pursuing money, power, fame or controlling everything and everyone—what Anne Wilson Shaef in *When Society Becomes an Addict* (1987) calls "process addiction." Even successful businessmen are not happy with their lives (Jan Halper, *Quiet Desperation,* 1989). As it takes more and more to maintain illusions about oneself, there will be more and more casualties. Americans will come to see that we need a new, more humane and responsive social order, and that all of the troubles are not due to the shortcomings of individuals.

While mainstream America continues to slide into illusions, the Afro-American subculture has historically put a premium on "telling it like it is." Black Americans could not have survived by living in illusions. Yet when it comes to the dreams and goals of our young people, we suddenly begin to tell stories. The fact of the matter is that we are asking our young people to enter a "burning house" for largely selfish, self-centered reasons. For example, the first story is "Work hard and you will be successful." But the truth is most will pay a price, work hard and still get nothing. A second story is "There are opportunities now as never before." The truth is that there are actually fewer opportunities open if you are Black and male because of continued discrimination and isolation. In prior generations young Black people were called upon to cultivate their minds. That knowledge could not be taken away, regardless of life conditions. Young people were also called upon to provide service. There was no greater privilege than to help others improve their minds, hearts and conditions. These are not the major themes young people are called to today. No wonder young Black men seem so poorly motivated to compete for admission into the mainstream. The messages they receive about it are mixed and confused. So they affirm neither where they are nor where we want them to be.

Tee Sweet is very perceptive to realize that young men who come out of spiritually and psychologically empty Black households (with good parents who worked hard) are more apt to abandon their culture and identity for so little. Black parents who uncritically push their children into the "burning house" are literally condemning them to spiritual bankruptcy. To be cut off from their roots and the folk wisdom of Black people's successful coping devices is to be condemned to invisibility and delusion in the larger world.

What is needed is a different dream and different goal, one worthy of the struggle Afro-Americans have waged to survive in and change America. That struggle is not simply to reform America so that the Afro-American middle class can be in on the profits and insanity as well. We need a vision of America transformed. And then we need to act to see that we do indeed build a better nation. This vision will not come from acting out of the same mind-sets that have characterized the thinking of oppressed people (Moss). It will require a turning within for self-examination and achieving a real spiritual centering. Then we will be able to look on our circumstances with fresh eyes and see that we have the keys not only to our own liberation, but to the nation's as well. This is not a call for better advertisers and public relations campaigns to improve the image of Black people or to further delude ourselves about the real sickness in this nation's heart and soul. The nation needs to be transformed in essence and substance, not simply in image.

The need to turn within and then act is now unavoidable. While White and Black Americans may be in denial about the gravity of the nation's economic and spiritual conditions, a radical transformation cannot be put off. The AIDS virus makes a coming together and change necessary for Black Americans as no other crisis we have faced (Fulliloves). If we do not act to transform our values, behavior and the present social order, we might very well die. New visions and action are needed as never before. Besides real opportunity and positive regard, vision and action are ultimately what young people need to motivate them and challenge them to affirm one another, to turn against drug trafficking, to respect and form families and to build rather than destroy the community. Young Black men will rise to this challenge and work hard to attain it if only they are shown the way.

Biographical Sketches

BENJAMIN P. BOWSER, Ph.D. is assistant professor of Sociology and Social Services at California State University, Hayward, associate editor of *Sage Race Relations Abstracts* (U.K.) and the new director of Multicultural Inquiry and Research on AIDS (San Francisco). He has held research and administrative positions at a number of universities. Dr. Bowser is co-editor of *Impacts of Racism on White Americans* (1981) with Raymond Hunt.

HARDY FRYE, Ph.D. is associate professor of Sociology and former associate dean of Social Sciences at the University of California, Santa Cruz. He is also a research associate at the Institute for the Study of Social Change, University of California, Berkeley. Dr. Frye is author of *Black Parties and Political Power* (1980) and is presently writing on local progressive governments.

MINDY FULLILOVE, M.D. is a psychiatrist and former director of Multicultural Inquiry and Research on AIDS (MIRA) in San Francisco. She is now director of the Substance Abuse Core at the HIV Center of Clinical and Behavioral Studies, New York State Psychiatric Institute. Her most recent publication is "AIDS Prevention Among Black Women: Toward Understanding the Gender Rules," *Journal of Sex Research* (1990).

ROBERT FULLILOVE, Ed.D. is former director of the Professional Development Program at University of California, Berkeley, and is now director of the Community Core at the HIV Center for Clinical and Behavioral Studies, New York State Psychiatric Institute. He is the lead author of "Risk of Sexually Transmitted Disease Among Black Adolescent Crack Users in Oakland and San Francisco, Calif.," *Journal of the American Medical Association* (1990).

LAWFORD GODDARD, Ph.D. is executive director of The Institute for the Advanced Study of Black Family Life and Culture (Oakland, CA.) and lecturer in Black Studies at San Francisco State University. He the author of "Black Teen Parenting" in Reginald Jones (ed.) *Black Adolescents*. Adolescents, substance abuse and AIDS prevention are his present research interests.

PETER HARRIS is founder and editor of *Genetic Dancers* the only magazine in the nation devoted to Black fathers. He is also a columnist in the *Baltimore Afro-American* and author of "Wherever Dreams Live" (folktales) and "Six Soft Sketches of a Man" (Poetry).

RONALD HUDSON, Ph.D. is a counseling psychologist and former assistant dean of Student Affairs and lecturer in Psychology at Stanford University. He is now assistant dean and director of Student Services at Los Angeles City College. He is continuing his interest in Black identity and self-esteem.

JOYCE KING, Ph.D. is associate professor of Education and director of Teacher Education at Santa Clara University. She and Carolyn Mitchell are authors of the recently published book, *Black Mothers to Sons* (1990). Dr. King's continued area of research is on teaching and parenting from an Afrocentric perspective.

ANTHONY LEMELLE, JR., Ph.D. is visiting associate professor of Sociology at Purdue University. He is a former probation officer who now specializes in community studies, social deviance and sociological theory. Dr. Lemelle has taught Black Studies and Race Relations at a number of universities.

GRACE MASSEY, Ph.D. is a lecturer in Afro-American Studies at the University of California at Berkeley where she is also coordinator for Afro-American student development. Doctor Massey is also research director of the Institute for Developmental Studies in Oakland, CA.—a direct service agency for Black teens. Her research focuses on families, children and the psychological stresses associated with racism.

FAYE McNAIR-KNOX, Ph.D. a lecturer in Linguistics and assistant director of the undergraduate Program in African and Afro-American Studies at Stanford University. She was a Senior Fulbright Scholar to Nigeria and her current research is on inter and intra ethnic variations in urban vernacular English.

CAROLYN MITCHELL, Ph.D. is associate professor of English at Santa Clara University and has taught the literature of religion and Afro-American spirituality at the Pacific School of Religion in Berkeley. Her specialities are also in African-American and twentieth century contemporary American fiction. Dr. Mitchell is author of "Henry Dumas" in the *Dictionary of Literary Biography.*

LOFTEN MITCHELL wrote the book for the hit Broadway musical, "Bubbling Brown Sugar." His plays include *A Land Beyond the River, Tell Pharaoh* and *Ballad for Bimshire.* His books are *Black Drama* (1967), and *Voices of the Black Theatre* (1975). He received a 1958-59 Guggenheim Award for creative writing in drama and the 1969 Harlem Cultural Council Award for Literary Contributions.

JAMES MOSS, Ph.D. is a psychoanalyst with a private practice in New York City. He is also co-director of the Association for Inter-Ethnic Studies. He is editor of *The Black Man In America* (1971), has published extensively in the *Journal of Human Relations,* and is the author of numerous articles on race relations, values and human rights.

DAPHNE MUSE is editor and publisher of *The Children's Advocate,* a nationally focused newspaper that provides comprehensive coverage and analysis of the issues affecting children, youth and families. She is also a multicultural children's literature author and consultant.

HERBERT PERKINS, Ph.D. is associate professor of Anthropology and associate dean of Students for Multicultural Affairs at Lawrence University in Appleton, Wis. He is former dean of Intercultural Studies at De Anza College. Dr. Perkins's research interests are in ethnographic studies, cultural criticism and semiotics.

ALVIN POUSSAINT, M.D. is associate professor of Psychiatry and associate dean for Student Affairs at Harvard Medical School. He is author of *Why Blacks Kill Blacks* (1972) and co-author of *Black Child Care* (1975). Dr. Poussaint is a script consultant to NBC's "The Cosby Show" and "A Different World." He also wrote the introductions to Bill Cosby's *Fatherhood* and *Time Flies.*

WALTER STAFFORD, Ph.D. is associate professor of Urban Planning and Public Policy at New York University and author of *Afro-American and Latino Men: New Dimensions of Institutional Bias* (1990) and "Political Dimensions of the Underclass Concept" in Herbert Gans (ed.) *Sociology in America* (1990). His current research focuses on the interaction of the state and institutional racism to economic markets.

ROBERT STAPLES, Ph.D. is professor of Sociology at the University of California, San Francisco. He is an author and editor whose books include *The World of Black Singles* (1981), *Black Masculinity* (1982), *The Black Family* (1986), and *The Urban Plantation* (1987). Dr. Staples has over 130 published papers and is on the editorial boards of *The Black Scholar, Journal Of Marriage And Family, Journal of Social and Behavioral Sciences* and the *Western Journal of Black Studies.*

H. TEE SWEET is director of the Family Development Center in San Jose, California, and former president of the San Jose Chapter of the National Association for the Advancement of Colored People. She has won numerous community service awards and spent most of her career as a teacher.

MUATA WEUSI-PURYEAR, Ph.D. is instructor of Mathematics at De Anza College and is president and founder of Edutek Corporation (Palo Alto, Ca.), an educational software development company for elementary school children. His current interests are in the history of mathematics and ancient numerical systems, in particular, Egyptian hieroglyphs.

OMANIKE WEUSI-PURYEAR is a part-time instructor of Intercultural Studies at De Anza College. She is an independent business woman and has had a long interest in Black literature. Her current interest is in Black women's literature. She is one of the founders of the Peninsula Book Club (Palo Alto, Ca.).

Name Index

Subject Index

D

E

S